K.I.S.S

DK

The Only Guides You'll Ever Need!

THIS SERIES IS YOUR TRUSTED GUIDE through all of life's stages and situations. Want to learn how to surf the Internet or care for your new dog? Or maybe you'd like to become a wine connoisseur or an expert gardener? The solution is simple: just pick up a K.I.S.S. Guide and turn to the first page.

Expert authors will walk you through the subject from start to finish, using simple blocks of knowledge to build your skills one step at a time. Build upon these learning blocks and by the end of the book, you'll be an expert yourself! Or, if you are familiar with the topic but want to learn more, it's easy to dive in and pick up where you left off.

The K.I.S.S. Guides deliver what they promise: simple access to all the information you'll need on one subject. Other titles you might want to check out include: Playing Guitar, Living With a Dog, the Internet, Wine, Managing Your Career, and many more.

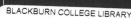

GUIDE TO

Pregnancy

FELICIA EISENBERG MOLNAR

Foreword by Dr. Miriam Stoppard

A Dorling Kindersley Book

LONDON, NEW YORK,
MUNICH, MELBOURNE, DELHI

Dorling Kindersley Limited
Project Editors Caroline Hunt, David Tombesi-Walton, Julian Gray
Art Editors Justin Clow, Simon Murrell

Managing Art Editor Heather McCarry
Managing Editor Maxine Lewis
Jacket Designer Neal Cobourne
Picture Researcher Franziska Marking
Picture Librarian Marcus Scott
Production Sarah Coltman, Heather Hughes
Category Publisher Mary Thompson

DK Publishing, Inc.
Editorial Director LaVonne Carlson
Series Editor Jennifer Williams
Senior Editor Jill Hamilton
Editor and Copy Editor Eve P. Steinberg

First published in 2001 by Dorling Kindersley Limited
80, Strand, London WC2R 0RL

2 4 6 8 10 9 7 5 3

A CIP catalogue record for this book is available from the British Library.

ISBN 0 7513 1241 X

Colour reproduction by ColourScan, Singapore
Printed and bound in Portugal by Printer Portuguesa

For our complete catalogue visit
www.dk.com

Contents at a Glance

CONTENTS

PART ONE The Exhilarating Early Weeks

CHAPTER 1 Am I Pregnant? 22

CHAPTER 2 Your Childbirth Choices 38

PART THREE Forty Weeks and Counting

PART FOUR Stages of Childbirth

PART FIVE The Early Days and Weeks

PART SIX You and Your Baby's Well-Being

APPENDICES

Foreword

PREGNANCY'S A SERIOUS business but that's no reason to make it more serious than it is. It's a natural event to be celebrated, which is why this K.I.S.S. Guide to Pregnancy is so welcome.

From the time you discover you're pregnant, there'll be a flood of questions you'll want answered. What should I be eating? (Do I need to take extra vitamins?) Can I continue exercising? (There goes my waistline!) What is happening inside my body and my precious baby's? (When can I hear a heartbeat?) What childbirth choices do I have? Now is the perfect time to read, absorb, and decide – with knowledge comes confidence.

It's a lot to take in, and because of the physical demands of pregnancy there will be times when you feel exhausted. It's important to know you're completely normal when you do. Pregnancy can be an emotional and physical rollercoaster. Don't get upset, but do talk it through, especially with your partner: I'm a firm believer in getting lots of support, encouragement, and help from your family and friends.

There's one thing I can guarantee: the second your baby is born, your relationship takes on new dimensions. You and your partner grow even closer if you take time out, with minimum interruption, to bond with your baby. The first weeks, days, months, perhaps more than any time, are very special indeed – and the bonding you do now with each other and your baby will set the seal for the rest of your life.

Sounds daunting? It doesn't have to be – not if you read as much as you can about pregnancy, including this refreshing K.I.S.S. Guide.

Good luck.

MIRIAM STOPPARD

Dr. Miriam Stoppard is known to millions through her bestselling publications and television appearances. A leading authority on pregnancy and childcare, her books on these topics have sold well over a million copies around the world. Further information and practical advice can be found at her web site, www.miriamstoppard.com.

Introduction

PREGNANCY IS A TIME of great wonder. You know, or are beginning to know, the questions well: Is everything going to be all right with my baby and me? Am I really going to be a mother? What is pregnancy and childbirth going to be like? In a world where information abounds, there is still a great need for a book in which you can find straightforward and reliable answers to the many questions that most naturally arise. The intention of this book is to bring together, simply, everything we know today about pregnancy to keep you informed, empowered, and reassured. Once you have this knowledge, you are in the best possible situation to make informed choices about your antenatal care and the birth of your child.

In the last 20 years, no other area of medicine has changed more drastically than obstetrics, whether in the field of antenatal care or actual childbirth. Today, as an expectant mother, you have so much more to learn than ever before. With all the complicated issues of maternity, anxiety, rather than peace of mind, can sometimes result. In writing this book it has been my intention to use clear, concise language that, I hope, will offer understanding on the subject of one of Mother Nature's most phenomenal and natural events without inundating you with too much information. It is also my hope that this book will bring you some measure of comfort and ease.

To be honest, pregnancy is not always 9 months of pure pleasure; there are challenges, too. I hope you can use the following chapters as a guide to this marvellous journey. With knowledge, practical advice, humour, and a few sensible notes of caution will come, I hope, the confidence to enjoy your pregnancy and the birth of your baby in good health and a positive state of mind.

FELICIA EISENBERG MOLNAR

Dedication

For Rita and Isabelle

F.E.M.

What's Inside?

THE INFORMATION in the K.I.S.S. Guide to Pregnancy is carefully arranged so that whichever stage you're at – from 2 weeks to 9 months – you'll have no problem finding the information you need to help you along the way.

PART ONE

"Am I pregnant?" is one of the most exciting questions you may ever ask yourself. And the possibility will no doubt send you into a dizzying combination of emotions. To figure out if you are expecting and what to do if you are, you need to know the facts firsthand.

PART TWO

Congratulations, you're going to have a baby! Get ready for shifts in feelings, mood, and energy levels, and appearance, too, but not yet. Your body is undergoing profound change, and right from the start you need to know about these changes.

PART THREE

One of the greatest wonders of the world, making a baby is fascinating and important for you to understand. At this time you may be asked to consider some antenatal testings to check that everything is okay. Part Three will guide you through all of this.

PART FOUR

Labour for most mere mortals is hard work and full of surprises, and although every woman describes her experience differently, three very specific stages always occur. Part Four tells you what they are and how to recognize them.

PART FIVE

The big day – and the arrival of a slippery baby. Gazing into your newborn's eyes sets you off on the trail of a love like you've never known before. But motherhood is a constant learning experience. Take one day at a time (with Part Five at your side).

PART SIX

Though the chances of anything going wrong with you or your baby are very slim, Part Six looks at some problems and their treatments. There's also a whole chapter devoted to complementary therapies and how they can help you through pregnancy and childbirth.

The Extras

THROUGHOUT THE BOOK, *you will notice a number of boxes and symbols. They are there to emphasize certain points I want you to pay special attention to, because they are important to your understanding of pregnancy and childbirth. You'll find:*

Very Important Point

This symbol points out a topic I believe deserves careful attention. You really need to know this information before continuing.

Complete No-No

This is a warning, something I want to advise you not to do or to be aware of.

Getting Technical

When the information is about to get a bit technical, I'll let you know so that you can read carefully.

Inside Scoop

These are special suggestions that come from my own personal experience. I want to share them with you because they helped me during my pregnancy.

You'll also find some little boxes that include information I think is important, useful, or just plain fun.

Trivia...
These are simply fun facts or anecdotes that I hope will give you a little insight into the pregnancy and childbirth process.

DEFINITION
*Here I'll **define** words and terms for you in an easy-to-understand style. You'll also find a glossary at the back of the book with all the relevant terms.*

INTERNET
www.dk.com

I think the Internet is a great resource for pregnant women and their partners, so I've scouted out some web sites that will help you on your magical journey.

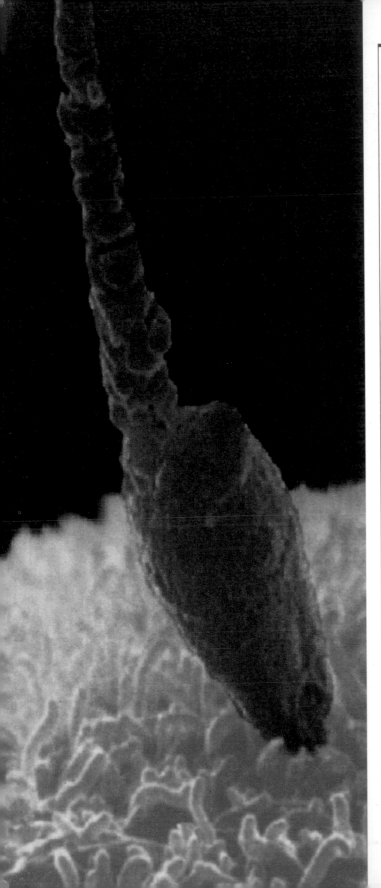

PART ONE

HOW IT ALL BEGINS: SPERM MEETS EGG

THE EXHILARATING EARLY WEEKS

AM I PREGNANT? This is one of the most *exciting* questions you may ever ask yourself. Whether you have been trying for months or even years, or are caught by surprise, the possibility will no doubt send you into a dizzying combination of *emotions*.

 Determining if you are pregnant can often take some patience and repeated testing. For others, just missing your period is enough of a sign. But it's not uncommon to experience a slight spotting around the time of your period even when you are pregnant. In order to figure out if you are expecting and what to do if you are, it's important to *know the facts* first-hand.

Chapter 1

Am I Pregnant?

WANTING TO HAVE A BABY is one of life's most powerful urges. Some women never doubt that motherhood will be an important part of their adult lives. For others, this feeling remains dormant until they find the right mate. Even if child-bearing and motherhood was once the furthest thing from your mind, discovering you are pregnant is surely one of life's most exciting moments.

In this chapter...

✓ Conceiving: the fundamentals

✓ The signs of pregnancy

✓ Proof positive

✓ Time to celebrate

THE ANTICIPATION IS ALWAYS EXCITING WHEN YOU'RE WAITING FOR THE RESULTS

Conceiving: the fundamentals

OH SURE, YOU LEARNED *all about the birds and the bees at school. But this time it's really about you, so pay attention and don't skip over this section. Your body's reproductive function is truly one of life's great wonders. You'll find yourself being the subject of much poking and prodding over the next 9 months, and understanding exactly how your body functions will become a focus of your waking hours. Trust me.*

A finely tuned sequence of events must take place for reproduction to occur. The entire process is regulated by an ensemble of hormones coursing through your body and orchestrating the ultimate release and nurturing of a healthy egg. Female sex hormones, mainly progesterone and oestrogen, determine when an egg is released and when your period arrives. This cycle, best known as the menstrual cycle, regulates your fertility.

You are probably at your most fertile for only a few days a month. And you thought getting pregnant was easy!

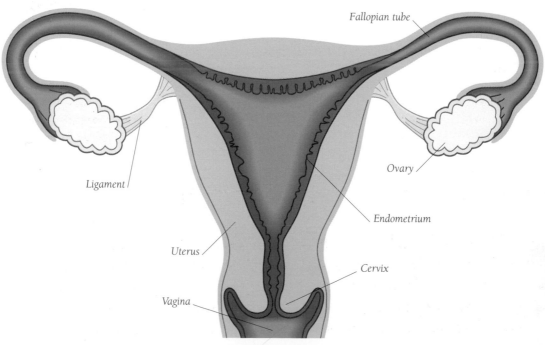

THE FEMALE REPRODUCTIVE SYSTEM

Fallopian tube

Ovary

Endometrium

Ligament

Uterus

Cervix

Vagina

The egg's journey

At birth, your ovaries contain about a million follicles or hollow balls of cells, each with an immature egg (ovum) at the centre. Once you have reached puberty, 20 follicles begin maturing every month, under the influence of hormones. A race ensues for one follicle to become the largest and to develop to about the size of a pinhead. Oestrogen then kicks in, triggering a surge of more hormones, causing the mature egg to burst through the ovary wall (about 14 days before your next period is due). Swept into the Fallopian tubes, this egg has just a few hours to makes its rendezvous with a lucky sperm. It then takes several days for the fertilized egg to travel to the uterus.

The embryo digs in

As soon as the fertilized egg burrows itself into the wall of the uterus, it begins releasing the pregnancy hormone HCG (human chorionic gonadotrophin). The presence of HCG sends an urgent message to the follicle casement, or corpus luteum, left behind by the egg in the ovary. The instruction to the corpus luteum is that it must continue releasing progesterone to nourish the uterine wall. The growing embryo is sustained by the nourishment of the uterine wall until the placenta is formed. In 3 months time the placenta will take over the life-supporting requirements.

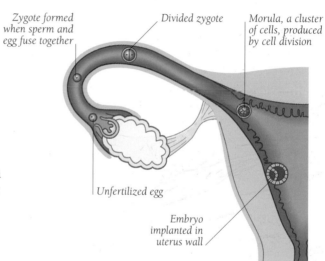

Zygote formed when sperm and egg fuse together

Divided zygote

Morula, a cluster of cells, produced by cell division

Unfertilized egg

Embryo implanted in uterus wall

■ **Following fertilization,** *the egg continues travelling down the Fallopian tube towards the uterus, doubling in cell number every 12 hours. By the time it implants in the uterus wall (above), the group of cells is called an embryo.*

The signs of pregnancy

APART FROM YOUR STRONG INTUITION, *the physical changes of early pregnancy are a simple gauge by which to confirm your inklings. As your body puts itself in high gear, much of what you may be feeling physically and emotionally is related to the rapid adjustments vital to ensuring a successful pregnancy. What follows is a simple guide to recognizing the common early warning signs.*

I missed my period

For me, the long break from my monthly cycle of bleeding, cramps, and tampons was one of the highlights of being pregnant. If your period occurs regularly, let's say every 28 days, and it hasn't come yet, chances are good that there is a baby growing in your belly. But you may have wildly infrequent cycles and never know when to expect your period. For you, missing a period is simply not the clue to trust.

You may notice a little spotting or light bleeding 9 to 10 days after fertilization, when the egg is implanting in the uterus. This is perfectly normal in pregnancy; it is not your period.

I'm nauseous

Feeling nauseous is not common to all pregnancies – it is not a requirement. If you are not nauseous, consider yourself lucky but not necessarily "not pregnant." For some women, nausea can hit within the first few weeks after conception. Vomiting, gagging, and turning green at the thought of food are just a few of the symptoms. And just in case feeling sick as a dog isn't enough, you may have an occasional voracious appetite or satisfy a specific craving which is then followed by vomiting. Simply torture! Even worse, some women suffer from a more extreme variant, *hyperemesis gravidarum*.

Not-just-morning sickness

Mistakenly referred to as morning sickness, nausea in pregnancy can occur any time of the day or night. There is a growing body of medical research indicating that morning sickness is Mother Nature's way of keeping mothers-to-be from ingesting anything that could be toxic to the fetus or harmful to the specially vulnerable pregnant woman. Thanks a lot for the vote of confidence, Madame Goddess! If you are terrified by all this misery, take solace in the knowledge that for the 60 to 80 per cent of pregnant women so afflicted, morning sickness usually passes by the end of the first 3-month period.

■ **Not much fun:** *Feeling nauseous, or indeed vomiting, at any hour of the day or night is probably most women's least favourite part of pregnancy.*

MOTHER'S CURES FOR NAUSEA

Try keeping something in your stomach at all times. Crackers, potato crisps, and ice cream are some favourites. Eat lightly throughout the day. Try small frequent high protein meals: soy milk, turkey breast, and slices of cheese may be good choices. Herb teas such as chamomile, ginger root, and peppermint also provide relief. The important thing to remember is to get calories in any way you can; even junk food is okay in these early months if it's the only thing you can keep down. You simply mustn't stop eating. Drinking lots of water, up to 12 glasses a day, may also give relief along with replacing fluid lost in vomiting. Many in the medical community believe that nausea between weeks 4 and 12 is caused by a contracted blood volume, and the above remedy is a good antidote.

■ **The need to** *keep something in your stomach at all times means that many women turn to light, easy-to-eat food such as ice cream.*

My bladder overrunneth

You knew to expect frequent urination in mid-pregnancy and beyond. But did you expect it within the first few weeks following conception? Surprise! Increased hormonal activity and a swelling uterus cause you to urinate more often right from the start of your pregnancy. Believe me, knowing your way to the nearest toilet for the next 9 months will be your first order of business whenever you are out. If you find yourself having to go to the bathroom a lot and wake up frequently during the night to pee, chances are good that you are pregnant!

My boobs hurt

Personally, when I think I may be pregnant, I always check my "boob meter." Sore breasts are one of the most common signs of a bun in the oven. Some women commonly suffer from tender swollen breasts at the end of their monthly cycles. Pregnant breasts, however, are often agonizingly sore, more sensitive, and puffy. This swelling occurs because the grapelike clusters of milk glands are beginning to enlarge and the blood supply to your breasts is increasing. You may also notice that your nipples and the area around them (areola) are darkening and plumping up. So if you suddenly find yourself blessed with a Pamela Anderson-esque bustline, chalk up another strong sign of pregnancy.

The amount of blood circulating in your body increases by 20–25 per cent in early pregnancy. And by the end of your pregnancy, you will have 40 per cent more blood than a non-pregnant woman.

I'm soooo tired

It's said that a pregnant resting body exerts the same amount of energy as a runner competing in a marathon. While your body is turning its attention to growing a baby, you may feel as though you have been bitten by the tsetse fly. When even the simplest everyday tasks become burdensome and fatigue takes over, you are feeling another physical sign of your impending 9-month journey.

■ **Even when resting**, *a pregnant body exerts so much energy that it may feel like you're running a marathon! Try taking it easy whenever possible – it's a long haul.*

My raging hormones

As I have already mentioned, hormones are strong orchestrators of your fertility and also of pregnancy. As they begin to increase exponentially in the early weeks following conception, these chemicals can wreak havoc on your emotions. Mood swings are as basic to pregnancy as missing your period. If you are feeling like a crazy woman or even just crazier then normal, this may be a strong indication that you are pregnant.

Proof positive

EVEN WHEN YOU HAVE a strong hunch and your physical body is showing signs of undergoing dramatic change, you may still be hesitant to believe that you are in fact pregnant. This is the time when you may rush off to the chemist for a two-pack of home pregnancy tests or schedule a medical appointment. To decide which is the right option for you, read on.

Should I take a home pregnancy test?

A home pregnancy test can be done as early as the first day your period would normally arrive. Many medical professionals agree that the array of over-the-counter home pregnancy tests available through pharmacies are 99 per cent accurate (as claimed by the manufacturers). The tests are generally easy to use and rely on the detection of high levels of the hormone HCG in urine. A box usually contains two test dipsticks and instructions for collecting your first morning urine, when HCG is likely to be most concentrated.

Once you have confirmed that you are pregnant you can start ensuring that your health, and therefore the baby's, is as good as it can be. That is why early diagnosis of pregnancy is important.

Avoid taking drugs, smoking, and drinking alcohol, all of which could harm the developing baby.

If you have any pre-existing conditions and take medications regularly, your usual doctor and the doctor or midwife who is managing your pregnancy must "talk."

■ **Home pregnancy** *test sticks are treated with a chemical that reacts with the pregnancy hormone HCG, which is found in urine. Once the stick and urine have come into contact, sit back and wait . . .*

Don't under any circumstances discontinue medications without your doctor's advice. And don't try any over-the-counter products or herbal medicines without medical approval.

It's rare to get a false positive pregnancy reading. If your test comes up negative, however, it could be an error. One reason for a false negative pregnancy result is that the test may have been done too soon, i.e., before the egg has had a chance to implant and start releasing HCG or before HCG has reached a level high enough to be detected in the urine. If that crucial second stripe or dot fails to appear in the window of the test stick, don't give up hope yet.

If you have a negative home pregnancy test, you may want to wait 3 to 5 days and then retest. The tests are most accurate at least 19 days post-conception.

When do I consult a doctor or midwife?

Whether your home test is negative or positive, you are perfectly normal if you still feel the need for absolute confirmation from a medical professional. As pregnancy is not seen as an emergency, some doctors may ask you to wait several weeks following the first day of your last month's period. Presuming you have a positive test on the day your period is due, waiting may seem agonizing. But doctors have good reasons to delay seeing you. If you have irregular periods, a long cycle with infrequent periods, or were on the Pill when you fell pregnant, your doctor will be able to date your pregnancy more accurately by looking at the size of the baby on a scan. This scan may not be accurate for some weeks following your *last menstrual period* (LMP).

If you still find yourself anxious, most doctors will happily oblige you with an immediate serum blood test. This test also relies on the detection of HCG in the bloodstream, but it is considered more sensitive than a urine test.

Hegar's sign is another early internal physical clue to pregnancy. This is the term used to describe the softening and slight enlargement of the cervix that your doctor can confirm during an internal exam.

Figuring out your due date

When your doctor pulls out one of those cardboard wheels to calculate your baby's expected birthday, you can feel certain that your life is about to change forever. The length of an average pregnancy is 266 days from conception. Your due date is determined by adding 280 days or 40 weeks to the first day of your last period. (Forty weeks for most of us equals ten monthly cycles, not nine, but then who am I to argue with one of mankind's most obvious oversights.) If you don't remember the first day of your LMP, let your doctor know. He or she will be able to assess your due date from an early scan.

WHEN IS YOUR BABY DUE?

Jan	Oct/Nov	Feb	Nov/Dec	Mar	Dec/Jan	Apr	Jan/Feb	May	Feb/Mar	Jun	Mar/Apr	Jul	Apr/May	Aug	May/Jun	Sep	Jun/Jul	Oct	Jul/Aug	Nov	Aug/Sep	Dec	Sep/Oct
1	8	1	8	1	6	1	6	1	5	1	8	1	7	1	8	1	8	1	8	1	8	1	7
2	9	2	9	2	7	2	7	2	6	2	9	2	8	2	9	2	9	2	9	2	9	2	8
3	10	3	10	3	8	3	8	3	7	3	10	3	9	3	10	3	10	3	10	3	10	3	9
4	11	4	11	4	9	4	9	4	8	4	11	4	10	4	11	4	11	4	11	4	11	4	10
5	12	5	12	5	10	5	10	5	9	5	12	5	11	5	12	5	12	5	12	5	12	5	11
6	13	6	13	6	11	6	11	6	10	6	13	6	12	6	13	6	13	6	13	6	13	6	12
7	14	7	14	7	12	7	12	7	11	7	14	7	13	7	14	7	14	7	14	7	14	7	13
8	15	8	15	8	13	8	13	8	12	8	15	8	14	8	15	8	15	8	15	8	15	8	14
9	16	9	16	9	14	9	14	9	13	9	16	9	15	9	16	9	16	9	16	9	16	9	15
10	17	10	17	10	15	10	15	10	14	10	17	10	16	10	17	10	17	10	17	10	17	10	16
11	18	11	18	11	16	11	16	11	15	11	18	11	17	11	18	11	18	11	18	11	18	11	17
12	19	12	19	12	17	12	17	12	16	12	19	12	18	12	19	12	19	12	19	12	19	12	18
13	20	13	20	13	18	13	18	13	17	13	20	13	19	13	20	13	20	13	20	13	20	13	19
14	21	14	21	14	19	14	19	14	18	14	21	14	20	14	21	14	21	14	21	14	21	14	20
15	22	15	22	15	20	15	20	15	19	15	22	15	21	15	22	15	22	15	22	15	22	15	21
16	23	16	23	16	21	16	21	16	20	16	23	16	22	16	23	16	23	16	23	16	23	16	22
17	24	17	24	17	22	17	22	17	21	17	24	17	23	17	24	17	24	17	24	17	24	17	23
18	25	18	25	18	23	18	23	18	22	18	25	18	24	18	25	18	25	18	25	18	25	18	24
19	26	19	26	19	24	19	24	19	23	19	26	19	25	19	26	19	26	19	26	19	26	19	25
20	27	20	27	20	25	20	25	20	24	20	27	20	26	20	27	20	27	20	27	20	27	20	26
21	28	21	28	21	26	21	26	21	25	21	28	21	27	21	28	21	28	21	28	21	28	21	27
22	29	22	29	22	27	22	27	22	26	22	29	22	28	22	29	22	29	22	29	22	29	22	28
23	30	23	30	23	28	23	28	23	27	23	30	23	29	23	30	23	30	23	30	23	30	23	29
24	31	24	1	24	29	24	29	24	28	24	31	24	30	24	31	24	1	24	31	24	31	24	30
25	1	25	2	25	30	25	30	25	1	25	1	25	1	25	1	25	2	25	1	25	1	25	1
26	2	26	3	26	31	26	31	26	2	26	2	26	2	26	2	26	3	26	2	26	2	26	2
27	3	27	4	27	1	27	1	27	3	27	3	27	3	27	3	27	4	27	3	27	3	27	3
28	4	28	5	28	2	28	2	28	4	28	4	28	4	28	4	28	5	28	4	28	4	28	4
29	5	29	6	29	3	29	3	29	5	29	5	29	5	29	5	29	6	29	5	29	5	29	5
30	6			30	4	30	4	30	6	30	6	30	6	30	6	30	7	30	6	30	6	30	6
31	7			31	5			31	7			31	7	31	7			31	7			31	7

■ **Using the chart:** Find the date of the first day of your LMP in the relevant shaded column. Look at the date immediately to the right (a pale yellow column) of your LMP date to find your expected due date. Example: An LMP of 7 March means a due date of 12 December.

Time to celebrate

YOU ARE PREGNANT *and you are going to be a mother. The pink lines on the home pregnancy stick and your doctor confirm it. Your hormones are raging; your tummy is growing. From the moment you know, there is no doubt that this is BIG news. Your first impulse may be to tell absolutely everybody you come into contact with that you are pregnant, especially if this is your first baby. Or you may simply be cautious and want only your husband or partner to know. Clearly, how we handle the news varies greatly from woman to woman, and I urge you to celebrate the news in your own way.*

Emotional adjustments

In the few moments, or days, following the momentous news that you are really pregnant, you may be hit by a flood of conflicting emotions. Joy and triumph in the form of "Wow! I did it", can be followed by fear, apprehension and doubt, even shock that while "Yes I wanted to get pregnant . . . it happened too soon. I'm not ready".

Let's be frank here. The emotional acceptance of your pregnancy is perhaps the most dramatic test following conception. For the first-time mother, pregnancy is the great unexplored territory. It is a mysterious, biological rite of passage. Even when a pregnancy is planned and truly desired, normal fears and conflicting emotions sometimes infringe on the joy of knowing a little seedling is growing inside you. Calm down. Don't worry. You are not crazy. You are not going to be a bad mother. Your feelings are very normal.

■ **Talking through** *your future as parents with your partner can be very exciting – and perhaps a little scary from time to time.*

It is normal to have mixed feelings about being pregnant, even if this is something you've been dreaming about for a long time.

New mother syndrome

I had always thought of myself as a reasonably well balanced 30-something woman. And then a few weeks into receiving the news of my first pregnancy, neurosis set in. This "new mother syndrome" will probably afflict you for most of the next 9 months and even after the baby is born. The thought, "Stop, I want to get off this high-speed train", is to be expected. You will come up with a dozen reasons why you are unfit for motherhood. You may feel the need to put your house on the market or start renovations. You'll wonder how you will be able to afford all the things a child needs. You may have dreams of giving birth to a gorilla. You worry that your pain threshold is too low. You will dread the embarrassing thought that you might lose control of your bladder or bowels during delivery.

■ **When you are pregnant** *life seems to fly past at hundreds of miles an hour. It can be difficult to feel in control of your life.*

Feelings of paranoia regarding the birth are not completely irrational. They are simply exaggerated thoughts about the real challenges facing you.

To cope and regain a sense of control, you may find it useful to talk with other mothers. Turning to the sisterhood of mothers – who you will learn to rely on hereon for wisdom and advice – is another one of those great benefits of your new status. It's also best to have a sense of humour with yourself. Please understand: pregnancy can make you behave oddly, especially as your hormones are fluctuating at high levels.

■ **Get the "inside story"** *by talking with women who have experienced the joys of motherhood.*

If you discover that you are pregnant, and this was not planned, you may also feel that life is treating you unfairly. Hopefully this pregnancy is not a disaster for you, and you can embrace the surprise of it in due time. This is a time for talking things through with your partner and with others who you feel will be helpful and not judgmental.

The expectant father

You may find yourself creating a romantic situation for sharing the wonderful news of your pregnancy with your husband or partner. One woman I know put the dipstick from her home pregnancy test into a baby bottle and set it on her husband's dinner table place setting. Such a metaphor would simply have gone right over my husband's head. He would have thought the bottle was some sort of fertility voodoo I read about on the Internet. Being unable to predict a man's first response is why I think we all feel a bit queasy with the prospect of breaking the news. Most men I know take the news cautiously at first. But hats off to the one who goes all out and buys you a huge bouquet of roses.

> ### Trivia...
> Some prospective fathers get into the pregnancy spirit so completely that they even experience morning sickness!

His emotional adjustments

If the roses don't arrive, or even if they do, remember that you are not the only one who has just crossed one of life's greatest thresholds. Besides helping to conceive, men also go through a series of emotional adjustments with the passage into fatherhood. Traditionally, this was a time in a man's life when he was thought to become a background fixture, hovering at the fringes of all the celebration with his role culminating in the job of passing out cigars at the end of 9 months. But these days, when men are taking on an active role in birth and parenting, it is important to be sensitive to the man's experience and feelings.

■ **Is this what you hope for** *when you tell your partner that you are carrying his child? Let the news sink in first . . . .*

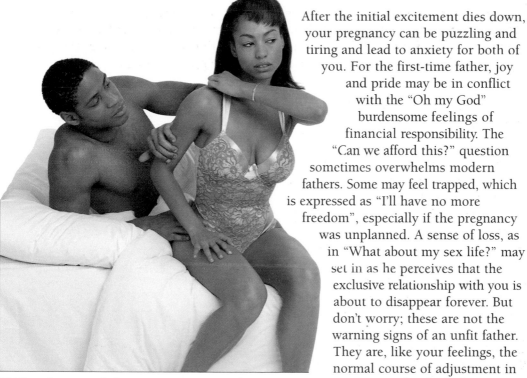

After the initial excitement dies down, your pregnancy can be puzzling and tiring and lead to anxiety for both of you. For the first-time father, joy and pride may be in conflict with the "Oh my God" burdensome feelings of financial responsibility. The "Can we afford this?" question sometimes overwhelms modern fathers. Some may feel trapped, which is expressed as "I'll have no more freedom", especially if the pregnancy was unplanned. A sense of loss, as in "What about my sex life?" may set in as he perceives that the exclusive relationship with you is about to disappear forever. But don't worry; these are not the warning signs of an unfit father. They are, like your feelings, the normal course of adjustment in preparation for the baby. Some say that's why Mother Nature gave us 9 months to gestate.

■ **Three's a crowd:** *It seems quite common for men to fear that the sexual intimacy they have with their partners will disappear once the baby is born.*

Single mothering

When the news of pregnancy breaks, some of us have a partner and some of us don't. Women on their own having babies do not fit into any one category. You may have made the choice to be a single mother, or circumstances may have put you into this position. Certainly you can successfully raise a happy, healthy child alone, but you do have more issues to face.

If you are a woman alone it is especially important that you seek out counselling from people who understand and share your situation and who may be able to put you in touch with other sources of help. Such organizations and people can help you cope with all the practical difficulties that can come up as well as with the emotional issues.

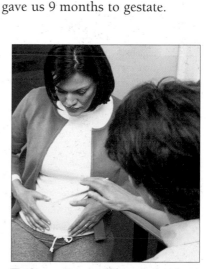

■ **If you are** *a single mother-to-be with no family living nearby, talk to a counsellor about your options.*

Should I keep my pregnancy a secret?

The news of pregnancy provides you with a splendid opportunity to catch up by telephone or e-mail with all your long-lost relatives and friends. Traditionally, people thought that a woman should not announce her pregnancy until the danger of miscarriage had passed, usually 3 months. If neither you nor a close friend or relative has ever experienced a miscarriage, the possibility of having one won't necessarily cross your mind. And some people just can't keep a secret. For others the decision to keep the pregnancy a secret from most friends and family for a time is a simple one.

About 10 to 20 per cent of all pregnancies end in miscarriage within the first 12 weeks.

A difficult phone call

With my first pregnancy, I did not hesitate to tell people from the moment I knew. I did the same with my second pregnancy, which unfortunately ended in a miscarriage at 8 weeks. For some weeks afterward, I received many very uncomfortable phone calls from unsuspecting well-wishers. This put us all in awkward positions. Basically, when to tell and whom to tell is your call and depends entirely on your comfort level. There simply is no one right time to break the news.

■ **If you choose** *to tell your friends and family straight away that you and your partner are expecting a baby, bear in mind that one of you might also have to share the sad news of a miscarriage – or risk being inundated with well-wishers for weeks to come.*

Dealing with unsolicited advice

As you will soon learn, complete strangers and even some of your kin will have no qualms about touching your belly without even asking your permission. These may be the same people who will serve up advice about your pregnancy, convinced that there is no way you could do it right on your own. Pregnancy seems to signal open season on your body and mind, as though you were merely a vessel for the continuation of the human species. So be forewarned. When you just can't take it any more, remember that it is your body and your baby. You are completely entitled to just politely step away.

A simple summary

✓ Your entire reproductive process is regulated by an ensemble of hormones or, simply, chemicals in the bloodstream and in the brain working together to ultimately release and nurture a healthy egg.

✓ The egg has just a few hours to make its rendezvous with a lucky sperm. It then takes several days for the fertilized egg to travel to the uterus, where it implants itself in the uterine wall. At this point, the human pregnancy hormone HCG is released to help keep the uterine wall well nourished for the growing embryo.

✓ The signs of pregnancy may include any of the following: a missed period, feeling of nausea, frequent need to pee, sore breasts, fatigue, and mood swings.

✓ To confirm your pregnancy you may choose to take a home test, which is generally easy to use and relies on the detection of high levels of the hormone HCG in urine. You may also make an appointment with your doctor or midwife who can administer a more sensitive blood test and ultimately confirm the pregnancy through an internal exam and ultrasound scan.

✓ With your pregnancy confirmed, it's time to celebrate. Choosing when to tell friends and family is really your choice. Remember, this is a very emotional time for both you and your partner.

Chapter 2

Your Childbirth Choices

APART FROM YOUR DECISION of whom to marry, the childbirth choices you make during pregnancy may be some of the most important decisions of your adult life. Today, childbirth is typically controlled by doctors and midwives, but we have more birth choices than ever before. There are many safe alternatives to consider when we choose our antenatal care and childbirth facilities. There is no decree that you must have a doctor and deliver your baby in a hospital. In this chapter, we will explore the options so you can make an informed choice.

In this chapter...

✔ Working out a birth plan

✔ Doctor or midwife?

✔ What is a midwife?

✔ Should I continue with my own doctor?

✔ Choosing where to give birth

Working out a birth plan

BIRTH IS AN INTIMIDATING *prospect for many of us, especially first timers. You may think, "There's so much to think about and do at this early stage of pregnancy. I'm just getting used to the idea of being pregnant; now you expect me to make a decision based on my feelings and beliefs about childbirth."*

Yes. It's important to work out as many of the details as early as possible because some doctors may be unwilling or unable to attend to you should you not choose a hospital birth. You'll want to make the decision of place of birth from the outset so that you don't have to change doctors or midwives midway through your pregnancy.

It's up to you

You are the best one to decide what kind of birth you want. That is not to say that the birth of your baby will actually follow your plan. Birth is full of surprises and no one can predict how it will proceed. The only thing we can be reasonably certain about is that in the majority of cases, a baby will enter your life. In general, the better you plan, the more likely you are to have the birth style of your choice.

Keep it simple

Keep the decisions simple now. Your birth plan can evolve over the next 9 months as you become more familiar with the nuances of birth, take classes, read books, and talk with other mothers. At this early stage, just try to come to some decision about where you would like to give birth, who you would like to be present, and how you feel you would like the birth to proceed.

■ **Writing it down:** *Start making notes about your birth plan as soon as possible. Think about all aspects of the big day.*

Your preliminary birth plan begins with choice of birthplace and choice of attendant. As you flesh out the plan, you may add a list of spectators, whether you want pain relief, consideration of a water birth, and thoughts about breastfeeding.

Doctor or midwife?

DURING YOUR 9 MONTHS *of pregnancy, regular monthly and later weekly check-ups are going to be a fact of life. Since you will be spending so much time with the person who directs your antenatal care and birth, it may be wise to sit down and think about what kind of antenatal care and which birth setting would make you most comfortable.*

Do be aware that you do not have to limit your delivery choice to your local hospital. Some GPs and midwives will attend births at private homes. You could even choose to give birth at a private birthing centre (although there are very few of these currently in the UK – ask your doctor or midwife if he or she knows of one).

A matter of style

It is a fact that most women feel safer when birth is medically supervised. Most women want a combination of high technology and personal care in which their opinions are considered and their decisions respected. Many of us, especially if we are pregnant for the first time, are convinced that being cared for by a specialist obstetrician in a hospital setting is our safest choice. We want to be certain that high-tech intervention and follow-through are available to deal with any complications or emergencies that may arise during birth. Through our fear of the unknown, we are also convinced that there is

no way we can survive the pain of childbirth without analgesia. So for us, a medical doctor and hospital birth seem on face value to be the right choice. And, in fact, a hospital birth is never wrong; it may just not suit your style and may not be necessary.

If you are decidedly braver than average or have successfully mastered at least one previous hospital birth, the romance of a home birth or alternative non-hospital birth may seem seductive.

■ **You might find it valuable** *to sit down with your partner and your doctor to discuss your antenatal and birthing options.*

What is a midwife?

NO ONE SAYS A DOCTOR has to deliver your baby. In fact, in the UK, the primary attendant at most births is a **registered midwife**. Historically, women having babies were attended by other women and most midwives are women, so for many women, midwife care is a natural choice. Women turn to midwives to provide nurturing, woman-centred care. Midwife care has been shown to produce excellent birth outcomes, generally with lower rates of intervention than births attended by doctors.

The assumption behind midwife care is that pregnancy and childbirth are normal life events, not pathologies. A midwife's duties can include monitoring the physical, psychological, and social well-being of the mother throughout childbearing; providing the mother with individualized education, counselling, and antenatal care; giving continuous hands-on assistance during labour and delivery; and offering support after the birth.

■ **The role of a midwife** in childbirth is long established, mentioned in the Bible books Genesis and Exodus. Midwives were also well-respected members of ancient Greek and Roman societies.

What it means

Most midwives practise within traditional medical practices and hospitals, but some now attend births at private hospitals, homes, and private birth centres. If working on her own, a responsible midwife will limit her practice to managing the maternity care of women whose progress through pregnancy, labour, and delivery promises to be normal and without complications.

Must a doctor also be present?

Midwives are trained to recognize any signs of trouble and will refer you to a specialist if you require special care. This means that a doctor need not be on site, but that one must be available as a back-up during birth in case there are any complications.

QUESTIONS FOR YOUR MIDWIFE

Here is a list of some of the most pertinent questions you should consider asking your midwife:

1. How soon do I need to decide between a home and a hospital birth?

2. If I choose a home or alternative birth, how do I arrange it?

3. If I opt for a hospital birth, how long must I stay in after delivery?

4. Is there any way of ensuring that I will see the same midwife throughout the whole of my pregnancy?

5. If I feel perfectly well, do I still need antenatal care?

6. Where do I get antenatal care?

7. When choosing antenatal care, what should I think about first?

8. Will my GP be able to attend the birth?

9. How soon do I need to inform the hospital of my wishes for attendees?

Working in the home

As I have already mentioned, some midwives are happy to attend births at private homes. Should you choose a home birth with a midwife, be aware that it may not work out exactly the way you have planned. Most midwives have plans for transporting you

to a hospital if any complications arise. A further option offered by some midwives is known as the Domino system. This involves a short stay in hospital for the birth, but you return home about 6 hours later if all is well. The midwife who has been tending to your antenatal care will then continue to visit you at home for the next 10 days or so.

■ **If home comforts** *are important to you, and you would rather be in a less clinical environment than a hospital, perhaps a home birth is for you.*

Should I continue with my own doctor?

A GENERAL PRACTITIONER *(GP) who cares for the medical needs of the whole family does have training in obstetrics. But family practitioners, because they care for such a wide range of patients and medical situations, do not have the specialized training of an* **obstetrician**. *You may choose your family doctor as your primary caretaker during pregnancy and to deliver your child if you want a home birth, but if you develop complications, your family doctor will refer you to an obstetrician.*

All doctors have the same basic training, and this includes some obstetrics and gynaecology. However, a GP will usually have had postgraduate experience and may have attained a diploma. A hospital doctor specializing in obstetrics and gynaecology will be a MRCOG and may eventually become a FRCOG.

Don't automatically assume that your family doctor is the right person to deliver your baby.

Assess your needs

Your needs from a doctor are different now from what they were before you were pregnant, and there is nothing wrong with shopping around. However, most NHS and private gynaecologists also practice obstetrics. Ask your family doctor for recommendations, but don't stop there.

When you first discover you are pregnant, your GP will probably refer you to a hospital. This is a good time to discuss with your GP the philosophies of specific consultants, if your GP knows them. You may also have a choice of hospitals available to you, depending on where you live. If you decide to give birth in a private hospital or birthing centre, follow referrals from other mothers. You may find that some doctor's names come up over and over. Narrow the list down to two or three. Credentials and specific skills being equal, there is nothing wrong with choosing the winner of a popularity contest.

Comparing notes

It's important that you and your doctor or midwife share the same expectations for your pregnancy and birthing experience. First make a list of what's important to you about the birth. Even if this is your first pregnancy and you don't know much about childbirth, you can ask questions and seek further information. Don't be afraid to ask questions about the labour and birth during your antenatal visits. Quiz your midwife on labour management, pain management, natural childbirth, and so forth. Sitting across a desk having an open discussion will give you ample information to make an informed decision about whether or not you are making the right birth choices for you.

■ **An excellent source** *of advice is other mothers. Now is the time to plug into this network and start building a list of your birthing requirements.*

Choosing where to give birth

JUST AS IT IS NOWHERE written that a doctor or midwife must deliver your baby, so too, it is not preordained that you must give birth in a hospital. In the minds of some women, hospitals are for sick people, and certainly pregnancy is not an illness. Some women choose a home or alternative birth after at least one experience in the hospital. They are generally looking for a more satisfying and relaxed environment, especially if their first experience of birth was normal and without complications. While many doctors still recommend hospital births, ultimately you have the freedom to choose. And if you do opt to deliver in a hospital, don't feel that all options are dictated. You will still have some degree of choice in the matter.

Hospital

In the old days women gave birth at home. Today, of course, modern hospitals are safe and secure places to give birth. For the vast majority of us, they are the place of choice, and we never have any second thoughts on the subject. Even before we find out that we are pregnant, we have probably made up our minds that a delivery without pain relief is inconceivable. We want to be sure that wherever we give birth, we have access to medication and a doctor. For us, a hospital birth is the only option.

Atmosphere and attitude are the basic requirements you should evaluate when trying to choose a birthplace.

The vast majority of births in the UK now take place in hospital. Indeed, if you are having your first child it is likely that your doctor will recommend a hospital birth so that expertise is at hand if needed. Hospitals today are certainly more accommodating and labour-friendly than they were in the past. Gone are the days when a mother was wheeled into a cold operating room to labour on her own and give birth while her partner paced in the waiting room.

For some women, all antenatal visits are at the hospital, as is the birth. But another common option these days is "shared care". Here, most of your antenatal procedures are carried out by your GP, with only a couple of visits to the hospital needed. The birth itself takes place at the hospital.

INTERNET

www.privatehealth.co.uk
/hosptls.htm

If you are interested in private care, you can find out where your local private hospital is by entering your town and postcode at this web page.

What to expect in a hospital

Most maternity wards feature pleasing decor with family-friendly labour rooms. Some even offer birthing pools, birthing chairs, and other "tools" to help make birth more comfortable for you. This is all to complement the high-tech medical assistance that is nearby should you or the baby experience any complications or require a surgical delivery. But decor and attractive surroundings do not in themselves make a good birth experience; people do. So don't be oversold on appearance. If you are unsure about a hospital birth, meet the maternity ward staff and check with your grapevine of mothers before you make any decisions.

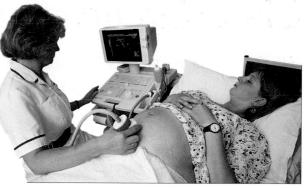

■ **If you find that** *you have no say in what hospital you give birth at, take comfort in the knowledge that they all have more or less the same facilities anyway.*

Making an informed choice when choosing where to give birth also requires that you evaluate a maternity department's policies surrounding labour and delivery and its options and routines for newborn care. Some hospitals restrict your freedom to move about and the positions you will be allowed in when giving birth. There may also be other hospital or departmental rules regarding visitors, food, music, fetal monitoring, and the baby's siblings. It's up to you to investigate what the regulations are in your hospital.

Specialist birthing facilities

Hospitals and **birth centres** both share the goal of safe and satisfying birth experiences, but their basic philosophies and environments achieve that goal in very different ways. Birth centres are created to care for families having normal, healthy birth experiences. By design, birth centres are very health conscious, and people who would prefer a natural birth might find hospitals too intervening.

> **DEFINITION**
>
> A **birth centre** is a privately run, out-of-hospital birthing facility. These are best used only if you are expecting no complications during delivery. There are, however, very few birth centres in the UK.

Another birthing facility option is a GP unit, although these are quite rare and most often found in rural areas. In a GP unit, a midwife will take care of you, and she will work directly with the GP. There tends to be less intervention than in a hospital, but you will not be able to request complex procedures, such as an epidural. Again, these facilities are designed for use only where a normal delivery is expected. Should any complications seem likely you will be transferred to a hospital.

If your pregnancy is classed as high risk, take your doctor's advice and have a hospital birth. Get a second opinion if you like, but don't dismiss the advice.

Do not stubbornly insist on a non-traditional birth setting if medical opinion is that it would put you or your baby at risk.

Alternative birthing facilities have the advantage of offering a lot of privacy and quiet for labour and delivery as well as personalized antenatal care. They also differ from hospitals in that their programme of care is based on the minimum of intervention unless medically necessary. In the US and some European countries, birth centres are becoming increasingly common. In the UK, there are still very few alternative birthing facilities available. But who knows what the future holds?

If you are thinking of a VBAC (vaginal birth after caesarean) you can still be a candidate for an out-of-hospital birth, as long as there are no other potential complications.

Any non-hospital birthing facility should have back-up systems, including transfers to the hospital, to deal with any problems you may encounter during labour and delivery. You might be interested to hear that about 12 to 14 per cent of the women who labour at birth centres in the US require hospital attention, though most are not emergencies. Only about 2 per cent go to the hospital as unforeseen emergencies. Thus women and babies are not put at risk if they require care above and beyond what an alternative centre can provide.

Of course, every deviation from the safety of hospital birth does entail some risk. Emergency transfer to a hospital, even if it's just across the road, does take some minutes, and just a few minutes of fetal oxygen deprivation can be enough to cause brain damage.

An alternative birthing centre is staffed mostly by midwives, and sometimes a doctor, and is off-site from a hospital, though it could be right across the road from one!

Home births

Since birth is a family affair, some people opt to give birth in what is the centre of family life, the home. In the UK, home births account for fewer than 1 per cent of all births. In Europe, home birthing rates are considerably higher, especially in the Scandinavian countries.

Women choosing a home birth are looking for a calm, peaceful environment that supports their own creative and unique ways of birthing their babies. A home birth is by nature focused on the family. At home, your children can assist with the birth and your partner can play the guitar if that's what you want – it's up to you! And you can deliver your baby squatting on the floor, in the bath, or in any way that you want to get your baby out. Many women have an innate feeling that birth is a natural, normal process, so for them a home birth is a very personal and spiritual decision.

The dominant issues of atmosphere, participation, empowerment, and control top the list for women choosing home births. Not surprisingly, few women who choose home births feel it is important for a doctor to be present, but most choose to have a midwife on hand, and there are still a few doctors who will attend home births. If you opt for a home birth, make sure that procedures are in place so that a hospital can be accessed quickly if necessary.

■ **A hospital** *may not be too keen to accommodate your partner's musical skills – even if they would help you relax!*

A simple summary

✓ You have a number of choices as to who will manage your antenatal care and help you deliver your baby.

✓ Discuss your hospital's policies on labour, birth, and postnatal care with your doctor or midwife – they vary from place to place.

✓ You are perfectly within your rights to request a midwife for all of your routine maternity care, instead of a doctor.

✓ You may choose to have your baby in a hospital, an alternative birthing facility, or at home.

✓ Your choice of birth place is generally a matter of personal preference and style, limited only by high-risk factors that might restrict you to a hospital.

Chapter 3

Am I Too Old for This?

Y OU'RE OVER 35 and pregnant. You are thrilled and excited but also aware that your biological clock is ticking away, forcing you to grapple with the reality that it's now or never. Maybe conceiving was easy for you, but for the vast majority of women in their late 30s and early 40s, fertility is an issue. The unfortunate truth is that as we reach our mid-30s our reproductive system slows down, and many in the medical community consider women over 35 to be at "high risk" for pregnancy complications. The best thing to do is to create a stress-free climate of confidence, take care of yourself, follow your doctor's or midwife's advice, and find support among other mothers your age. Relax and enjoy the prospect of motherhood. Don't worry about the things that you can't control.

In this chapter...

✓ Pregnancy after 35: facts and fictions

✓ Common age-related conditions

✓ Age, fertility, and conception

✓ Balancing the pros and cons

THERE ARE POSITIVE POINTS ABOUT LATER PREGNANCIES, TOO

Pregnancy after 35: facts and fictions

INCREASINGLY, WOMEN ARE *choosing to have babies into their mid-to late 30s or beyond. Many of us feel that we are better educated and more ready emotionally and financially to raise a child than we were in our 20s. At this point of our lives, we probably have a stable relationship and home life. We've done our globetrotting and spent some time in the fast lane, so to speak. Social science studies suggest that you will raise a child more likely to do well in school and be a professional. Not that you couldn't do a good job when you were younger, but the likelihood of "successful" child rearing gets higher with age. It's not unusual at this time to start planning a family in your late 30s or even in your 40s. You are part of a growing trend. You have lots of company.*

It's a good time

There has never been a better time in human history to become pregnant after the age of 35. Today's older mothers have a lot of advantages over older mothers of a generation ago. The science of fertility has improved so dramatically in the last few years that there is a good chance for conceiving and carrying a baby to term even at the age of 48. Through tests, drugs, and interventions, medical science can today screen for birth defects and control other complications such as preterm labour. As the frequency of older women bearing children has zoomed, so too have knowledge, experience, and advances in reducing reproductive risks after 35.

Despite what the medical textbooks write, age by itself is not necessarily a determinant of high risk. The medical community has made great strides to improve the odds of your having a healthy baby. Add to this the steps you take to boost the odds. Exercise, diet, and good prenatal care can take years off your scientific-based pregnancy profile, giving you the chance of delivering a healthy baby right up there with a much younger woman.

■ **Over 35?** *Don't let them convince you that you're too old! You have a great chance of a successful birth.*

Common age-related conditions

THERE'S NO BETTER WAY to traumatize and terrify a pregnant woman than to talk about all the things that might go wrong. With all the benefits of medicine and high-tech diagnostic instruments, comes a lot of angst for those of us on the receiving end. In the past, it was believed there were too many complications for women to risk becoming pregnant after age 35.

Today, thanks to early recognition and management of higher-risk pregnancies, better prenatal care, improvements in obstetrical procedures, and the general trend of women taking better care of themselves, many of the problems associated with pregnancy for this age group have been reduced. In most cases, a normal pregnancy and baby can be expected.

It's not just age

Recent studies have shown that maternal age alone is not a definitive risk factor. So if you're not prepared for all the worry associated with knowing too much about what might go wrong, then be my guest and skip this section. But for those of you who must be well informed on how age might affect your pregnancy, then please, read on.

■ **Keeping fit** *is important even if you are not pregnant. Indeed, a good health regimen will increase your chances of a trouble-free pregnancy later.*

Putting yourself under unnecessary stress can endanger your baby.

Don't obsess about possible problems. Constant preoccupation and worry cannot reverse any potential problem, but the stress of the worry can interfere with hormone release and can raise your blood pressure.

Keeping up with your doctor's or midwife's advised prenatal testing can maximize your odds of having a normal pregnancy and baby.

Age, fertility, and conception

THERE ARE PHYSICAL CHANGES *that speed up as we start heading into our late 30s. One clear fact is that there are fewer viable and healthy eggs. We are born with our lifetime supply of eggs. By middle age the numbers have dwindled, and time has taken its toll on the remainder. In fact, it may not be our inability to conceive at an older age that causes fertility problems, but rather the odds of a fertilized egg's surviving implantation. So while you may be conceiving frequently, there may be a hormonal imbalance or other physical problems preventing your body from sustaining the embryo. Also, the "old" eggs themselves are thought to be increasingly less able to survive after fertilization.*

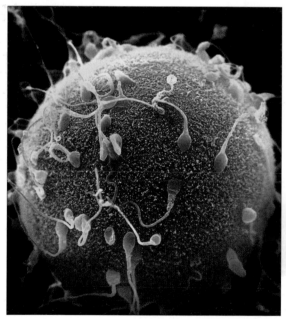

■ **The fertilization** *of the egg – usually by a single sperm despite many others' attempts – marks the beginning of pregnancy, and the egg subsequently implants itself in the uterus wall. But it seems that as you get older, you have fewer eggs that are healthy enough to survive fertilization or implantation.*

Difficulty with conception is probably the most common age-related problem for women over 35. As we age, our stock of healthy eggs diminishes, and our hormones to support pregnancy and fertility also start to fail us. As mentioned in Chapter 1, in order for an egg to have a chance to develop, implant, and mature, our hormones must be released in a well-orchestrated manner. It is not uncommon for older women to have a problem with progesterone production in the latter phase of the menstrual cycle.

Some doctors prescribe a natural version of progesterone, available in cream and pill forms, in order to maintain healthy progesterone levels for optimal ovulation and implantation.

Age and chromosomes

Chromosomal disorders are probably the most common issue in pregnancies for women over the age of 35. Some chromosomal problems are inherited, but most are caused by an error that occurs at the union of sperm and egg. Extra, missing, or incomplete *chromosomes* usually cause serious health problems for the baby and account for many of the incidences of miscarriage. The risk of having a child with a chromosomal disorder is always present and it rises with the age of the mother. If you are 35, the chances of bearing a child with a chromosomal disorder is about 1 in 200. But the risk really does jump after the age of 40. For a 40-year-old woman, the chance is about 1 in 60. However, if you pass at least two normal diagnostic ultrasounds, your risk is reduced to about 1 in 80. The good news is that the statistical chance is 79 in 80 that your baby won't have a chromosome disorder.

Age and Down's syndrome

Although **Down's syndrome** was first identified 130 years ago, the last 20 to 30 years have brought remarkable progress in understanding the genetic basis and risk factors for this condition.

> **DEFINITION**
>
> **Chromosomes** *carry our genes and are the basic units of heredity. Chromosomes determine physical features such as eye and hair colour. Each cell in our body carries 46 chromosomes arranged in 23 pairs. There are two exceptions to this rule – egg cells and sperm cells have 23 chromosomes each instead of 46. When the nucleus of an egg fuses with the nucleus of a sperm, the newly fertilized cell contains 46 chromosomes, like every other human cell.*
>
> *But sometimes things go wrong. In the case of Down's syndrome, there is an extra copy of chromosome number 21. This is called trisomy 21.*

> **DEFINITION**
>
> **Down's syndrome** *is a chromosomal disorder characterized by various degrees of mental retardation. Down's syndrome babies often have loose muscle tone and other physical and mental problems.*

Recently, chromosome 21, the one responsible for Down's syndrome, was decoded by a team of Japanese and German scientists. Identifying this chromosome and understanding when and where it operates could lay the basis for devising gene therapy for the syndrome in the future.

Down's syndrome is one of the most common effects of a chromosomal defect. But in eight out of ten cases, Down's babies are born to younger women with no risk factors, not to older women. Probably this occurs because women under the age of 35 do not routinely undergo prenatal screening tests and therefore unknowingly carry through Down's pregnancies. But only 10 per cent of children diagnosed with a risk of Down's syndrome are severely handicapped. Some can learn to read and write, are extremely loving, and can become self-reliant. So if you do receive news that you are carrying a baby with Down's syndrome, there is no reason why you cannot choose to continue the pregnancy, though many choose not to.

Expectant parents should do the research and discuss their options with professionals and parents of Down's syndrome children. Older women often elect to terminate the pregnancy if an abnormality is discovered. Although researchers are experimenting with ways to test a woman's likelihood of suffering an improper chromosome division, there is currently no test for Down's syndrome risk prior to conception. The medical community still relies on maternal age as one of the indicators for the risk of carrying a Down's syndrome baby.

Today, parents and physicians are also better able to identify the risk of having a child with Down's syndrome earlier in pregnancy. Improved prenatal diagnostic tests such as amniocentesis and chorionic villi sampling procedures provide highly accurate identification of Down's syndrome-related genetic abnormalities. There is also a non-diagnostic blood test available; see p. 138 for full details of this triple screen test.

INTERNET

www.43green.freeserve.
co.uk/uk_downs_
syndrome/ukdsinfo.html

A great resource for parents of Down's syndrome children.

If you are especially concerned about your risks of carrying a child with birth defects, you might consider seeking genetic counselling before you become pregnant. A genetic counsellor can give you a realistic perspective about your risks and options and may calm your fears. It's your decision whether or not to have genetic counselling. Some find it reassuring. Others would rather not know. If there is a history of birth defects in your family, it may be a good idea. Chapter 9, Prenatal Testing, will give you further information on testing for genetic disorders and birth defects and on genetic screening and counselling.

WEIGHING YOUR RISKS WITH AGE

MOTHER'S AGE	RISK OF DOWN'S SYNDROME	RISK OF ANY CHROMOSOMAL DISORDER
20	1 in 1,667	1 in 526
25	1 in 1250	1 in 476
30	1 in 952	1 in 385
35	1 in 378	1 in 192
40	1 in 106	1 in 66
41	1 in 82	1 in 53
42	1 in 63	1 in 42
43	1 in 49	1 in 33
44	1 in 38	1 in 26
45	1 in 30	1 in 21

Age and miscarriage

While the chance of miscarriage is higher in women over the age of 35, it is a common complication of all pregnancies, no matter what the age. Between 10 and 20 per cent of pregnancies end in miscarriage within the first 6 to 12 weeks following conception. It is thought that a large percentage of early miscarriages are due to defective embryos with abnormalities that would not allow them to survive after birth. Sometimes there is no development beyond the early division when sperm meets egg. As we reach middle age, a higher percentage of conceptions ends in miscarriage. For women in their 40s, the miscarriage rate is believed to be 50 per cent, most of which are not detected. Miscarriages are nature's way of selecting out unhealthy offspring. Late miscarriages, after 12 weeks, are three times as rare as early ones, and are also more likely to occur in older women. There are many possible reasons, such as an incompetent cervix or failed placenta.

Unlike women, who are born with their full complement of eggs, men continually produce fresh sperm throughout their reproductive lives. Therefore, while we can speak of "old" eggs, we must rethink our terminology and refer to "the sperm of older men" when discussing the contribution of age to miscarriage.

It is not certain just what is the exact cause of the increase in miscarriages in older women. There is speculation that a women's ability to nurture an egg is compromised as she gets older. In the medical community, it is also thought that as men age the sperm contribute to an increased risk of fetal loss.

Age and other risks

Other risks depend on your health. Some studies indicate that older women are at an increased risk for fetal growth problems, preterm labour, high blood pressure, pre-eclampsia (high blood pressure combined with excessive fluid retention and/or protein in the urine), and diabetes. These complications may not stem from age alone but may be a result of conditions unrelated to pregnancy but more common with age, such as weight problems and cardiovascular disease. If you are in good health, your risks appear to be not much higher than those of a younger woman. Your doctor will still be watching you a little more closely for problems, but you will have normal care unless some complication shows up during a routine visit.

■ **Regular routine checkups** *with your doctor or midwife will help to bring any unforeseen complications to light.*

Balancing the pros and cons

IF YOU TEND TO FOCUS *on the risks of pregnancy, trust me, it doesn't matter if you are 21 rather than 40. There are always risks, no age barred.*

If you've made up your mind to start a family and you have successfully conceived, your best bet is to stay informed, take care of yourself, and be positive. Looking for something to go wrong is the job you entrusted to your doctor or midwife. Your job is to think positively. Nobody can predict any pregnancy's outcome. These days, with all the advances in maternal science and medical discoveries, the chances are great that you will give birth to a healthy baby in 9 months.

It's not all bad!

The positive side of a pregnancy at this stage of your life is that you are likely to be wiser and more mature and to have greater patience. You are probably better focused and already accomplished in your career and ready for "the next phase." And with your financial stability (and perhaps job flexibility), you may be able to enjoy being a full-time or at least part-time "at home" parent. On the flip side, the naysayers may argue

PREPARING FOR A HEALTHY BABY AFTER 35

If you are over age 35, there are several points that you would do well to consider in advance of your pregnancy – and during, too. These points include:

1 **Ask yourself** *some important questions, like: "Am I emotionally and physically strong enough to handle raising a child?"*

2 **Plan ahead financially** *or you may face the expense of raising a child in your retirement years.*

3 **Remember:** *Babies bring change and demand lifestyle adjustments. Be realistic about how a baby is going to fit into your current lifestyle, and be honest with yourself about how flexible you can be.*

4 **Exercise and eat right:** *Good nutrition is essential for a healthy pregnancy and baby. Stop smoking, eat healthfully, take in folic acid, and avoid alcohol – this is all good advice whatever your age.*

5 **Be aware of age discrimination:** *Some people may not be very accepting of women over 40 having children, but may accept older men having children. Be prepared for these reactions with a straightforward – but non-defensive – response to make things easy on yourself.*

that you will have less energy than a younger woman. In sum, the pros and cons are not straightforward. What matters at any age is your ability to parent, and this simply comes down to you as an individual – your maturity, personality, and values.

Simply enjoy it

Now is the time to simply be excited about your pregnancy. You will find that you may be more tired than when you were 20, that you have more aches and pains, and there will be days you wonder why you did this. Parenting at 20, 40, or even later takes three basic things: nurturing, love, and a sense of humour. Overall, I would bet that you will be the mature, stable mother every child needs.

A simple summary

✓ As to whether a 45-year-old can have a healthy pregnancy, the answer is, "absolutely!" Much depends on the woman's medical and physical condition before pregnancy – a healthy, fit 45-year-old will likely do better than an unhealthy, overweight 20-year-old smoker.

✓ Of course, there are risks to both mother and baby as mother gets older. Foremost is the increase in genetic defects. As a woman and her eggs age, it is more likely that the eggs will be damaged.

✓ The risk of miscarriage is higher in older women. Early miscarriage is directly related to the increased chance of a chromosomal defect. Increased chance of late miscarriage is also age-related, though the causes are not well understood.

✓ Older women are more likely to have pre-existing medical problems, like diabetes and high blood pressure. Again, with good prenatal care, these conditions can be detected and treated without significant consequences to either mother or baby.

✓ With early, good prenatal care and commitment to a healthy lifestyle (no smoking, no alcohol, no illicit drugs, a well-balanced diet, and moderate exercise), you and your child will more than likely do fine.

Chapter 4

Oh My, I'm Pregnant Again!

S O YOU'RE PREGNANT AGAIN. But don't expect a repeat performance of your last pregnancy – chances are this one will be different. Or it might be a carbon copy. You simply can't predict! Furthermore, in the world of maternity, things change fast.... Let's have a look.

In this chapter...

✓ The second time around

✓ Can I have a vaginal delivery after a previous surgical birth?

✓ What's my risk of miscarriage this time?

✓ Do I need to go to childbirth classes again?

✓ Can our older children be present at the birth?

A SECOND PREGNANCY CAN BE A GREAT TIME FOR SHARING

The second time around

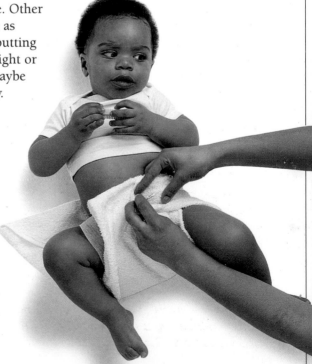

IT IS UNUSUAL THESE DAYS for families to choose to have more than three children. So instead of pregnancy being a frequent, commonplace occurrence in a woman's life, it has become a special thing. When your second pregnancy may well be your last, you will probably be paying as much attention to what is happening to your body this time as you did the very first time.

Certainly you've changed a lot since your first pregnancy. Now you know how to change a nappy. You know what it feels like to stay up all night with a sick child, and your body no longer resembles its svelte pre-first-pregnancy self. The mystery of childbearing is not so mysterious anymore, and you made it through labour and delivery one way or another. With all this experience and built-in confidence, the exciting news is that you will probably be more assertive and want to take more control of this pregnancy.

Is there an optimal spacing between pregnancies?

Some people argue that it is better to get all the nappies out of the way as soon as possible. Other people want to have as much quality time as possible with their previous child before putting a new baby into the picture. There is no right or wrong here. You are free to choose – or maybe you were surprised by this new pregnancy.

For those of you who follow up one pregnancy with another, you should understand there might be a little price to pay when it comes to your physical health. If in your last pregnancy you delivered via a caesarean section, many doctors recommend waiting at least a year for your body to recover before considering a subsequent pregnancy.

■ **If you are content** *to spend several years changing nappies, you may choose to have very little time between pregnancies.*

Jumping the gun is not wise; your body will suffer. In general, conceiving before you have had time to fully recover from your last pregnancy is not a great idea. Your body has gone through a lot during labour and delivery.

It's not that common for women to become pregnant in the first 3 months after delivery, especially if breastfeeding only – Mother Nature's own birth control – however it has been known to happen. Conceiving within this time may put you at a nutritional disadvantage because your body will not have had time to replenish its store of nutrients. If you are surprised by an early sudden pregnancy, just take it in stride. Your baby will probably be born perfectly healthy, and though you may be a bit worse for wear, you will ultimately bounce back in fine condition if you take good care of yourself. It's probably a good idea to consider weaning your baby as soon as possible if you find out you are pregnant again. Trying to sustain the nutritional demands of a pregnancy and breastfeeding can be a trying and probably losing battle.

For some couples the next child is a surprise; for others, deciding when to have the next child is simply a matter of preference. Though many people try to second-guess the perfect spacing between siblings, there does not seem to be any conclusive evidence that 2 years is better or worse than 4 or 5 years. Ultimately, good family dynamics are the result of confident parental leadership. The right sibling spacing is just a matter of timing and personal choice.

■ **If you are breastfeeding** *it is very unlikely that you will become pregnant again within the first 3 months.*

Should I have a big family?

You might think that the more childbearing experience you have under your belt the better – but that's not totally true. Women who have more than five children have for a long time been considered by the medical community to be putting themselves at higher risk for complications. But with today's advances in prenatal care and obstetrical science, not to mention the fact that women are taking better care of themselves during pregnancy, there is no reason that you cannot choose to have a large family.

Trivia...
In primitive societies, where women generally breastfeed for as long as 4 years, siblings are usually spread further apart than they are in western cultures.

According to some studies, there is a slight increased risk in the fifth or subsequent pregnancies for Down's syndrome, multiple birth, and other problems, so you may want to consider prenatal testing, especially if you are 35 or older.

In general, if you find yourself pregnant and already have a large family, you would be wise to get lots of help, teach older kids to pitch in, and not exhaust yourself. Also, you need to be extra vigilant about your diet and weight; your body needs extra special care with each pregnancy.

Rest more than you think you require.

Having other children makes it hard for pregnant women to set their priorities straight and take good care of themselves. Let some work and chores go. Have your partner pitch in.

■ **It is important** *that you get plenty of rest while pregnant. Your partner should willingly help out with chores – but if not, be sure to make it clear that you would like some assistance.*

Should I change doctors or consider having a home birth?

You have changed since your last pregnancy. You are no longer an anxious, inexperienced woman waiting to hear the instructions of a medical authority. You have more of a sense of yourself, and you want to play a greater role in decisions about your prenatal care and childbirth procedures. This time around you may wish to consider a home birth. You may want to fully understand the pros and cons of episiotomy, epidural anaesthesia, and fetal monitoring before you make the decisions – not like last time, when you probably just went along with your doctor's or midwife's recommendation. Some women who had a perfectly smooth delivery but found the inflexible style of their doctor or hospital birth unsatisfying elect to have an alternative birth with their subsequent pregnancy.

But beware of becoming too smug. Just because you had a picture-perfect labour and delivery the first time around, it might be foolish to count on hitting the jackpot again. Just as one complicated pregnancy doesn't guarantee another, practice in childbearing does not guarantee anything except, perhaps, wisdom. No pregnancy or birth is exactly the same. Having said this, now that you have one sort of experience under your belt, you should feel free to explore your options. Consider writing a birth plan about how you would like this experience to differ from your last, and feel free to share it with your health care practitioner.

If you didn't breastfeed your first baby, this is a great opportunity to try something new. Breastfeeding is good for you and your baby, and making this innovation is comparable to changing birthing methods.

Why do I keep gaining weight with each pregnancy?

Your body undergoes additional changes with each subsequent pregnancy. There is a tendency to add a few more pounds with each baby, but this weight doesn't have to be a permanent fixture in your life if you watch your weight and eat healthy foods. Stay away from nutritional losers such as sugars and fats, and you should be able to stay healthy and not retain the added weight once the baby is born. Pregnant women with other children tend to be too busy to take care of themselves, taking meals on the run and generally wearing themselves down with family matters. You should be sure to make time to relax and give yourself some needed rest breaks. You will also need to allow time to exercise to keep in shape. Brisk family walks with your other children could prove to be an excellent exercise routine for all of you and a chance for togetherness at the same time. This should help keep the unnecessary weight at bay and allay your guilt about occasionally having a break from your other youngsters while you take a nap.

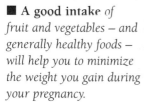

■ **A good intake** *of fruit and vegetables – and generally healthy foods – will help you to minimize the weight you gain during your pregnancy.*

MATTERS OF WEIGHT

The average weight gain during pregnancy is 10 to 15 kilograms (25 to 35 pounds). Of course, check with your doctor or midwife to find out what your appropriate weight gain really is, especially if you are starting out over- or underweight. Here's what all those extra pounds should roughly add up to:

1. Baby: 3.4 kg (7½ lb)
2. Amniotic fluid: 900 g (2 lb)
3. Placenta: 700 g (1½ lb)
4. Fluid and blood: 3.6 kg (8 lb)
5. Breast growth: 900 g (2 lb)
6. Uterus: 900 g (2 lb)
7. Body fat/nutrient stores: 3.2 kg (7 lb)

Total: 13.6 kg (30 lb)

Can I have a vaginal delivery after a previous surgical birth?

ONCE A CAESAREAN, *always a caesarean is no longer the obstetrical mantra. Most women who have had a previous caesarean birth can now choose to deliver vaginally, sometimes known as a "VBAC" – vaginal birth after caesarean.*

The old rule was based on the medical community's fear that a previously operated-on uterus couldn't withstand the stress of contractions and might rupture during labour. If this were to happen, both mother and baby could die. But that was in the days when they made a vertical incision, from the belly button down. Today, the incision is usually made horizontally, in the lower part of the uterus. The "bikini cut" is considered unlikely to rupture, especially if the woman has waited at least a year before conceiving again.

You can improve your chances of having a vaginal delivery by:

1. Making sure you have a supportive doctor or midwife

2. Checking out hospital policy

3 Educating yourself about your options

4 Employing a labour assistant, such as a doula

Research has shown that up to 80 per cent of women who have had caesareans in the past can go on to have successful vaginal births. This is true even for women who have had more than one caesarean, unless the incision was a vertical one.

If you have had a caesarean due to a complication not likely to repeat itself, such as fetal distress, the chances are good that your doctor or midwife will encourage you to go for a vaginal delivery this time.

But if you have a chronic condition such as high blood pressure or an uncorrectable problem such as an oddly proportioned pelvis, then you will probably require a repeat caesarean. For safety's sake, you should plan on a hospital birth in case a repeat surgical delivery becomes necessary. Find out if there are classes in your area that help prepare expectant mothers who want to try for a vaginal delivery after a previous caesarean.

INTERNET

www.midwifery.org.uk

This web site provides great information for those considering a VBAC

You should also be aware that women giving birth vaginally for the first time after an elective caesarean should expect labour to last as long as a typical first-time labour regardless of how many babies they may have previously had by caesarean section.

Should I schedule a surgical delivery?

Some women I know who had long, painful labours that ultimately resulted in a caesarean can't bear the thought of another marathon session and decide to schedule a caesarean in advance.

Many repeat caesareans are requested by mothers who can afford private care and want to avoid another prolonged and agonizing labour.

But doctors will not suggest a caesarean just so you can avoid the pain of labour. A surgical delivery entails many more risks than natural labour, and your risks actually increase with each subsequent caesarean. There is also a chance that your labour will be easier and shorter than last time. Do you remember that long and painful recovery period following your caesarean? Well, that can be avoided if you at least give yourself the opportunity to try for a vaginal delivery. Even if your labour is a typical "first-time labour," once it's over, it's over, and recovery from vaginal delivery is a piece of cake compared to recovery from a c-section.

Should I worry about a surgical delivery if I had a vaginal birth before?

Well, I guess worrying is part of being pregnant. So who am I to tell you not to worry. Your chances of having a normal, vaginal delivery are good. However every pregnant woman has a 20 per cent chance of having a caesarean, even if she had a normal vaginal delivery with her last pregnancy. The best possible birth is the one that results in a healthy baby, so take good care of yourself, think positively, and don't worry too much about your small chance of having a caesarean.

Don't worry. Don't fret. Don't put yourself under unnecessary stress.

It's important that you maintain a steady heart and respiration rate, do not artificially elevate your blood pressure, and get plenty of rest and sleep. The odds are heavily in favour of a routine pregnancy and birth and a healthy baby. Do yourself a favour – relax!

What's my risk of miscarriage this time?

HAVING HAD A PREVIOUS successful pregnancy does not seem to affect your risk for spontaneous abortion or for any miscarriage, neither positively nor adversely.

The chance of having a miscarriage remains constant with each pregnancy: about a one in five chance. Many miscarriages are not detected, and most women who have one go on to have a normal pregnancy next time. Again, this is an event that is mostly outside of your control, so think positively.

> **DEFINITION**
>
> **Spontaneous abortion** *is another name for early miscarriage, that is, miscarriage that occurs in the first trimester. Miscarriages that occur in later pregnancy are always called miscarriages.*

Do I need to go to childbirth classes again?

THERE ARE A NUMBER OF *good reasons for reacquainting yourself with the breathing and relaxation tips offered in childbirth classes. No doubt some time has passed, maybe a lot of time, since you last gave birth. It would be a good idea to refortify yourself with the exercises and advice these classes offer.*

If you attended hospital or health authority antenatal classes last time, you might choose a smaller, more intimate class such as those run by the National Childbirth Trust (NCT). These classes aim to help ease the pain of birth and give you a sense of confidence and control. A refresher course is useful if you had a less than fulfilling experience last time.

WHAT IF MY TODDLER COMES DOWN WITH AN INFECTION?

Children bring all sorts of wonderful things home from nursery including infections, and you may be the recipient of some of these gifts. Fevers are especially worrisome during pregnancy. If you run a fever, contact your doctor or midwife and try to bring it down quickly. Some children's diseases can prove harmful to the fetus while others have no effect whatsoever. Other diseases are harmful only during very specific segments of the pregnancy, usually the early months.

Your unborn baby can't catch chickenpox from a third party, only from you. Chances are that you had the infection yourself as a child and are immune. Check with your doctor to confirm your immunity through blood tests. You will then be advised about what other precautions are necessary. Chickenpox is a worry for expectant mothers who are not immune because this infection can cause birth defects. A recently developed vaccination may be recommended within 96 hours of exposure if you are not immune, so the possibility of your becoming ill is slim.

If you are not immune to rubella, you should get vaccinated before getting pregnant. However, about 75–80 percent of women are immune due to exposure or immunization.

Trivia...

In the years before the mumps vaccine, a friend in her sixth month who had never had mumps called her doctor in a panic when her two small sons both came down with mumps. The doctor's reply was, "Go ahead and have the mumps". She didn't.

Can our older children be present at the birth?

SOME PEOPLE ARGUE THAT *allowing their older children to share in the birth experience is a good way to help them bond with the new baby and assuage possible rivalry. If you choose to have your children present at the birth, and they want to be there – an important angle to this question – you have to prepare them for the experience.*

■ **If you're having a home birth,** *it is easy for your other children to be present, but some progressive centres and hospitals may also accommodate kids. However, be sure to check with the hospital in advance.*

If siblings are present at the birth, make sure you have another caretaker there who can be responsible for the children in case they need to be escorted away or are disturbed by the experience. For many people the question of including their children in the birth is one that never crosses their minds. But if you are keen, you might read the book *Children at Birth* by Margie and Jay Hathaway for a more in-depth look at this question.

If you want your children at the birth, it might be a good idea to find out if there are any sibling-preparation classes in your area. Such classes address what it means to have a new baby in the house, what kinds of changes to expect, and the role of the big brother or sister. This is another fine way of including your other children in the experience of your pregnancy and preparing them for the new member of the family.

A simple summary

✔ Since each pregnancy is unique in some way, your second pregnancy will most likely be quite different from your first. Some of these differences will occur within your body, and some will come about through changes you make.

✔ You will face new instructions and new prohibitions. In the world of maternity, things change fast. New tests are introduced, new health hazards are discovered, and controversies you never dreamed of before are at the forefront of the news.

✔ There is no right or wrong spacing of children. Some people choose to get all the nappies out of the way as soon as possible and raise a sibling group that is close in age. Other people want to have quality time with each child before putting a new baby into the picture.

✔ Breastfeeding is good for mother and baby, but consider weaning your baby as soon as possible if you find out you are pregnant again. Sustaining the nutritional demands of a pregnancy and breastfeeding can be a trying and probably losing battle.

✔ If you had a smooth delivery but found the style of your doctor or hospital birth unsatisfying, you might elect to have an alternative birth or at least change doctors the second time around.

✔ "Once a caesarean, always a caesarean" no longer holds true in all cases. Most women whose caesarean was caused by a problem with the baby, perhaps a breech presentation, rather than a problem with the birth canal, can now deliver vaginally. This is good news for women who have had surgical deliveries.

PART TWO

YOU'LL BE AMAZED AT THE CHANGES TAKING PLACE!

SO YOU'RE GOING TO BE A MOTHER

CONGRATULATIONS, YOU ARE GOING to have a baby! Over the next 9 months you will undergo a sea of *change* in feelings, appearance, mood, and energy levels. Pregnancy is bliss for some and a great *challenge* for others. But when you finally meet the child now growing inside you, your pregnancy will all make sense.

Although there won't be any obvious physical changes at the beginning, your body is undergoing profound change. It's important, right from the start, that you *understand* these changes, as well as learn the best way to go about caring for yourself and your baby.

Chapter 5

Taking Care of Yourself

TAKING CARE OF YOURSELF is the first and best way to take care of your future child. Your most important role during pregnancy is looking after your own well-being and maintaining a healthy diet to provide for the needs of the little one growing inside. If you've never paid an ounce of attention to your diet, now is the time to start.

In this chapter...

✓ Nutrition for two

✓ Healthy eating

✓ What should I eat?

✓ Should I take any vitamins?

✓ What foods should I avoid?

✓ How much weight gain is okay?

✓ The big no-no's

KISS JUNK FOOD GOODBYE AND START ENJOYING A HEALTHY DIET

Nutrition for two

A WELL-NOURISHED MOTHER is more likely to produce a good-sized baby who is active and mentally alert. As you move through your pregnancy, your appetite will probably increase to ensure that you eat enough for yourself and your baby. Eating more does not mean eating twice as much. Your energy requirements will increase by approximately 15 per cent (500 *calories* per day). You simply need to make sure that everything you eat is good for the health and well-being of both you and your baby. A balanced diet helps keep pregnancy problems at bay and will certainly make it easier for you to return to your pre-pregnancy figure.

> **DEFINITION**
>
> A **calorie** is a unit for measuring the energy value of food.

Healthy eating

EATING HEALTHILY is essential in meeting the rapid growth needs of your baby, maintaining your health, and preparing you for breastfeeding. As a pregnant mother, you should eat a variety of foods from three important food groups, namely:

1. Carbohydrates (e.g., brown rice, wholemeal bread)

2. Proteins (e.g., eggs, meats, fish)

3. Fats (e.g., olive and sunflower oils)

You need all three because each food group offers a different type of nutrition. For instance, meat is rich in protein and iron but has no vitamin C. Broccoli has lots of calcium and vitamins but no protein.

■ **Make sure that each meal** *comprises a variety of foods so that you get the right balance of nutrients in your daily diet.*

An unhealthy diet during pregnancy has been linked to stillborn babies, low birth weight or premature babies, babies with brain damage and lower intelligence, and children who get sick easily.

Simple dietary adjustments

This is time to fine-tune your diet. If you feel as if you've been a nutritional loser for your whole life, now's the time to change. There are plenty of myths and misconceptions about what is good to eat during pregnancy and what isn't, and about which vitamins you must or needn't take. Even if you already eat well, you'll need to increase your intake of protein and of certain vitamins and minerals, such as folic acid and iron, during pregnancy. If your eating habits are poor to begin with, you'll want to make the transition to eating nutritious, well-balanced meals. Limit junk food, since it offers little more than empty calories. Try not to eat takeaways or convenience food. Firstly, these tend to contain too much fat, salt, and sugar, and not enough of the nutrients you and your baby need. Secondly, the fat and sugar will probably stick on you as maternal fat and be hard to lose after the baby arrives, even if you breastfeed.

Quality not quantity

Eating better does not mean eating more, at least not much more. Surprisingly, in the first trimester your additional caloric needs are slight (equivalent to about an 8-ounce glass of milk). In your second and third trimesters, you need only an additional 300 calories per day over your pre-pregnancy needs (for most non-pregnant women, that's between 1,800 and 2,200 calories per day). Adding just 300 calories on top of what you normally eat isn't difficult to accomplish, but making them count is. Three hundred calories from two doughnuts is not as nutritionally valuable as 300 calories from a turkey and Swiss cheese sandwich. So choose wisely.

Your caloric intake may vary according to your pre-pregnancy weight and health. All expectant mothers should discuss their nutritional and caloric needs with a midwife or doctor.

This is especially true for women who are underweight or overweight and for women carrying multiple foetuses. The caloric needs of teenagers are also different during pregnancy, so teenage mothers should seek nutritional advice.

■ **The extra calories** *you need in the first 3 months are equivalent to one glass of milk. So, don't kid yourself that you need those extra doughnuts!*

What should I eat?

GOOD NUTRITION FOR TWO *means that every single day you should eat: five or more servings of fresh fruit and vegetables; two to four servings of protein- and calcium-rich foods; four to six servings of wholegrains, pulses, and iron-rich foods; and even some high-fat foods.*

MEETING YOUR DAILY REQUIREMENTS

High-calcium foods

2 TO 4 SERVINGS DAILY
(LOW FAT IS BEST)
250ml (9fl oz) milk or yogurt
325g (13 oz) cottage cheese
40g (1½ oz) hard cheese
250ml (9fl oz) fortified soy beverage
300g (10 oz) ice cream
1 cup calcium-fortified fruit juice

Choose low-fat cottage cheese and yoghurt

Hard cheese is rich in calcium

Protein foods

2 TO 4 SERVINGS DAILY
(LEAN IS BEST)
75g (3 oz) cooked meat, fish, or poultry
2 eggs
75g (3oz) cooked beans
4 tbsp nut butter (try almond or cashew instead of peanut butter)

Most types of fish are a good source of protein

Breads and grains

4 TO 6 SERVINGS
(WHOLE-GRAINS ARE BEST)
1 slice bread (25g/1 oz)
1 small tortilla
75g (3oz) cooked cereal

Choose wholegrain breads as part of your carbohydrate intake

Why protein?

Protein provides the necessary building blocks for the growth and repair of body tissues such as those that make up the muscle, heart, lungs, eyes, and skin of your developing baby. Protein is also essential for the proper functioning of the hormones that regulate pregnancy and for the blood clotting factors critical during delivery. Good sources of protein can be found in both animal products and vegetable products such as tofu, soya milk, nuts, and beans.

Fruit is rich in fibre and fluids so don't skimp on the servings

250g (3oz) cold cereal
75g (3oz) cooked pasta
50g (2oz) cooked rice
½ muffin
½ small bagel

INTERNET

www.cyberdiet.com

You'll find great advice on pregnancy and nutrition at this site.

Fruits and vegetables

5 OR MORE SERVINGS DAILY
(FRESH ORGANIC PRODUCE IS BEST)
250g (9oz) raw fruit or vegetables
75g (3oz) cooked vegetables
1 medium piece fresh fruit
1 cup green salad
50g (2oz) dried fruit
50ml (2fl oz) fruit or vegetable juice

A slice of avocado will provide you with essential oils

Fats and oils

2 TO 3 SERVINGS DAILY
(UNSATURATED IS BEST)
⅛ avocado
1 tsp vegetable oil
(olive oil is best)
1 tsp mayonnaise
6 almonds (7g/¼ oz nuts)
20 cashews
1 tbsp sunflower seeds

Stick to the unsalted variety of nuts

While it's not a good idea to get all your protein from one source, lean organic meats serve as a common and straightforward avenue to meeting this daily requirement. Vegetarians often derive complete proteins through food combining.

Organically grown fruit and vegetables are raised without chemical fertilizers, growth hormones, or pesticides that might possibly prove harmful to mother or fetus.

What about fats?

Fats such as butter and oils are another source of energy. However, they should be taken in moderate amounts. Excessive intake of fat will lead to weight gain and some health hazards. Polyunsaturated fats such as olive oil are the healthiest fats. In general, it is best to minimize your intake of animal fats such as lard and butter.

Why carbohydrates?

Carbohydrates provide energy. Some examples of carbohydrates are rice, bread, potatoes, oats, and breakfast cereals. The amount of energy a pregnant woman needs varies with age, weight, and activity level. Try to vary your choice for each meal. Most women require up to six servings a day.

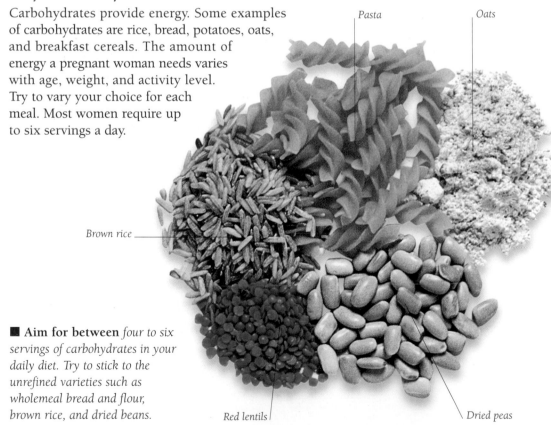

Pasta

Oats

Brown rice

Red lentils

Dried peas

■ **Aim for between** *four to six servings of carbohydrates in your daily diet. Try to stick to the unrefined varieties such as wholemeal bread and flour, brown rice, and dried beans.*

Why calcium?

You need more calcium in pregnancy to maintain your own calcium level and to develop your baby's bones and teeth. The most ideal sources of calcium are leafy green vegetables, citrus fruit, broccoli, tinned sardines, fortified soya milk, and, of course, dairy products such as milk, yoghurt, and cheese.

What about snacks?

First, think smart snacking. Try a banana milkshake rather than ice cream, or fresh fruit and cheese instead of crisps. Go ahead and give in to an occasional treat; a biscuit once in a while won't kill you.

REMINDERS FOR A HEALTHY DIET

1 Eat a wide variety of nutritious foods

2 Choose vegetable, rather than animal, fats

3 Ensure you have a good intake of calcium

4 Eat plenty of salad, vegetables, and fruit (preferably raw)

5 Be sensible about sweet and fatty foods

6 Drink water and fruit juices to keep up your fluid intake

7 Drink tea and coffee substitutes such as herbal tea and decaffeinated coffee

■ **Make sure you drink at least eight** *glasses of fluids a day to keep your kidneys working efficiently and to prevent constipation.*

Should I take any vitamins?

IN AN IDEAL WORLD you would get all your vitamins and minerals from the foods you eat, and you wouldn't be nauseous or turned off by the smell of cheese. But in the real world, a vitamin-mineral supplement is good insurance to help you meet your nutritional needs, especially if you are experiencing any aversions. While vitamin and mineral supplements for pregnant mothers are readily available, it is most important that you check with your doctor or midwife prior to taking any supplements. Keep in mind that more is not always better. Avoid large doses of vitamins and minerals that could be harmful to your developing baby.

What's all the fuss about folic acid?

Pregnancy doubles a woman's need for folic acid (folate or folacin). Folic acid helps you make extra blood and is necessary for cell growth and cell reproduction. A deficiency in folic acid can also cause you to be anaemic. Studies have shown that folic acid, when taken before conception and early in pregnancy, can also help prevent neural tube defects in babies.

Doctors recommend that all women of childbearing age have 0.4 mg of folic acid daily and a higher dosage of 4 mg daily if planning to conceive or pregnant. You can get additional folic acid by eating green leafy vegetables, yeast, eggs, nuts, whole-grain cereals, and oranges. If you have trouble getting the extra folic acid in your diet, most antenatal supplements can help.

■ **One good source** *of folic acid, which helps prevent birth defects, is cabbage. Others include spinach and broccoli.*

What about iron?

Like folic acid, iron is essential during pregnancy for the production of extra blood and the formation of healthy red blood cells. The need for iron is so great during pregnancy, especially in the last trimester, that it may be difficult to get enough of it from foods alone. Without enough iron, the fetus will draw its supply from you, often leaving you anaemic and feeling exhausted. An iron supplement can help prevent this condition. But check with your doctor or midwife before taking this important mineral.

What foods should I avoid?

SOME FOODS ARE NO-NO'S *when you are pregnant. You'll want to steer clear of raw seafood (such as oysters or uncooked sushi), unpasteurized milk or soft cheeses (such as brie or camembert), pâté, and raw or undercooked meat and poultry. All are possible sources of bacteria that can harm your unborn child.*

Steer clear of sugar and processed foods

To prevent excessive weight gain, you should also avoid sugary food such as cakes and sweetened drinks, which, by the way, have zero nutritional value. It is also best to avoid fried foods since the cooking process usually removes any trace of vitamins and minerals, not to mention piling on the extra fat. Try not to eat any processed foods (particularly cheese and meats), because they contain chemicals, additives, and salt. Also stay away from preserved foods such as smoked fish, meat, and cheese, and from pickled foods and sausages. These contain nitrates – chemical additives that can reduce the oxygen-carrying power of your blood.

FOOD HAZARDS DURING PREGNANCY

Certain foods may contain bacteria that can cause illness, particularly in pregnant women and babies. Some bacterial infections that can be harmful include:

a Listeriosis – caused by the bacteria *Listeria monocytogens,* sometimes found in unpasteurized milk, soft cheeses, pâtés, cooked chilled foods, rare meat, and pre-prepared coleslaw.

b Toxoplasmosis – caused by an infection from a parasite called *Toxoplasma gondii,* sometimes found in raw or rare meat, particularly lamb.

c Salmonella – the salmonella bacteria is traced to eggs and chicken. It's therefore advisable to avoid foods that contain raw egg and always cook chicken and eggs thoroughly. Wherever possible, purchase free-range eggs and chicken.

d Botulism – the *botulinum* toxin is found in improperly tinned or preserved food such as cured ham or pork.

What about my cravings?

Appetite cravings during pregnancy may well be a reflection of your body's changing nutritional needs. If you crave a glass of milk or a steak, pay attention: you may be in need of calcium or protein. Such cravings may arise partly from the nourishment demands of the fetus and be partly responsive to other physiological changes that are linked to our absorption and metabolism of nutrients. These physical adjustments help ensure normal development of the baby and fill the subsequent demands of breastfeeding.

What about my aversions?

Food aversions during pregnancy are signs from our bodies that may be worth heeding. Some people speculate that pregnant women have aversions to foods that may not be good for them, such as alcohol and caffeinated drinks. You should also take seriously the stuff that turns you off: it may not be good for you. Another theory is that aversions are related to all the hormones coursing through your veins. These may create a heightened sensitivity to smells, which then translates into aversions to food. I, for instance, couldn't walk into a butcher shop when I was pregnant for fear of smelling all that raw meat. I met my protein needs in other ways.

Think before you give in

While you need to ensure that you eat well during pregnancy, you may not feel like following normal eating patterns. Use your mind when dealing with your cravings and aversions. If all you crave is a giant multilayered chocolate cake, it would be better to find a suitable substitute. On the other hand, if you are craving a protein shake, you may be in need of a boost. Listen to your body, use your intelligence, and try not to put your baby's nutritional needs at risk.

Trivia...

You may think that "pickles and ice cream" stories are great entertainment for the masses, but they are true. Whether the source of these cravings is merely psychological or whether they are based on physiological needs, they do indeed occur. Go ahead and indulge, but not to excess.

■ **Simply irresistible?** *You may not want to find an alternative to a slice of chocolate cake but such high-fat, high-sugar foods won't benefit you or your baby.*

How much weight gain is okay?

WEIGHT GAIN *is one of the most positive signs of a healthy pregnancy. Recommended weight gains are based on your overall body mass, which is a calculation based on weight and height. If you began the pregnancy at a desirable weight, a total weight gain of 11 to 16kg (25 to 35lb) is usually recommended.*

Your pattern of gain is considered much more important than the amount of weight you put on over 9 months. Weight gain should be at its lowest during the first trimester, and should steadily increase, with the mother-to-be gaining the most weight in her third trimester, when the fetus and placenta are growing most rapidly. You should put on about 1 to 2kg (3 to 4lb) in the first 3 months and 1 to 2kg (3 to 4lb) a month during the rest of the pregnancy.

Simply eat well

Approximately 3 to 4kg (6 to 8lb) of the total weight is the baby. The remaining weight consists of increased fluid volume, larger breasts and uterus, amniotic fluid, and placenta. Some women have a hard time putting on weight in the first trimester, especially if they are suffering from morning sickness. Some women even lose a little weight during this time. Try not to worry, but do try to keep eating well. Not gaining weight early on may be okay as long as you start gaining and keep gaining in the last 6 months. In short, the theory behind putting on weight is simple. If you eat well and gain the appropriate amount of weight for your body, you are more likely to have a healthy baby. If you are eating fresh, healthy foods and putting on weight, relax: you are supposed to be getting bigger. Just remember to gain the weight gradually.

Trivia...

How much you eat has little bearing on the size of the baby. Putting on extra weight will not guarantee a plump, cherubic baby. Gaining less weight than expected will not yield you a smaller baby. Besides, labour is not made easier if your baby is small and underweight.

■ **Weight gain** *should be a gradual process throughout your pregnancy. Try not to worry about the increased weight, but concentrate on eating wisely.*

Dieting and pregnancy

It is very important not to diet or skip meals while you're pregnant – your baby grows all day every day and will suffer if you diet or deprive yourself of adequate calories.

Now is not the time to battle with your weight. Dieting during pregnancy is potentially hazardous to you and your developing baby. If you've gained too much weight in the first trimester, you shouldn't try to turn back the clock by dieting. Your baby still needs a consistent supply of calories and nutrients. You must never cut back on your food intake without your doctor's or midwife's direction. A weight-loss programme could leave you low on iron, folic acid, and other important vitamins and minerals. Again, if you are eating a well-balanced diet of good foods and staying away from sweets, you won't have to really worry about the weight you are putting on. You may be surprised at how easily you shed the pounds after the baby arrives, especially if you breastfeed.

The big no-no's

STANDING ON MY SOAPBOX telling you to eat your vegetables is one thing. Maybe you will, maybe you won't. However, when it comes to the big no-no's of pregnancy – smoking and alcohol – I become emphatic. If you partake of smoking and alcohol, you are simply exposing your baby to unnecessary poisons and risks. I hope you will stop. Here are the reasons.

Smoking

When you smoke during pregnancy you are putting not only your own health at risk but that of your baby as well. Imagine your womb filling up with noxious smoke. This is the environment you are creating for your baby when you light up. Each puff subjects you and the fetus to harmful chemicals such as tar, nicotine, and carbon monoxide, and lowers the amount of oxygen reaching you both. Nicotine crosses the placenta, constricting the baby's blood vessels, thereby depriving him or her of nourishment and oxygen. Second-hand smoke is considered just as dangerous. Try to stay away from smokers and avoid smoke-filled rooms.

Finally, smoking also puts you at risk for problems like miscarriage and premature delivery. Your best bet is to quit smoking during pregnancy, and if you can't quit, talk to your doctor or midwife and at least cut back. By the way, the ban extends beyond tobacco to pot. Your baby is too young to smoke anything, marijuana included.

Alcohol

Pregnancy is the time when you are better off giving up drinking altogether. There may be a difference between one glass of wine and alcohol abuse, but nobody really knows. It's unethical and therefore impossible to do such studies on real pregnant women. There has been no end to the debate as to whether there is a safe level of alcohol intake during pregnancy. Drinking excessive amounts of alcohol during pregnancy is known to cause physical defects, learning disabilities, and emotional problems in children.

Women who have the occasional glass of wine a week don't appear to have any more problems than women who don't drink at all. However, women who drink more regularly may be causing problems for themselves and their baby. Though much is known about alcoholic mothers and the devastating effects on their babies (fetal alcohol syndrome), we still don't really know the implications of drinking even the smallest amount of alcohol. Best bet – be wise and refrain.

■ **If you're a smoker and drink alcohol** *regularly you should stop, ideally, before conception but, more importantly, as soon as you find out you're pregnant. Where once you may have had that glass of wine and a cigarette, you should now try to refrain completely. It's not worth the risk to your baby.*

Caffeine

And you might also want to skip caffeinated beverages, especially early in your pregnancy. That may be no problem for women who are suddenly revolted by the stuff during their first trimester. But for the "java junkies" who can't seem to live without the stuff, be warned! Some studies suggest that drinking more than four cups of coffee a day may increase the risk of miscarriage. The stimulant caffeine, which is found in coffee, tea, soft drinks, and chocolate, can also interfere with iron utilization. You can switch to decaffeinated coffee or try something more nutritious like a protein shake or freshly-squeezed fruit or vegetable juice. Herbal tea is a good substitute for the caffeinated version. And don't forget about water.

■ **Try to cut down** *or, even better, find a substitute for those daily cups of fresh coffee. If you really can't live without the taste why not drink decaffeinated instead.*

Drugs and medications

Medical advice is simple on this topic. Consult with your doctor or midwife before taking or stopping any medication. Both categories of drugs – prescription and over-the-counter – can be dangerous to your baby during pregnancy.

Do not expose yourself or your baby to medications without first checking with your doctor or midwife.

As it is ethically impossible and irresponsible to conduct studies on the effects of drugs on pregnant women, no one really knows for sure if certain ingredients, including some in over-the-counter remedies, will have a detrimental effect on your developing baby.

Common medications to avoid during pregnancy include certain antibiotics, antidepressants, antihistamines, antinausea pills, aspirin, cortisone, cough syrup, diet pills, tranquillizers, vitamins in excess quantities, and a lot more.

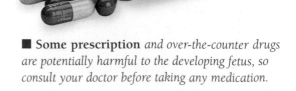

■ **Some prescription** *and over-the-counter drugs are potentially harmful to the developing fetus, so consult your doctor before taking any medication.*

If your doctor or midwife tells you to take any medication at all during pregnancy, discuss the side effects and the possibility of limiting use to the smallest effective dose. You should always understand the risk to the baby in relation to the benefit to you.

Street or recreational drugs such as cocaine and heroin are dangerous substances at the best of times and can cause permanent damage to babies whose mothers underestimate the implications of taking drugs during pregnancy.

Still and premature births, retarded growth, learning disabilities, and behaviour disorders are just some of the possible complications that illegal street drugs can cause if taken during pregnancy.

A simple summary

✔ Good nutrition for two includes daily intake of five or more servings of fresh fruit and vegetables, two to four servings each of protein- and calcium-rich foods, and four to six servings of carbohydrates.

✔ Eating for two does not mean eating twice as much. A vitamin-mineral supplement is good insurance to help you meet your nutritional needs.

✔ One simple rule sums it all up: when it comes to good nutrition and taking care of the two of you, make every calorie you put in your mouth count.

✔ Stay away from possible food sources of bacteria that can harm your unborn child, specifically: raw seafood (such as oysters or uncooked sushi), unpasteurized milk or soft cheeses (such as brie or camembert), pâté, and raw or undercooked meat and poultry.

✔ Don't smoke, drink, or take any illegal drugs. Discuss any prescription and over-the-counter medications with your doctor or midwife.

Chapter 6

Staying in Shape

STAYING IN SHAPE is good for you at any time, whether you're pregnant or not. You probably already know that staying active during pregnancy is better than sitting on the couch for the next 9 months. Next to eating well, not smoking, and avoiding alcohol, regular exercise is one of the simplest things you can do to take care of yourself and your baby. No amount of exercise is guaranteed to make labour easy, but studies show that women who exercise while pregnant not only have more comfortable pregnancies than their sedentary counterparts, but they have an easier time of labour and recover more quickly after birth.

In this chapter...
✓ Can I still work out?
✓ Modifying your routine
✓ What exercises are best when I'm pregnant?
✓ Pelvic floor exercises

TAKE THE ACTIVE ROUTE FOR A HEALTHY PREGNANCY

Can I still work out?

IF YOU HAVE BEEN FOLLOWING a regular exercise programme prior to your pregnancy, you should be able to maintain that programme, with some modifications, throughout the next 9 months. But first you will want to get the approval of your doctor or midwife. If you are in good health, quite fit, and feel up to it, you will probably find all sorts of support and encouragement to keep exercising. If you have a medical condition, exercise could be harmful to you or your baby. So please, a green light from a medical authority first.

In general, when planning your work-outs, consider your pre-pregnancy fitness and activity level. If you are physically fit, you should be able to continue most activities at or slightly below levels prior to pregnancy. You should never try to exceed pre-pregnancy levels. Overall, it's best if you can exercise regularly and consistently, about three times a week. But if you exercise more frequently, alternate your work-outs.

Modifying your routine

YOUR BODY WILL PROBABLY take the initiative in telling you to scale down your exercise routine, especially in the first and last trimesters. In addition, you must make some pregnancy-specific modifications.

Exercises to avoid

After the first trimester or beginning of your fourth month, you will need to eliminate all exercises that are performed while lying flat on your back. Exercising on your back puts pressure on your enlarging uterus and can interfere with the blood and oxygen flow to the baby. You also want to avoid exercises that require you to stand in one place for long periods, as this too can reduce blood flow to your womb.

■ **Switch to fast walking** *around the park – jogging can put unnecessary stress on your body.*

When you exercise, drink plenty of fluids, especially water, to avoid becoming dehydrated. Your thirst level actually lags behind your level of dehydration, so you should take a break every 15 minutes for a drink, even if you don't feel thirsty.

Don't wear yourself out

In general, you should never exercise to the point of exhaustion or "go for the burn," as athletes like to say. Stop when you are fatigued. Listen to your body. It will naturally give you signals that it is time to reduce the level of exercise when you are overexerting yourself or putting yourself or the baby at risk.

There simply should not be any pain when you exercise during pregnancy. If your joints are screaming, your feet ache, or your head is spinning — stop!

If you wish to exercise for long time periods, it is best to alternate light with vigorous exercise. It is also a good idea to monitor your heart rate. Follow this incredibly simple rule of thumb: if you can't comfortably carry on a conversation while exercising, slow down. You must also make sure that you never become overheated.

If your core body temperature rises above 37° Centigrade (100° Fahrenheit), your baby can suffer developmental harm. If you feel you are becoming too hot, decrease your exercise intensity. Avoid exercising outside during the hottest part of the day, and make sure indoor areas are well ventilated.

During pregnancy, all the connective tissue in the body becomes more lax. To help prevent injury, avoid overextension of the joints and excessive activities that require jumping or jarring motions or rapid changes in direction.

■ **Always perform** *a few gentle stretches before you start exercising; this will relieve tension and prevent your muscles from overstretching.*

Simple common sense

As your pregnancy progresses, your centre of gravity will shift, making it easy to lose your balance and fall – both an embarrassing and potentially harmful experience. So be careful and prudent.

When doing floor exercises, rise gradually to avoid a sudden, rapid decrease in blood pressure, which may result in a momentary blackout. Cool down by walking after rising from exercise. Stop exercising immediately if you experience dizziness, shortness of breath, or vaginal bleeding, or if you feel faint, have difficulty walking, or have *Braxton-Hicks contractions* or cramping. If you have any questions regarding your work-out routine, you might want to engage the service of a qualified exercise instructor to determine your specific needs and to suggest other pregnancy modifications.

DEFINITION

Braxton-Hicks contractions *are painless contractions of the uterus that occur in late pregnancy. They are not real labour, though the first time you feel them you may be frightened into thinking you are going into labour. Though perfectly normal, if these contractions increase markedly during exercise slow down or stop completely. If they continue or are painful, notify your midwife.*

KEEPING YOUR ABDOMINALS IN CHECK

If you are exercising regularly, you should make it a habit to check your abdominal muscles weekly, starting in your fifth month, to determine if the rectus abdominus muscle has separated. Normally this muscle consists of two loosely connected strips that run down the centre of your belly. Like all muscles, they stretch, but they can stretch only so far. When the uterus grows too large or you overextend yourself during pregnancy, they actually separate and move out of the way.

You can easily check if they have separated by lying on your back with knees bent and feet flat on the floor. Place your fingertips in the centre of your abdomen just above the navel. Exhale and lift your head off the floor as you press your lower back into the floor. Gently press your fingertips into the gap between the two sides of the muscle. A one to two finger-width gap is considered normal. A gap of more than two finger widths requires corrective exercise to prevent further muscle trauma. If this is the case, consult with a medical professional or licensed trainer.

INTERNET

www.fitnesslink.com

Go to this site for exercise ideas during pregnancy.

Can I start a whole new exercise routine?

If you are just starting an exercise programme as a way of improving your health during your pregnancy, you should start very slowly and be careful not to overexert yourself. Below is a list of exercise programmes you might want to consider. Once you've decided to start, remember to go slowly and follow the guidelines above to ensure the safety of you and your baby.

What exercises are best when I'm pregnant?

THE MOST COMFORTABLE *exercises for pregnancy even for those not currently participating in an exercise program are walking, yoga,* Pilates*, swimming, water aerobics, low-impact aerobics, stationary cycling, tennis, golf, and rowing machine. All are considered good, safe activities during pregnancy, as long as you don't overdo it.*

> **DEFINITION**
>
> **Pilates** *is a form of exercise using special machines with tensioned ropes. It is a non-impact strengthening and muscle-building technique first developed to keep dancers, specifically ballerinas, in top form. Pilates classes are becoming more popular all over the country.*

Do yoga

Yoga is a wonderful age-old activity to take up during pregnancy. It offers techniques that both strengthen your body and relax your mind. It can be especially useful in preparing you for labour and delivery. Yoga is challenging, yet gentle, with no jerky movements or undue joint stress. Yoga has also helped many of my pregnant friends deal with lower back troubles. Almost every yoga asana, or position, provides you with an opportunity to confront what you think are your physical limitations. Yoga challenges us to keep breathing and to move with our pain. And believe me, the experience of childbirth will challenge you beyond your wildest dreams. Many yoga studios and teachers offer special classes for expectant mothers. So check it out.

■ **Practise a little yoga every day** *to increase your suppleness, reduce tension, and help you focus on your breathing.*

Tone your tummy

Keep your stomach muscles in shape. Get on all fours, like a cat, and contract your stomach muscles. Do repetitions of 25 at a time, for as long as you can, at least once a day. The more the better!

Go swimming

Swimming is one of the best forms of exercise when you are pregnant. When you swim your weight is supported by the water, and it is difficult to strain muscles and joints. When I was feeling more whale-like than human in those last few months, I loved to slither into the pool and take advantage of my added buoyancy.

Lots of gyms and fitness centres offer special antenatal swimming and aqua aerobics classes. You might even be lucky enough to find a midwife-led aquatics class for expectant mothers.

■ **Swimming is one of the activities** *that tones the muscles and is excellent for improving stamina, and, since the water supports the weight of the body, it is almost impossible to strain your muscles and joints.*

Pelvic floor exercises

YOU MAY BE SURPRISED to learn that pelvic floor exercises are not done on the floor. Your top priority for any exercise program during pregnancy has to include a simple routine for the muscles of your pelvic floor. If you've never heard of these muscles before, it's time to learn about them. These muscles are crucial to your present and future health, not to mention your sex life. Well that got your attention, so keep reading.

Curbing incontinence

You may notice, especially towards the end of your pregnancy, a bit of urine leakage when you laugh, sneeze, or otherwise strain. This happens because your expanding uterus is putting downward pressure on your bladder and your pelvic floor muscles. These muscles form the base of support for your reproductive organs as well as for your bladder and bowel. They appear as a kind of hammock, slung between the vagina, anus, and urethra. And they become very, very stretched during pregnancy and especially during delivery.

A very loose hammock and excessive sagging of these muscles over a long period of time can result in problems such as incontinence and other structural changes. It's like a chair losing its seat. Your uterus can actually fall through your vagina.

Less serious problems include trouble retaining a tampon, vague aches, and heaviness. You could also find that sexual pleasure for you and your partner is reduced – a common complaint of many women following childbirth. But there is a very simple solution to prevent all this chaos between your legs. You must keep these muscles in tone before, during, and after pregnancy with a very simple exercise. It's not hard to learn or do. Trust me.

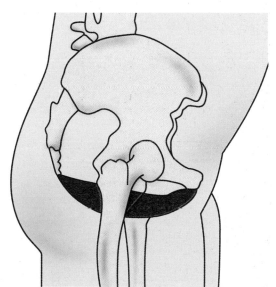

■ **The pelvic floor** *is the hammock of muscles that supports the uterus, bowel, and bladder. During pregnancy these muscles tend to soften and relax.*

97

The exercise for any time or any place

Pelvic floor exercises are simple. All women can benefit from them, and they can be performed any time and in any place. I like to do them when I am driving the car or sitting at the computer. You can do them standing or lying on your back (but not after your fourth month). You simply pull up and tense the muscles around your vagina and anus, hold for 8 to10 seconds or as long as you can, then slowly release the muscles. Do at least 25 repetitions at various times throughout the day. It's never too late to learn how to contract the pelvic floor muscles. If you don't heed my advice now, and later find you are experiencing some impairment, this exercise can always be of some value. But, I'm warning you, the process of learning and toning is more difficult following delivery when the muscles are very stretched and slack. So do your pelvic floor exercises now, and do them for the rest of your life. And learn to love them.

PELVIC TUCK-INS

Try this exercise for strengthening the pelvic floor muscles. If you learn to move your pelvis easily during pregnancy, you're more likely to find the most comfortable position during labour.

Buttock muscles clenched

Knees 30cm (12in) apart

1 **Kneel down on all fours**

Get down on the floor, and kneel with your knees about 30cm (12in) apart. Tighten your buttock muscles and tuck your pelvis in so that your back arches upwards.

2 **Hold the tuck-in**

Maintain this position for about 30 seconds and then release. Make sure that you don't let your back sink downward. Try practising the same movement while rocking your pelvis up and down.

WHICH SPORTS ARE STRICTLY OFF LIMITS?

Make sure you avoid all sports with a high potential for hard falls or ones where you might be thrown off-balance. These include contact sports, vigorous sports, horseback riding, downhill skiing, and water-skiing. You might even want to consider giving up cycling after the second trimester, even if you're an experienced cyclist, because of the potential for falls. Even mild injuries to the tummy area can be serious when you're pregnant.

A simple summary

✓ Next to eating well, not smoking, and avoiding alcohol, regular exercise is simply one of the most important things you can do to take care of yourself and your baby.

✓ Your doctor or midwife must approve any continuing physical activity or any new exercise programme you propose.

✓ Start your exercise regime slowly, being careful not to overheat or overexert yourself, and drink plenty of water to avoid dehydration.

✓ After the first trimester or beginning of your fourth month, do no exercises that must be performed while lying flat on your back.

✓ Choose your sports sensibly, selecting those that are fun and safe and avoiding those that present the danger of falls and hard jolts.

✓ Be sure to include exercises for the muscles of your pelvic floor in your daily exercise routine.

Chapter 7

Feeling Attractive and Looking Good

ALL PREGNANT WOMEN have to grapple with body issues. The concept of being seen in public with an oversize middle is daunting. But there's no reason why you can't have sex appeal or fashion goals. When you are pregnant, people don't give you a hard time for having a big belly. You may think you look overweight, but everyone else sees a woman who is going to have a baby. Here are the simple facts: you are pregnant; your belly and body are expected to grow big. The times have changed and privately or publicly, many modern pregnant women are starting to think of themselves – and their condition – as sexy. To them, the tighter the clothes, the better. It's all about being excited about pregnancy, feeling attractive, and looking good.

In this chapter...
- ✔ *Fashion advice*
- ✔ *Personal beauty care*
- ✔ *Now let's talk about sex!*

WHY NOT FEEL GOOD ABOUT YOUR CHANGING BODY?

Fashion advice

WE CAN ALL USE *a little fashion advice now and then, but remember, it's important to do what feels right to you. Look for clothes that make you feel special and good about yourself. When you feel confident, strong, and beautiful on the inside, you will probably look great on the outside, too.*

My wardrobe

Maternity and fashion are two words that, when strung together, make most of us laugh. Maternity shops still seem to subscribe to the credo that "Thou shalt not look sexy, funky, hip, or cool" during pregnancy. I find most of the clothes on the racks to be unspeakably tacky, as though the designers are having a great laugh at our expense. Expect to find navy dresses with polka dots and shoulder pads you can serve hamburgers on. Most of the fabrics are wrinkle-proof polyester, designed to make sure your skin never breathes an ounce of real air. Pink, spearmint, and tiny floral patterns are preferred in dresses with a requisite bow under the bosom.

Do pregnant women really want to look like the baby they are about to have, you may wonder? If you just can't forego the experience of entering the sacred realm of a maternity wear shop, consider yourself forewarned. Most are hugely overpriced, especially for clothing that gets worn for such a short time and that you can't wait to throw out at the end of 9 months.

■ **It's not only the celebs** *who can look hip and trendy when they're pregnant – you too can avoid maternity wear that strips you of your true personality.*

Simple versatility

Luckily, today you are free to develop your own pregnancy style. While maternity clothes are designed to cover you up, I'm a great advocate of body acceptance and natural beauty. I prefer to dress in comfortable clothes that reveal to the world my growing body and baby. Before you go spending money on maternity clothes, I suggest you closely examine your own closet (and your partner's – a trade secret!). You will be surprised at the number of options you already own. If this is your first pregnancy, you'll probably be able to make do with your normal wardrobe for the first few weeks, although you might find that the button on your jeans needs opening at the end of the day. Loose-fitting shirts with leggings can take you a long way. There are also a few good lines of maternity wear that offer you the basics for today's lifestyles, so shop around. Try searching on the Internet for some inspiration: you'll find a surprisingly good selection of sites selling maternity wear for all occasions.

INTERNET

bloomingmarvellous.co.uk

swell.co.uk

These two sites display a wonderful selection of maternity wear. You can even pick up tips for improvising or creating your own clothing.

Staying cool and comfortable

Once you do find the clothes you are most comfortable in, no doubt you'll wear them over and over again. As your pregnancy moves on, look for leggings with a waistband that cradles the belly or is big enough to stretch over it. Try to avoid wearing restrictive clothing, especially tight belts.

Thanks to fluid retention, you will find your feet growing too. And of course your centre of gravity is changing, striking some problems with your sense of balance. Needless to say, this is not the time to be strutting around in stilettos. Choose flats or shoes with wide, chunky heels instead. Slip-ons that eliminate the problem of reaching your feet down below that bulging belly are also great.

My rule of thumb when it comes to your maternity wardrobe is to go slowly, be creative, don't overspend, and resist the temptation to buy too much too soon. We all grow unpredictably so be conservative and fill in as needed.

■ **For the high-powered** *pregnant mother, smart but comfortable suits and shoes are still an option.*

■ **Choose cotton** *leggings and loose-fitting T-shirts for comfort around the house.*

Maternity underwear

Comfortable, well-fitting underwear is important during pregnancy and this, along with a bathing suit, might actually be one thing you march down to the maternity wear shop to buy. Bikini briefs with a band just above the pubic line and below your belly are good for some. I preferred the hugely ungainly granny cotton briefs that covered up my belly with the elastic band resting just below the bra line. Bottom line, no pun intended, is to make sure whatever you choose has a cotton liner. Your undies do not have to be a fashion statement. Believe me they'll be tossed in the bin when this is all over.

Breasts and bras

Invest in a few good bras. Your breasts will swell during pregnancy. Some women go up as much as three cup sizes. Look for bras made of 100 per cent cotton with wide straps and bands to support growing breast tissue. A good nursing bra will have several rows of adjustable hooks in the back to accommodate your expansion. You should buy maternity bras as soon as you are no longer comfortable in your regular bras. Size your maternity bra so that it fits you on the tightest hook. Then you can get more mileage out of it as you grow.

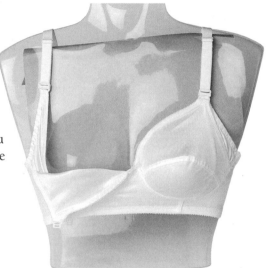

You don't need to buy nursing bras until the last month of pregnancy, when the size of your breasts is closest to what it will be when your milk comes in.

■ **Nursing bras** *come in all different styles for ease of opening – the cups of this one unclip from the bra strap. Buy one just before your due date when your breasts start to fill with milk.*

A nursing bra typically has a few hooks or velcro at the top of the cup for easy opening. This fastener affords you the ability to adjust the tightness of the cup. Some styles are just meant to pull off to the side. Some even come with pockets to hold nursing pads. Whichever style you prefer, be sure to get a good fit – you can even get professional help with this if you feel you need it. A nursing bra that is too restrictive may clog your milk ducts and interfere with your milk supply.

Maternity bathing suits, while not a necessity, offer a pregnant body a bit more coverage both behind and up front, as well as additional support for those growing boobs. If you are hugely pregnant in the heat of summer or if you are getting some of your exercise in the pool, this is a good reason to make a trip to the maternity wear shop.

Personal beauty care

PREGNANCY IS A GREAT TIME to treat yourself to a new beauty routine and perhaps even to a day at a health centre if it is not too much of a strain on the budget. During delivery there will be lots of people at your feet, so a pedicure as you approach your due date would be a nice touch and give a boost to your self-image. Make-up is okay during pregnancy, and there is no need to give it up if it's part of your normal routine. No doubt you will find yourself making some adjustments; your hair and your skin are also undergoing tremendous changes as your pregnancy proceeds.

Trivia...

Oh those hormones. How they wreak havoc with your sense of smell, heightening your sensitivity to odours, both pleasant and noxious. A friend of mine who began a pregnancy in early spring found herself turning the same colour as the new-mown grass that nauseated her so. Good luck avoiding odours that sicken you.

What about my hair?

One of the most impulsive things women do during pregnancy is changing their hairstyle and colour dramatically. Sometimes they regret it all too soon. Your hair is also subject to great change during pregnancy thanks to the influence of changing hormone levels. You may notice the texture changing, becoming thinner or thicker. And yet, your hair may seem to be the only thing you feel you can control when the rest of your body feels so out of your control. So, go ahead and play with your hair; just don't chop too dramatically or too impulsively.

Can I dye my hair?

The question that tops the list of most pregnant women is whether it is safe to colour hair during pregnancy. While there are no conclusive studies on the subject, experts suggest that you consider waiting until after your first trimester. No one really knows whether using chemical dyes during pregnancy is completely safe or not. Ultimately the decision is yours. If colouring your hair makes you feel good, go for it. If you do choose to colour your hair while expecting, wear gloves and work in a well-ventilated space to minimize your exposure to the harsh chemicals used in the colouring process. Some of my friends recommend vegetable dyes as a good alternative to synthetic chemical agents during pregnancy.

■ **If you notice a change** *in the quality of your hair try switching to a mild shampoo and avoid permanent colourings, especially in the first 3 months.*

Simple, pure henna, is a great alternative to chemical hair dyes. Henna, which comes in a number of colours, is a semi-permanent vegetable dye considered to be very safe, though not everyone loves the tones.

In sum, be prudent with your hair, especially when you are experiencing a momentary pregnancy fashion crisis.

What's happening to my skin?

Pregnant women are beautiful, no doubt about it. But in addition to that telltale rosy glow (which is actually caused by increased blood flow in your body), pregnancy can also stimulate some less desirable changes in your skin. You probably expected the bloating and weight gain, but did you also know that your skin could become blotchy or oily, prone to acne, and more susceptible to sun damage? More signs of the internal hormonal changes your body is going through. Make-up can help camouflage blotchy or uneven areas. If you're into foundations, try a yellow-toned one with a pink blush and lip colour.

■ **Pay extra special care** *to your skin, adjusting your daily routine if you find an increased tendency for spots, oily skin, or dry patches.*

Now let's talk about sex!

IT'S EMBARRASSING, I KNOW. Nothing raises more eyebrows than the subject of sex during pregnancy You should be pleased to know that, unless you have been advised otherwise for medical reasons, it is safe to have sex while pregnant. In fact, you may find sex is better than ever.

With a normal pregnancy, there's no reason you can't keep having sex right up until your water breaks. But as with any activity during pregnancy, it's always prudent to check with your doctor or midwife.

For many women, pregnancy adds a new dimension to their sex lives. Hormones are amazing things, and some women never feel more alive, sensual, and sexy. You are finally free from worries about conception and contraception. Pregnancy can also be a time of intense closeness for a couple. Most men find their pregnant partner more attractive than ever. Add the allure of the new "Big Berthas" in your maternity support bra, and this can really be a very exciting time for many couples.

SEXUAL POSITIONS IN PREGNANCY

Experiment to find which positions are most comfortable for sex at each stage of your pregnancy. Here are some suggestions:

a Lie sideways. Having your partner on top can be uncomfortable as your tummy swells. But lying partly sideways allows your partner to keep most of his weight off your uterus.

b Lie side-by-side in the spoons position, with your partner entering from behind, as this allows for only shallow penetration. Deep thrusts can become uncomfortable as the months pass.

c Get on top of your partner – try sitting on his lap as he sits on a chair.

Communicating your concerns

With other couples, a sex life and pregnancy may not be so compatible. Sometimes you may feel too tired or nauseous for much sex, especially in the first trimester. Your desire may wane again in the third trimester as birth, labour, and your belly loom large, or you may simply feel unattractive. Some men worry that having sex may cause problems for mother and child. A man's desire may be dampened by concerns for his partner's health and fear that sex can hurt the baby. It's nice to get the fears out in conversation and, hopefully, pass beyond them to physical intimacy. Let me assure you, once the baby is born your sex life can really sink to an all time low. Do try to enjoy it now. The best approach is to be open with one another about your feelings, needs, and expectations.

■ **Intimacy and understanding** *should be foremost in your sex lives during the changing months of pregnancy, so why not explore other forms of sensual pleasure with your partner if you don't feel like intercourse?*

During those last few weeks of pregnancy when you're convinced that the baby will never, ever come out, sex can be medically useful. Semen deposited near the cervix can help soften and loosen things up, and nipple stimulation and orgasm can sometimes induce labour. This is a great way to pass the time while you wait!

If sex becomes a difficult issue for either you or your partner, this may be an ideal opportunity to explore other ways of giving each other pleasure. The best way to overcome any difficulties is to spend time talking. Try to build security and a feeling of closeness by focusing on your love for each other rather than just your sex life (or lack of it). Chances are if you feel intimate and close, more intimate and satisfying lovemaking will follow.

Can we hurt the baby?

You won't hurt the baby by making love, even with your partner on top. The thick mucus plug that seals the cervix helps guard against infection. The amniotic sac and the strong muscles of the uterus also protect your baby. Though your fetus may bounce around a bit after orgasm, it's because of your pounding heart, not because he or she knows what's happening or feels pain.

Normal oral sex won't harm you or your baby. But, don't let your partner blow air into your vagina, and don't insert any sex aids.

When sex is not okay during pregnancy

Always check with your doctor or midwife before having sex if you're having any problems with your pregnancy. There are some important circumstances under which you may be advised not to have intercourse: if you have a history of premature birth or labour; if you have *placenta praevia*; if your water has broken; if you are currently experiencing bleeding; or if you or your partner has an active sexually transmitted disease.

> **DEFINITION**
>
> **Placenta praevia** is a condition in which the placenta is set low in the uterus. A complete placenta praevia completely covers the cervix, a partial one partially covers it. A woman with placenta praevia normally has her baby delivered by caesarean section.

Sex after pregnancy

After you've had a baby, the idea of having sex is nothing short of simply horrifying for the next few weeks. Your stitches (if you have any) are killing you, haemorrhoids are your new worst friend, and the thought of something tiny going in where something so big just came out is mortifying.

Take your time; wait until you're ready. Don't worry, your libido will return. Doctors usually clear you for intercourse after a few weeks. For some this is still way too soon. When you do decide it's time, go slowly.

A simple summary

✔ All pregnant women have to grapple with body issues. The concept of being seen in public in your swollen state is daunting. But pregnancy is normal; there is no reason why you can't have sex appeal or fashion goals.

✔ Look for clothes that make you feel special and good about yourself. When you feel confident, strong, and beautiful on the inside, you will probably look great on the outside, too.

✔ Comfortable, well-fitting underwear is important during pregnancy. Your undies do not have to be a fashion statement, but be sure to choose panties with a cotton liner. Invest in a few good maternity bras and have them fitted in a maternity wear shop or maternity department. Don't be alarmed at the cup size; this is temporary.

✔ Your personal beauty care can be spiritually, physically, and emotionally uplifting. Don't make impulsive changes to hair colour or style, but do indulge in beauty treatments and give special attention to skin and hair. Make-up can make you feel more attractive.

✔ With a normal pregnancy, there's no reason you can't keep having sex right up until your water breaks. But as with all activity during pregnancy, check with your doctor or midwife.

✔ After you've had a baby, you'll have a few weeks in which the idea of having sex is nothing short of horrifying and a few more weeks in which sex is still not recommended. Then, take your time; wait until you're ready.

Chapter 8

Preparing for Birth

NOBODY REALLY LIKES to talk about it, but – let's face it – birth is painful. From your friends you'll probably hear birth stories ranging from "it wasn't that bad" to "never again". But these assessments of the event will do little to educate you on what to expect during birth and how best to deal with it. In decades past, a pregnant woman simply showed up at the hospital when her contractions started. She often laboured alone while the expectant father took up a chair in the waiting room. But times have changed. Women and their mates are today expected to enter the birth arena well prepared and then to take an active role in the birth of their children.

In this chapter...

✓ Choosing a childbirth class

✓ Developing a birth plan

✓ Your birth support team

✓ Your baby's doctor

✓ The circumcision decision

PLAN THE BIG DAY TOGETHER

Choosing a childbirth class

THE QUESTION THAT CONFRONTS *all first-time pregnant women and their partners is whether or not to attend a childbirth preparation class. After all, having a baby is supposed to be a natural process. What can there be to learn? "Millions of women have done it before", you think, "I'll just roll with the punches". Well, you're right, it is natural. But today most of us do not go out and squat in the woods, nor, more importantly, do we give a hand at or even witness the births of friends and relatives. Instead, high technology has entered the childbirth picture and has made the natural event much more complicated. So in place of our mothers and sisters teaching us about what to expect, we now have formal childbirth classes.*

What happens in a hospital childbirth class?

There are many different childbirth, or antenatal, classes offered by an equally bewildering number of instructors based in hospitals or in the community. The most simple, straightforward route is to take the antenatal classes offered by your hospital. Hospital courses generally enroll expectant mothers and fathers in the last few weeks of pregnancy.

Hospital classes may also give you more information about exactly what to expect from that hospital's obstetrical and perinatal routines. Some may

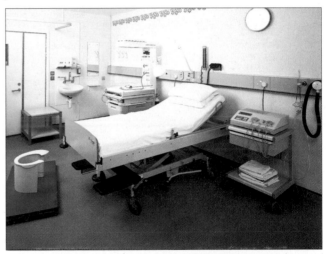

■ **A tour of the delivery room** *can help demystify the whole labour process and give you a chance to ask all the questions you need to get a clear idea of the hospital's birthing procedure.*

include a tour of the labour ward and maternity unit. This tour will give you an opportunity to see what the areas look like, the kind of equipment you can expect to see, and a general sense of what to expect when you are admitted in labour. For many of you, this will be your first experience as a patient in a hospital, and actually seeing what to expect can be soothing.

Benefits of a childbirth class

One of the biggest advantages of attending a childbirth preparation class is learning how you can help yourself break the fear-pain cycle during labour. Most of the popular methods teach guided imagery, rhythmic breathing, and other relaxation techniques that give you a sense of control and mastery over what may be seen as an uncontrollable event. These classes also usually offer basic instruction on how to know when you're in labour and when to go to the hospital, and teach labour support techniques for birth partners.

■ **Antenatal classes** *provide instruction for the essential breathing and relaxation techniques needed for labour, as well as create a venue for pregnant women and their partners to come together and discuss their experiences.*

Another great advantage to attending classes is the contact with other pregnant mothers sharing your experiences, fears, and joys. You can share and compare notes and develop a telephone support system for those last uncomfortable weeks of pregnancy. The benefit you get out of taking antenatal classes directly relates to what you put into them. The classes can be a fun experience for both you and partner (who will soon be your coach), or it can be a chore – it's up to you.

When enrolling in a non-hospital childbirth class, always check the credentials of the teacher.

If you are not having a hospital birth (or even if you are), you might consider finding a private teacher or classes that aren't too large. The National Childbirth Trust holds a range of smaller, private antenatal classes run by qualified teachers. Branches can be found all over the country.

YOU AND YOUR ANTENATAL CLASS

Expecting a baby can be an exciting, often confusing, and sometimes stressful time for the mother-to-be, her partner, and her family. So being able to talk about your concerns, ask questions, and find solutions in the company of others going through the same experience can be very helpful. Finding out what is likely to happen during the birth and in the weeks immediately following delivery can really boost your confidence and help you make the decisions that are right for you.

■ **You'll be far more relaxed and confident** *about the impending birth if you thoroughly prepare yourself for what is to come.*

What do classes cover?

Antenatal classes come in various forms but all have the same aim – to help prepare you for labour and childbirth. Those run by midwives or at your local hospital are free, but you may have to pay for other types, such as National Childbirth Trust classes and Active Birth Centre classes. The content of the classes will vary but should include the following:

- Information about the processes of labour and childbirth.

- "What-to-expect" details of medical procedures and interventions.

- Suggestions about possible physical preparations for labour and childbirth.

- Advice on relaxation techniques.

- The opportunity to learn about and experiment with different birth positions.

- A guide to pain relief choices.

- The chance to try out massage skills and breathing techniques.

- Some indication of the changes you might experience after the birth and into early parenthood.

Different types of classes

Health authority classes

You can find out from your midwife, GP, or health visitor about the free classes in your area. These are usually run by midwives with some input from health visitors and physiotherapists. They often vary considerably in styles – for example, there may be between three and six sessions of different lengths in the afternoon or evening, or the course might take place over a weekend. The classes on offer could include: early pregnancy classes that cover topics on nutrition and exercise for a healthy pregnancy; women-only classes for single women or for those who don't want their partner there; couples' classes for first-time parents; and refresher classes aimed at women who have already had children.

National Childbirth Trust (NCT) classes

NCT classes are run by qualified antenatal teachers who hold a License to Practice certificate that is annually renewed. They offer support, information, practical skills, and resources to help parents make informed choices for themselves and their babies. However, they do not offer medical advice and parents are asked to take any questions about the medical care of mother and baby to their midwife, doctor, or health visitor.

INTERNET

www.nct-online.org

Click here for the National Childbirth Trust's web site.

Active Birth Centre Classes

These classes have different formats but the emphasis tends to be on positive physical preparation and active participation in the birth. Other mothers may be able to recommend good classes in your area. The Active Birth Centre runs antenatal yoga classes in London, and you can contact them for a list of active birth teachers outside the capital (see Appendices).

Aquanatal exercise classes

Aquanatal exercise classes are, as the name suggests, exercise-based classes that take place in a pool. The classes are fun and provide you with an opportunity to exercise and socialize with other mothers-to-be. The exercises are particularly good for pregnant women because they don't strain your body – the water supports your body and makes you buoyant. An added bonus for some, is that you don't have to be able to swim to partake in these classes, since the water is only hip-deep. Aquanatal exercises are suitable from early pregnancy until your waters have broken. However, make sure you check that your teacher is a qualified aquanatal instructor and not simply a water aerobics teacher.

Breastfeeding classes

Many women are shocked at how difficult breastfeeding can sometimes be, especially in the first few weeks, so most antenatal classes will cover the subject in great detail. You'll be introduced to a breastfeeding counsellor, whom you can contact once your baby is born, you'll be shown the different feeding techniques, the potential problems and solutions, and the enormous benefits to your baby. Learning how to successfully breastfeed before the baby arrives will allow you to meet the challenge head on and have some coping tools in your back pocket for those first overwhelming weeks when you and the baby are getting to know each other.

Sibling classes

Preparing your other children for the arrival of a new brother or sister is not always easy. In the months leading up to the birth make time to explain to your other children what it means to have a new baby in the house, the kind of changes they can expect, and the role of a big brother or sister. If you feel there may be a problem bringing a new baby into your household you can suggest having a discussion group at your antenatal class and find out how other parents have coped with the situation. There are also lots of books about childbirth specially written for young children, so why not pick one for the appropriate age and interest of your child.

■ **Breastfeeding** *can be more challenging for some women than for others, so learning about breastfeeding before the birth may help you to succeed.*

■ **Brotherly love:** *Every parent dreads the possibility of jealous reactions from their older children towards the new baby. If you're worried about how to prepare your other children why not discuss it at your antenatal class.*

Developing a birth plan

BY WRITING A BIRTH PLAN you can detail the kind of birth you want and organize your thoughts and wishes for your doctor or other birth attendant. Do you want to be free to walk during your contractions? Whom would you like at the birth? Do you want your friends and family visiting you if you're having a home birth? Do you want an epidural or would you prefer an unmedicated birth? You can list the props you desire – pillows, showers, labour stools, and so forth. Would you like to bring music, or do you prefer quiet and dim lights? Of course these are all negotiable desires, and they will undoubtedly change as the circumstances warrant. Finally, when your birth plan is complete, you will want to share it with your midwife or doctor. Be careful at this time to present it in a positive way so as to gain maximum cooperation from busy professionals whose focus is legitimately on other aspects of the birthing process.

Don't get fixated on exactly how your birth "should be" from beginning to end.

Much happens in the course of a birth, and any number of circumstances from fetal distress, to slow progress of labour, to just plain excruciating pain can cause your birth attendants or you yourself to alter the planned scenario.

It's best if you recognize from the beginning that there is no such thing as a perfect childbirth experience. Some of us put ourselves through terrible guilt trips if we don't "succeed" at what we set out to do in our birth plan: give birth "perfectly and naturally". Many couples expect too much and are disappointed when events don't proceed exactly as they have planned. Birth is a physical experience. You're not in complete control of what happens – your body and your baby are. The most important point is that both of you are healthy when the whole thing is over.

■ **By making a plan** *of how you want the birth to be you'll be playing more of an active role in the birth of your child.*

Your birth support team

YOU HAVE GREAT FREEDOM *to make the birthing experience yours. You are about to learn about a few of your options for choosing the cast of supporting characters who can help make the journey of birth easier and more satisfying. The role of the support person or persons during labour and birth is to provide emotional support and physical comfort to the mother (helping with relaxation and breathing techniques, massage, and taking care of needs like thirst) and to help communicate with the hospital staff.*

In many hospitals, birth is now viewed as a family event. In these hospitals, and even more likely in a birthing centre, your partner and others will be able to see as much or as little of the birth as you wish. Maybe, for you, more than three is a crowd; or perhaps you like the idea of having your mother, children, and in-laws present. I'll lay out some pros and cons below. These should help you make an informed decision when choosing who should attend your birth.

Your mate's role

Today it is often assumed, even expected, that your partner will play a primary role in the birth of your child. Having the father on hand for comfort and support is good news for labouring mothers. In the best case scenario, there should be no mandates about the expectant father's role. Some fathers love being the coach. Others find this role to be awkward and even embarrassing. A father should be free to find his own way of participating in his baby's birth. It might be unfair to expect your Tom Cruise observer-type partner to turn into a Tom Hanks coach overnight. One thing is certain: each father is as unique as each labouring woman.

■ **Allow your partner** *to provide support and understanding in the way he best knows how, and don't expect him to be the "ideal" type you've read about in magazines or seen in the movies.*

One role many fathers do feel comfortable with is serving as advocate for their partners during a hospital birth. By understanding medical procedures and knowing a mother's rights, they can help you get the attention and care of usually busy and overworked hospital staff. It's the old "squeaky wheel gets the grease" routine. Some men really get off on this role. The idea of storming the hospital and fighting for what they want can be fun. Other men are absolutely terrified by the thought of doing battle with medical professionals.

Being a support without being there

Though rare, some partners decide not to attend labour and birth at all. And some women are absolutely fine with this. If the father is dead set against being there, forcing him can only add to the stress of delivery. Surely, under these circumstances, the father's presence is actually counterproductive. There are other ways he can support the mother, especially by taking an active role in caring for the mother and baby after the birth, even before they leave the hospital.

Each father is unique and cannot simply be addressed in a predetermined, formulaic way. Trust your mate's intuition and deep caring. If he wants to be present and involved, there is a unique niche that he can fill during the birth; if not, he will fill other important roles.

Forget the expectations; you may both be disappointed. In the final analysis, the most important role for any partner may just be loving the mother.

Recruiting help

In many cultures, women labour with the assistance of a female birth companion, often referred to by the Greek word *doula*. The doula is not a nurse but is usually a woman who has given birth herself and who is specially trained to help labouring women. The doula is not there to replace the midwife, nurse, or even the father, though she can do the father's coaching job. A doula's main role during labour is to remain with the mother continuously and to provide both physical and emotional support along with acting as a liaison with the hospital staff and the primary care giver. Doulas can be especially useful if the father must travel as part of his job and may not be able to reach the bedside in time to support you during labour and the birth experience.

DEFINITION

*The word **doula** comes from the Greek for "in service of" and, in our culture, denotes a person who provides continuous emotional and physical support for the labouring mother.*

In addition, if you choose to involve your older children in the birth experience, the father cannot be expected to support both the mother and the children. Professional doulas are able to bridge these gaps and provide the support and guidance necessary in each individual case. This female support is particularly popular in the US and is gradually being recognized as an important part of the childbirth process for some labouring women in the UK.

FEMALE SUPPORT AND REASSURANCE

Will this birth be a family affair?

Having a baby is a family affair. But people interpret this statement in many different ways. I have heard stories of women inviting mother, mother-in-law, family, and friends to attend the birth of their baby. My own personal style is to shy away from the grandstand effect of a large crowd, especially when I am not expecting to look my best or be on my best behaviour. Having my husband present along with my fabulous doctor and the midwives was all the company I found I needed. Hats off to you, though, if a gathering of friends and family is your idea of a perfect birth environment in which to welcome in your new baby.

INTERNET

www.bestdoulas.com

Check out the unique role of the doula and pick up tips on all aspects of the birth.

Sometimes older children want to be at the birth of their new sister or brother. If you choose to have your children present, check the rules and regulations of the hospital or birth centre, designate a caretaker to be responsible for the children at all times, and most of all, prepare the kids for what to expect when you are going through labour so they are less likely to be spooked.

■ **If any of your children** *express a desire to be at the birth make sure you brief them so they are sufficiently prepared to see their mother in labour.*

Your baby's doctor

IN MOST CASES your baby's doctor will be the same as your own GP. However, if one of the partners in your practice has a particular interest in paediatrics, or usually performs developmental screenings you may choose to make an appointment with him or her to discuss your child's health.

Generally, after the birth your baby will be routinely checked by a paediatrician before you're both discharged. If there are any problems with your newborn you'll be allocated a paediatrician who will be on call if there are any further problems, otherwise your baby is not likely to see a consultant or other child specialist. Once you are home find out as much as you can about your local practice in regards to child development and care. Ask about your baby's routine checks and immunizations, and whether they will be carried out by your GP or if you'll have to go to a different clinic.

If you are happy for your own doctor to assume the care of your new baby, then you are all set. But do investigate the alternatives if you feel it's necessary.

If you'd like your child to be seen by a doctor whom you feel is more experienced in childcare, enquire at your local surgery to see if this is possible. Get recommendations from other mothers about the other doctors in your local practice.

Picking the practice

With a new baby at home it won't simply be the suitability of your GP that you'll have to consider but also the practice itself. You'll suddenly find that with a new baby in the house your priorities in these matters will change, so ask yourself a few questions. Does the surgery have emergency appointments for babies and young children? How far away is the surgery? Are there adequate parking facilities?

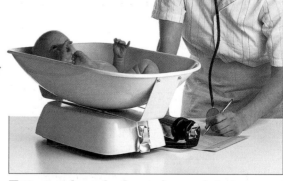

■ **Having the right doctor** *for your baby is a blessing: over the coming years you'll find that a familiar face and sparkling personality can do wonders for a sick child.*

Consider how child-friendly your own practice is. Ideally there should be a child's play area in the waiting room, and change facilities for waiting mothers and babies. A surgery that is too smart will not be conducive to a screaming baby or a sick young child.

The circumcision decision

UNLESS YOU KNOW that you are giving birth to a girl, you might be in a position to consider **circumcision** before the baby is born. If you are Jewish, the decision is religiously determined. Likewise, if you practice Islam or belong to any number of other religious or ethnic groups that practise ritual male circumcision you will be considering this option. The US is the only country in the world that circumcises its male infants for non-religious reasons, with nearly 1.2 million newborns undergoing circumcision each year. In the UK, this operation is not performed routinely or at a parent's request – it is only carried out for religious reasons or medical conditions.

> **DEFINITION**
>
> **Circumcision** is the surgical removal of the foreskin of the penis, the flap of skin that covers the glans (head). In some cultures, circumcision is a routine operation for infant boys in the belief that removal of the foreskin would improve hygiene. However, there is no longer any evidence that this is so and in the UK circumcision is only carried out for religious or medical reasons.

Are there any health benefits?

Advocates of this operation say that there are health benefits ranging from fewer penile infections to a lowered risk of penile cancer. Critics, however, say that researchers don't know whether it's circumcision or cultural risk factors that account for the varying health benefits. Indeed, Denmark, where males are overwhelmingly uncircumcised, has a lower penile cancer rate than does the US. The studies tend to yield contradictory and inconclusive results. Taken as a whole, the health benefits of circumcision seem to be negligible. So this is truly a personal decision.

For parents wishing to have their son circumcised for religious reasons, there has been a surprising recommendation made recently by experts and doctors – a call for pain relief during surgery. Traditionally, doctors didn't think there was enough pain or that the procedure took long enough to merit medication. Even today, parents shouldn't assume that there will be any pain relief.

Babies do of course feel pain and the foreskin is laced with sensitive nerves. So ask. And if you are having a religious circumcision, be aware that all mohels are not equal. Check credentials, get recommendations, and interview before entrusting your little boy to anyone.

A simple summary

✔ Most childbirth preparation classes will provide you with knowledge, breathing and coping techniques, tips for coaches, and medication and analgesia information – everything needed to make informed choices. Whichever type of antenatal class you choose to take you will be taught how to deal with pain during labour and delivery.

✔ Most antenatal classes devote a session to the techniques of breastfeeding; this is usually led by a professional breastfeeding counsellor.

✔ Today it is often assumed, even expected, that your partner will play a primary role in the birth of your child, generally as labour coach and giver of moral encouragement. Some partners, however, shy away from the scene of blood and pain. That's okay too. The most important role for a dad at the birth may just be loving the mother.

✔ If you wish to have additional physical and emotional support as well as a liaison with the hospital staff and the primary caregiver, you might consider recruiting a doula or other birth attendant.

✔ Review your choice of GP to make sure they are still appropriate for you in your new role as a mother as well as for your baby.

✔ If your religious beliefs require your baby son be circumcised, make sure you talk to your doctor about the operation.

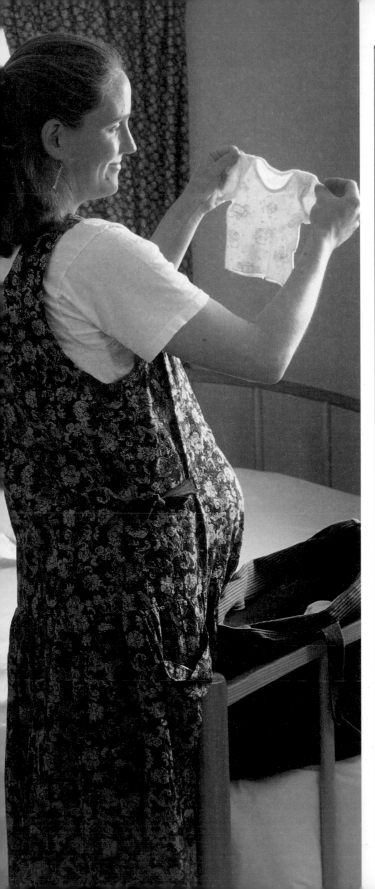

PART THREE

YOU'LL BE PACKING A BIRTH BAG BEFORE YOU KNOW IT

FORTY WEEKS AND COUNTING

OVER 9 MAGICAL MONTHS, the simple meeting of a sperm and egg is transformed from a mass of cells into your child. As one of the greatest wonders of the world, the making of a baby is fascinating to follow and important for you to understand so that you can provide the best environment for this event to unfold. With such explosive *growth* in such a relatively short time, your body is working overtime to nurture and grow your baby.

Meanwhile, you may be asked to consider some *prenatal testing* to make sure everything is proceeding along normally. When you are up-to-date on the events taking place in your body and with your baby during each of the trimesters of pregnancy, you will undoubtedly have a more satisfying experience – even if you do have morning sickness for 3 months or more!

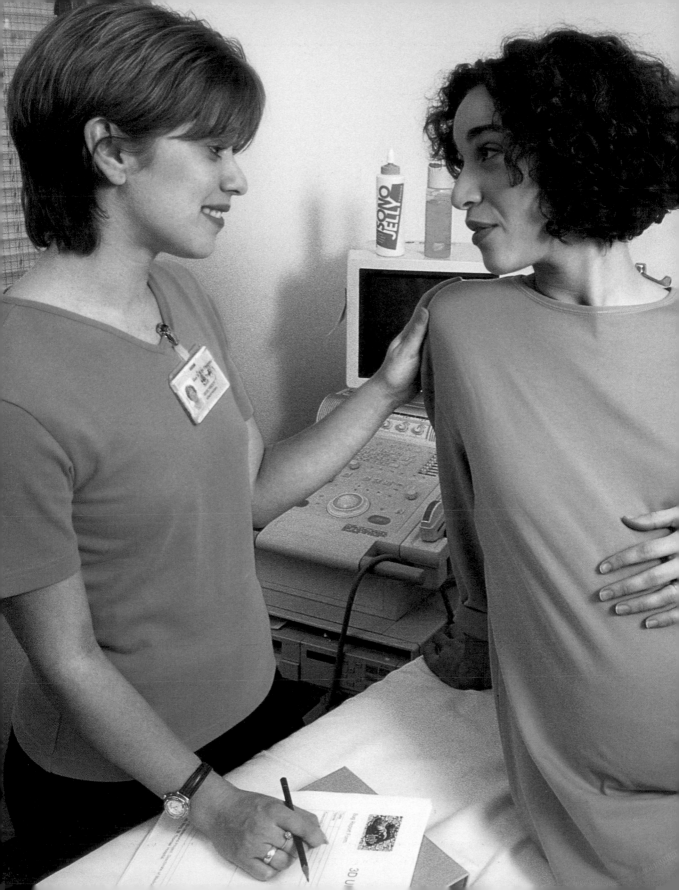

Chapter 9

Prenatal Testing

I F YOU THOUGHT A PREGNANCY TEST was the only test you would be
subjected to over the next 9 months, then you've got another think
coming! No matter how young or healthy they are, mothers-to-be face a
variety of routine and elective prenatal tests to monitor the health of
their babies and of their pregnancies. At times, it may appear that your
midwife or doctor is nothing more than a vampire trying to suck every
last drop of blood from you. But there is more for you to do than just be
the subject of all this poking and prodding. Read on....

In this chapter...

✔ An overview of the
  prenatal testing scene

✔ What routine tests
  may tell you

✔ Genetic screening

✔ Genetic testing

A CLOSE RELATIONSHIP WITH YOUR BIRTH TEAM WILL MAKE THE PROCESS ENJOYABLE

An overview of the prenatal testing scene

PRENATAL, OR ANTENATAL, TESTING is used to monitor the health of you and your unborn baby. Routine tests such as blood tests may be repeated several times during pregnancy. These tests are meant to spot problems such as **iron-deficiency anaemia**. Other, special tests may not be offered unless you or your baby are at increased risk of complications. The most common of these special tests are **chorionic villus sampling** and **amniocentesis**.

DEFINITION

Iron deficiency anaemia, in which the level of iron in the blood is insufficient, is common during pregnancy because the mother's blood is diluted by the increase in its volume and because it has to supply iron to the fetus. If you're anaemic, your doctor will probably prescribe iron supplements and urge you to eat iron-rich food.

DEFINITION

In **chorionic villus sampling,** *a tube is inserted, usually through the cervix, and a small sample of tissue from the edge of the placenta (chorionic villi) is removed by gentle suction. In* **amniocentesis,** *a hollow needle is inserted through the abdominal wall into the uterus to extract a sample of amniotic fluid. Both tests are used to detect genetic defects such as Down's syndrome and to determine the baby's sex.*

Where you decide to have your antenatal care largely depends on the kind of birth you want and what is available in your area. If you want a hospital birth but do not want to attend the hospital for each antenatal visit, you could choose shared care. In this system the checkups are shared between the GP's surgery and the hospital. If you choose community midwife care, you will be seen by specific midwives who care for you through the antenatal tests, the birth, and after delivery – even if you decide to give birth at home. Women with medical problems require hospital only care. In this system, all checkups after the initial GP visit take place at the hospital, as does the birth itself. GP units are usually only available in rural areas. In these units, care is provided by midwives who work in conjunction with GPs.

What if a prenatal test detects a problem?

If a test detects a problem in the mother, such as iron deficiency anaemia or diabetes, the condition can be treated early before complications occur. That's why it is so important to attend all of your antenatal appointments even if you feel healthy. If a test detects a problem with your baby, you will have some very difficult decisions to make, depending on the nature of the problem. You may need to choose between continuing your pregnancy and having a termination. If you would never consider a termination, you may choose not to have any special antenatal tests. However, even if your results do point to a problem, this news can be useful in helping you secure special care in advance, as your pregnancy continues. Also, medical science is coming up with more and more interventions to minimize or even prevent certain birth defects.

Are prenatal tests totally accurate?

To put it simply, no test is guaranteed 100 per cent accurate. You should know that a birth defect can go undetected. There may be a problem that the test you had was not designed or able to find. For some problems no detection test yet exists. In a word, normal test results cannot guarantee that a baby will be normal. The test may be inaccurate or the abnormality may be one that does not show up on that test. And we've all heard stories of false positive results, ending with a baby that was perfectly normal even though the mother's prenatal tests showed something wrong. This is possible, but exceedingly uncommon.

How do I decide which test is right for me?

To decide which of these tests are right for you, and you may want more than one, it's important to carefully discuss with your doctor or midwife what each of the various tests is supposed to measure, how reliable the test is, the potential risks, and your options and plans if the results hold bad news.

If you and your partner would continue with the pregnancy even if the test showed a problem, then the value of a diagnostic test like amniocentesis or CVS might not be worth the risks and trouble to you. The test might be worthwhile, however, if you would consider terminating the pregnancy or if you want to be prepared in advance should you be carrying a child with special needs.

■ **When it comes to deciding** *which tests are right for you, sit down with your partner and your doctor, discuss your family histories, and assess your risks and needs.*

How do I know if I am a candidate for special tests?

A doctor or midwife will take a detailed medical and family history at your initial antenatal visit. During this visit, he or she is assessing your need for special antenatal tests. If you are 35 years old or older on your due date, you are at a higher risk of having an infant with a chromosomal problem such as Down's syndrome, which increases with the woman's age. So, depending on the results of your ultrasound scan, you may be offered amniocentesis. But again, the choice to have the test is entirely yours.

Couples who have already had a child with a birth defect or who have a family history of certain birth defects or diseases are also candidates for tests that fall outside of the normal routine. Pregnant women with other abnormal genetic test results or medical problems may also require special tests.

What routine tests may tell you

ROUTINE ANTENATAL TESTS *help your doctor or midwife assess your health and monitor your pregnancy for signs of possible problems.*

For most women, the first and longest visit occurs between weeks 8 and 12 of pregnancy. Check-ups are then at monthly intervals until week 28, then every other week until week 36. After this you'll be seen once a week until the birth. You may need more check-ups if you have any complications. Routine tests include blood and urine tests, ultrasound scans, blood pressure measurements, and physical examinations.

Blood tests

During your regular visits to your doctor or midwife, samples of your blood will be taken for analysis. Initial tests will determine whether or not you are immune to rubella; assess your haemoglobin and blood-cell concentrations; and, hopefully, rule out sexually transmitted diseases such as syphilis and hepatitis.

Your blood will also be examined to determine your blood type and *Rh factor.* The Rh factor does not affect a person's general health. It can, however, cause problems during pregnancy. If you have Rh negative blood and the baby's father is Rh positive, you may need injections containing antibodies to the Rh factor at 28 weeks and possibly again following delivery.

DEFINITION

Just as there are different major blood groups, type O, type A, and type B, there is also an **Rh factor** *– protein on the red blood cells. Most people have the Rh factor and are said to be Rh positive. Others do not have the Rh factor and are considered Rh negative. Today, a simple lab test quickly determines whether an individual is Rh positive or Rh negative.*

THE BENEFIT OF TIMING

How lucky we are to be having our babies after so many amazing medical advances. Before the development of preventive drugs, some (about 8 per cent) Rh positive babies of Rh negative mothers developed erythroblastosis, a life-threatening battle between the baby's blood and antibodies received from its mother, and had to undergo an exchange transfusion immediately after birth. All of the baby's Rh positive blood had to be rapidly replaced by Rh negative blood to ensure the baby's survival. The procedure was a dangerous one, and was not always successful.

This inoculation helps in preventing a condition called isoimmunization. In this condition, a mother can potentially make antibodies against her unborn child's blood cells, resulting in severe anaemia and possibly threatening the child's life. Isoimmunization can occur only if an Rh negative mother is carrying an Rh positive baby. Since an unborn baby's blood type is unknown, many Rh negative women receive the injections as a precaution.

In many hospitals, blood is now tested routinely for HIV infection. This is done only with your consent. If you are HIV positive but you are otherwise well, your pregnancy will not necessarily be affected. The disease can be transmitted to the baby, but there are ways of reducing this risk at or after the birth. Ask your doctor or midwife for advice.

Your blood may also be tested for immunity to toxoplasmosis, a condition caused by a parasite that lives in some cats' faeces. This parasite has been found to be the cause of some neurologic damage in developing babies. You will only be tested if there is a high risk that you have been exposed to the illness.

Don't touch the kitty litter when you're pregnant.

Have your partner or kids change the cat litter instead. But don't worry: you can still play with and stroke your kitty. The parasite is in the faeces, not on the cat itself.

■ **Although contact with cats** *is absolutely fine during pregnancy, you must not change their litter. Take the opportunity to teach others in the household responsibility for the pets.*

If you, or any of your ancestors, originate from certain parts of Asia or Africa, the laboratory might also be asked to assess your blood sample for the type of haemoglobin you have. This test is called a haemoglobin electrophoresis, and it tests for the presence of certain disorders in which the blood cells are abnormal such as sickle-cell disease, thalassaemia major, and thalassemia minor.

It's very important that all black women know their sickle-cell status.

If you are uncertain of your sickle-cell status or have never been tested, consult with your doctor or midwife.

Urine tests

Besides helping to confirm a pregnancy, urine tests during pregnancy will be a regular feature of all your routine office visits to the doctor or midwife. You'll be asked for urine samples so that your practitioner can look for signs of kidney infection, glucose (a sign of diabetes), and albumin (a protein that indicates pre-eclampsia, which is pregnancy-induced high blood pressure).

■ **Sickle-cell anaemia** *is a recessive genetic disorder that can be passed on to your child if you and your partner are both carriers. It occurs primarily in people of black ancestry.*

Ultrasound

Everyone loves to see the baby on the ultrasound. It's our modern window on the world of your unborn baby, and it's the one exam most fathers can be persuaded to leave work for. If the fetus happens to be positioned just right, it is often possible to determine the baby's sex. However, the purpose of the ultrasound is to provide the doctor with a good survey of the baby and of conditions in your uterus. Ultrasound can confirm the date of your pregnancy, assess your risk of certain problems and, in conjunction with other tests and exams, determine proper treatment if any problems are detected. It can enable your doctor or midwife to monitor such problems more closely.

Ultrasound is energy in the form of sound waves. By reflecting off internal organs and being "read" by scanners, the sound waves create pictures of the fetus.

A simple ultrasound can provide a wide array of valuable information about the age of the fetus, location and size of the placenta, whether the size of the fetus is right for its age, rate of growth, amount of amniotic fluid in the uterus, and number of fetuses – no more surprise multiple births. At the end of the exam, you will usually be provided with a black-and-white printout photo of your baby in the uterus. Generally, two scans are done during pregnancy. The first, carried out at around 12 weeks is done to date the baby. In many centres, the first scan also involves a nuchal scan.

The nuchal scan measures the thickness of a pad of skin at the back of the neck. If this scan shows that the risk of having a Down's baby is high, you may be offered amniocentesis.

The second scan, at 18 to 22 weeks, checks the development of the baby's organs. Further scans may be recommended if there are complications or other medical reasons for more scans. Certain high-risk situations, such as gestational diabetes, warrant more scans to ensure that the baby is thriving. Your doctor or midwife will discuss with you how often ultrasound should be done to best suit the well-being of you and your baby.

Sometimes vaginal ultrasound is used during pregnancy to find the cause of bleeding or pain, to diagnose an ectopic pregnancy (in which the fertilized egg has begun to grow in a place other than inside the uterus, such as in a Fallopian tube) or to find certain types of birth defects in the fetus early in pregnancy.

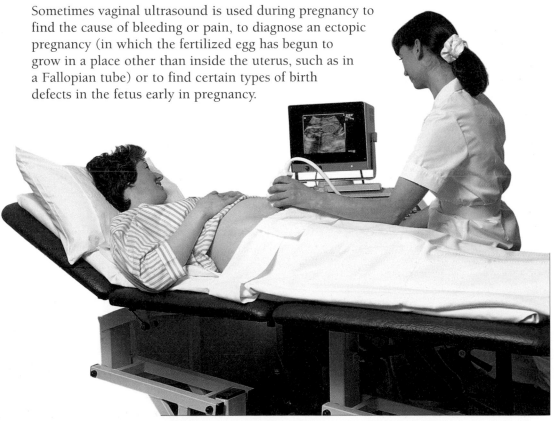

■ **Taking shape:** *The majority of people derive great pleasure from their ultrasound scan; it gives them the chance to see their baby looking more and more human. And you can take a photo away with you!*

Screening for diabetes

Usually conducted between weeks 20 and 26, the sugar test is an optional test during pregnancy. The sugar test is a very important screen for gestational diabetes (pregnancy-induced diabetes), which can result in an overly large baby, difficult delivery, and health problems for mother and baby. This condition occurs in about 2–3 per cent of all pregnancies. Women who are older than age 35, who are obese, or who have a family history of diabetes are at increased risk of gestational diabetes. If this is your situation, or if your baby is very large for its date, your doctor or midwife may advise you to take this test.

The test is simple: you drink a liquid containing lots of sugar (usually 50–60 grams flavoured with orange or lemon-lime), and 1 hour later your blood is drawn to see how your body handles sugar. If the reading is high, which happens about 20 per cent of the time, you'll take a more sensitive glucose-tolerance test in which you drink a glucose solution on an empty stomach and have your blood drawn once every hour for 3 hours.

Women who develop gestational diabetes are at an increased risk for developing diabetes later in life, having larger than normal babies, and most importantly, giving birth to a still-born fetus. The risk is small if the diabetes is controlled.

If you develop gestational diabetes, your diet will be altered, you will need to test your own blood sugar at home, and several ultrasounds will be performed to check your baby's weight and overall well-being.

■ **If you are diabetic,** *or are diagnosed with gestational diabetes, you will have to pay close attention to what you eat and drink and undergo more regular checks on your unborn baby.*

And finally ...

A number of physical examinations will be carried out by the doctor or midwife. On your first antenatal visit the doctor will check your heart, lungs, and general health. You'll be weighed and your height will be recorded. On subsequent visits, your breasts will be checked to make sure there are no lumps, and if your cervical smear tests are not up to date a smear may be taken. Your blood pressure will be taken on your first visit, and subsequently at every antenatal check-up.

Don't worry if your blood pressure drops slightly in the middle of the second trimester, since this is normal in many pregnant women and will probably rise again in final weeks. However, if there is a marked rise in your blood pressure, it may be the first sign of pre-eclampsia in which case you'll be closely monitored (see p. 293).

Throughout your pregnancy your abdomen will be regularly measured to check the height of the top of the womb (fundus), and on some visits you'll be given an internal examination; both tests help to assess how well the baby is growing. Your baby's heartbeat will also be measured regularly – if you're able to listen to this, it will probably be one of the most amazing sounds you'll ever hear!

INTERNET

www.ukparents.co.uk

Check out this web site for useful tips on many aspects of pregnancy and parenting. The site includes advice on why you should see a doctor or midwife during pregnancy.

Genetic screening

GENETIC SCREENING *is used to find out which diseases or birth defects a child may inherit from its parents. If you are concerned about heritable illnesses or disabilities in one or both of your families, you might consider undergoing genetic screening before you even think about becoming pregnant. Genetic screening may also be carried out at your first antenatal visit or even later in your pregnancy if you are at increased risk.*

You can request genetic screening recommendations from your doctor or midwife. A genetic counsellor will ask for a detailed family history of diseases, disorders, and birth defects. Some blood tests may also be done. If you are already pregnant when you go for counselling, tests to examine the baby's condition and chromosomes may be performed.

To prepare for genetic screening, find out the medical history of all family members, including details of any inherited diseases in either your family or your partner's family.

Ask your parents and your partner's parents if there have been any children with mental or physical disabilities, or other abnormalities among any of their relatives. Also be prepared to report the following personal information which, while not genetically related, may have a bearing on the development of your fetus: any past miscarriages; exposure to chemicals, radiation (including x-rays), or other environmental hazards (such as through your work or hobbies) before or during pregnancy; history of drug or alcohol overuse; prescription or over-the-counter drugs taken by you before you became pregnant or before you knew you were pregnant.

REASONS FOR GENETIC SCREENING

The following list contains some of the most common reasons for couples to elect to undergo genetic screening:

a The mother will be 35 years old or older at the time of delivery.

b The couple has already had a child with an inherited disease or birth defect.

c The mother has had stillbirths (babies born dead after 28 weeks of pregnancy) or has had several miscarriages.

d An abnormality, such as an abnormal level of serum alpha fetoprotein (AFP) or too much or too little amniotic fluid around the fetus, has been found.

e The family has a history of thalassaemia. Thalassaemia is most common in people from Southeast Asia, China, and the Mediterranean countries, such as Italy and Greece.

f The family has a history of other inherited disorders such as Tay-Sachs disease, a brain disorder that can cause early death. This disease is most common in Jews who have Eastern European (Ashkenazic) ancestry.

g The family has a history of inherited disorders such as haemophilia (a blood clotting disorder), cystic fibrosis, or sickle-cell anaemia.

Genetic testing

A GENETIC COUNSELLOR *will suggest which, if any, special antenatal test you should consider taking. If any problems are uncovered, your doctor, midwife, or genetic counsellor will discuss your treatment options. They will define these clearly and discuss them at length with you.*

Maternal serum screening

Maternal serum screening is composed of two parts, alpha-fetoprotein (AFP) screening and the triple screen test. Maternal serum screening provides preliminary information about whether you may be at risk of having a baby with certain birth defects, such as Down's syndrome or spina bifida.

The maternal serum screening is not a diagnostic test; it can be performed whether or not there are symptoms or known risk factors present.

As a screening test, it can only show whether you may be at risk of having a baby with a certain birth defect. It does not show that you are carrying a baby with a defect. If your screening test shows a higher-than-average risk, further tests may be required for a confident diagnosis. Be reassured however, that most women with abnormal screening tests have normal babies. If you have no known risk factors, this test is unlikely to be offered to you.

Your doctor or midwife may, however, suggest some tests if you have the following risk profile: you are 35 years old or older when the baby is due; you have a family or personal history of birth defects, or you have previously had a child with a birth defect, or you already had insulin-dependent diabetes prior to pregnancy.

Alpha-fetoprotein (AFP) screening

The maternal serum screening tests your blood for the presence of alpha-fetoprotein (AFP), a protein produced by a growing fetus. This protein is present in amniotic fluid, in fetal blood, and, in smaller amounts, in the mother's blood. Abnormal levels indicate the possibility (not existence) of Down's syndrome or a neural-tube defect such as spina bifida. Further investigative tests can then be carried out. The AFP test is usually performed at 15 to 20 weeks of pregnancy, at which time the test is most accurate.

Triple screen test

Adding certain tests to the AFP test can give more information than the AFP test alone about your risk of having a baby with Down's syndrome. Besides measuring AFP, a triple screen measures other substances in the mother's blood that come from the pregnancy. Two substances that might be measured are Human chorionic gonadotropin (HCG) and oestriol. HCG is a hormone produced by the placenta. Levels of HCG are higher than normal in most pregnancies carrying a fetus with Down's syndrome. Oestriol is produced mostly in the placenta and in the liver of the fetus. Oestriol levels are lower than normal in most pregnancies with a fetus with Down's syndrome.

A triple screen is performed at 15 to 16 weeks of pregnancy. As in the AFP test, a small amount of blood is taken from a vein in the mother's arm. Usually the same blood sample is used for both parts of the maternal serum test mentioned above. Results are usually available within a week. About 3 to 5 per cent of women who have the screening test will have an abnormal reading, but only about 10 per cent of those women will have a child with a genetic problem.

If all these genetic tests sound confusing, talk to your doctor or midwife about your concerns and questions.

Maternal screening and ultrasound

The triple screen test is usually carried out in conjunction with an ultrasound scan. The combined readings from the blood test and the scan give a more accurate indication of the risk of your baby being affected. The procedure may be able to pick up a substantial portion of Down's syndrome cases. But, as with all screening methods, the results of the combined test are not absolute, and a more complete diagnostic technique such as amniocentesis would need to be carried out to confirm or rule out that the baby has the condition. Your doctor will use the test results to advise you about your specific risks and whether or not a further, invasive test is recommended.

Amniocentesis

Amniocentesis is the most common procedure used to test for birth defects. This optional diagnostic test is usually performed between 14 and 26 weeks for women who are 35 or older, have a higher-than-usual risk for genetic disorders, or whose AFP test, triple screen test, or nuchal scan results raise suspicion. In the procedure, a sample of amniotic fluid is withdrawn through a needle from the amniotic sac that surrounds the fetus. Amniotic fluid contains cells from the fetus and can be tested in a lab culture. An amniocentesis is performed in a hospital; you do not need to stay overnight. The procedure takes 10 to 20 minutes.

For the procedure, you will be asked to put on a gown and lie down with your abdomen uncovered. A little curtain may be placed just under your breast line so that you do not

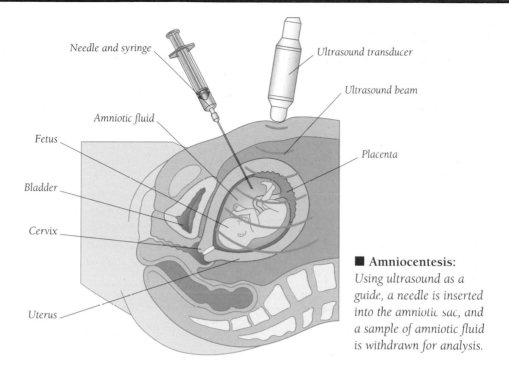

Needle and syringe

Ultrasound transducer

Ultrasound beam

Amniotic fluid

Fetus

Placenta

Bladder

Cervix

Uterus

■ **Amniocentesis:**
Using ultrasound as a guide, a needle is inserted into the amniotic sac, and a sample of amniotic fluid is withdrawn for analysis.

have to watch the needle if you are especially queasy. An ultrasound then shows the doctor where to insert the needle to avoid touching the fetus. The doctor carefully guides the needle through the abdomen and the uterus into the amniotic sac. A small sample (about 25 g, or 1 oz) of fluid, which looks golden in colour, is withdrawn. (If you're up to it, take a look at the sample of your amniotic fluid. I found it quite magical.) If you are carrying twins, the doctor will need to take a sample from each sac. Don't worry, your body will produce more amniotic fluid to replace the fluid that is removed.

The amniotic fluid is sent to a lab. There the cells are grown in a special fluid for several days. It may take about 2 weeks for enough cells to grow and tests to be performed. One such test is the alpha-fetoprotein (AFP) test, which is also sometimes tested from samples of your blood. AFP is a protein made by every growing fetus. Small amounts of AFP pass into the amniotic fluid. Too much AFP in the amniotic fluid can be a sign of fetal defects, such as open neural tube defects or openings in the fetus' abdomen. The lab can also accurately determine the baby's sex at this time.

Although amniocentesis is fairly safe, there are some risks involved.

Side effects that may occur include cramping, bleeding, infection, leaking of amniotic fluid after the procedure, and miscarriage. Miscarriage is not a great risk. Fewer than 1 in 200 women who have the test will have a miscarriage that they would not have had otherwise. Injury to the fetus from amniocentesis is rare. After the procedure you will be advised to go home and rest for a day.

This is important for letting your body repair and for preventing any leakage of amniotic fluid.

Most women expect to experience some pain with this procedure. At most there is a little discomfort, but I didn't feel a thing.

Chorionic villus sampling (CVS)

CVS can be performed earlier in pregnancy than amniocentesis, but it is considered riskier. It is an invasive procedure usually done about 10–12 weeks from the woman's LMP, allowing for earlier detection of birth defects. Like amniocentesis, CVS is performed in a hospital and does not involve any overnight stay. When CVS is performed, a small sample of cells is taken from the placenta where it is attached to the wall of the uterus.

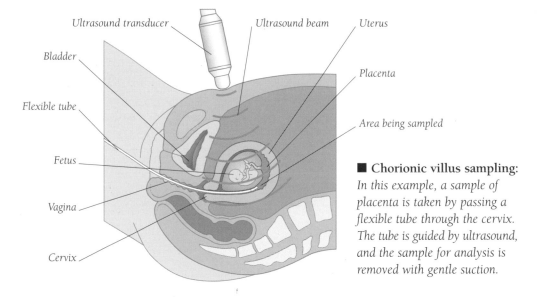

Ultrasound transducer *Ultrasound beam* *Uterus*

Bladder

Placenta

Flexible tube

Area being sampled

Fetus

Vagina

Cervix

■ **Chorionic villus sampling:**
In this example, a sample of placenta is taken by passing a flexible tube through the cervix. The tube is guided by ultrasound, and the sample for analysis is removed with gentle suction.

Chorionic villi are tiny parts of the placenta. Villi are formed from the fertilized egg and have the same genes as the fetus.

There are two ways to collect cells from the placenta: through the vagina or through the abdomen. To collect cells through the vagina, a speculum is inserted just as for a cervical smear. Then, a very thin, plastic tube is inserted into the vagina and up through the cervix. With ultrasound, the tube is guided to the placenta. A small sample is removed. To collect cells through the abdomen, a slender needle is inserted through the woman's abdomen to the placenta, much as in amniocentesis.

The sample of chorionic villi is then sent to a lab, where the cells are grown and tested.

CVS can detect most of the same defects as amniocentesis. One defect that cannot be detected by CVS is a neural tube defect. If you have CVS, you may want to consider having a blood AFP test later in the pregnancy to screen for neural tube defects. The results of CVS can be obtained earlier in pregnancy and more quickly than with amniocentesis. Most women get their results within 10 days.

CVS may carry a slightly higher risk of miscarriage than amniocentesis, probably because CVS is done earlier in pregnancy, when the risk of miscarriage is higher anyway. Infection can also be a complication of CVS. If a CVS procedure is recommended to you, you should discuss any concerns or questions you may have with your doctor or midwife.

A simple summary

✓ No matter how young or healthy you are, you will face batteries of routine tests and be offered a variety of elective antenatal tests to monitor the health of your baby and your pregnancy.

✓ About 97 per cent of all babies are born healthy. Despite this, we all worry about birth defects. Thanks to modern science, huge advances have been made in detecting fetal abnormalities and even in correcting some of these before delivery.

✓ Routine tests such as urine and blood tests will be repeated several times during your pregnancy. They offer reassurance that everything is going smoothly.

Many of them are meant to spot problems, such as iron deficiency or diabetes, that can be treated before complications occur.

✓ Genetic counselling is useful in helping you to decide the extent of your risk of having a handicapped baby and in educating you as to the available tests and options for dealing with their results.

✓ To decide which of these tests are right for you, it's important to carefully discuss with your doctor or midwife what each of the various tests is supposed to measure, how reliable it is, the potential risks, and the implications of the results.

Chapter 10

First Trimester

FOR THE NEXT 40 WEEKS, counting from the first day of your last menstrual period, your pregnancy will be referred to in three parts, called trimesters. The first trimester lasts 12 weeks, the second from week 13 to the end of week 27, and the third from week 28 to week 40. Throughout the whole pregnancy, no matter what you're feeling, one thing is certain: your baby is growing by the minute, hour, day, and week. In this chapter we'll explore the physical changes in your body in the first trimester, how you may be feeling, how the baby is developing, and some common concerns during this period.

In this chapter...
- ✔ My changing body
- ✔ Why do I feel this way?
- ✔ I don't feel anything
- ✔ Hey baby, what are you doing in there?

My changing body

MAKING A BABY IS HARD WORK. When you are pregnant, your body undergoes a radical overhaul. Once the embryo has implanted in your uterus, it triggers a number of chemical changes that in turn send signals to other parts of your body. In response, these parts of your body immediately start to change. It's amazing how fast this happens. Breasts begin to grow, your ovulation cycle stops, your uterus softens, and your immune system is adjusted so your body won't reject the baby. And these are just some of the events that occur in the first few weeks of pregnancy.

Understanding the changes taking place in your body and the development of the fetus during the first 3 months of pregnancy will help prepare you for what to expect in the weeks to come. You must know what is normal and also how to recognize signs of trouble if they should occur.

You may find yourself with a stuffy nose. Nasal congestion and nosebleeds are fairly common during pregnancy. Try using a vaporizer or humidifier to help lessen the symptoms.

Many of the physical changes that occur during the first 3 months are not visible. Your metabolic rate is increasing because all the systems in your body must work harder to accommodate the developing baby and to grow the *placenta*.

What goes on?

During these first weeks, your body begins to produce more blood to carry nutrients to the fetus. Your heart multiplies its efforts to accommodate this increased blood flow, and your pulse quickens by as much as 10 to 15 beats per minute. Your pulse rate will continue to rise until the middle of the second trimester. Your body changes the way it uses water, protein, carbohydrates, and fat. You will also be breathing more rapidly because the fetus needs more oxygen, and there is more carbon dioxide to exhale. The combined effect of these profound physical changes sometimes translates into feeling fatigued. This feeling is understandable: your body has a lot of work to do. While in the beginning you may not look or even feel pregnant, soon all those hormones coursing through your veins will affect you profoundly.

The changes you experience during pregnancy may not all be annoying or uncomfortable. If you have hay fever or allergies, you may find that these miraculously disappear during your pregnancy.

Your body is making lots of hormones that are in turn needed to "grow" a baby. The action of oestrogen and progesterone will make your breasts grow, enlarge your uterus, and cause the muscle fibres of the uterus to thicken.

Your growing uterus will then cause you to urinate more frequently as it presses on your bladder, but you probably won't notice your waistline expanding until the end of this trimester. You may also have cravings or hate foods you used to like. These food fetishes are commonly associated with the increased amounts of hormones in your system.

Growing the placenta

Perhaps the most important task for your body during the first 3 months is growing the placenta, the life support organ for the baby. The placenta begins to form the moment the fertilized egg attaches to the lining of the uterus.

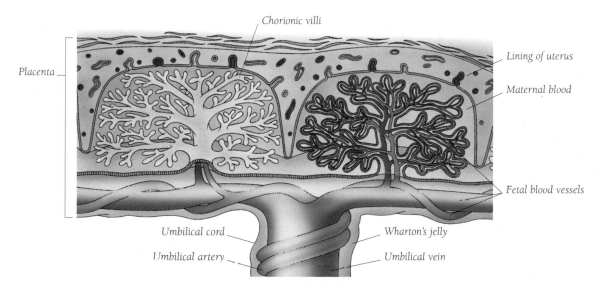

■ **The umbilical cord** connects the placenta to the fetus and contains three intertwined blood vessels. Surrounding these blood vessels (two arteries and one vein) is a jelly-like substance known as Wharton's jelly.

The placenta starts out as small finger-like projections growing from the wall of the fertilized egg. These projections, called chorionic villi, form fetal blood vessels and tap into the maternal blood vessels. Though the mother's and baby's blood systems are in close contact, they never mix. The two bloodstreams are separated by a membrane that allows substances to be diffused from one bloodstream to the other. The placenta is attached to the umbilical cord, which connects to the fetus at the navel.

My breasts

After a few weeks of pregnancy, you may not recognize your breasts. Not only are they enlarging and very sore and tender, thanks to the increased amount of progesterone and oestrogen your body is producing, but you will probably notice other changes as well. The areola (the pigmented circle around the nipple) is darkening and spreading and may be spotted with even darker areas. You may also notice little bumps on the areola. These are sebaceous glands that become more prominent at this time, but fade back to normal after pregnancy. And a map of blue veins may appear streaking across your breasts due to the increased volume of blood and other nutrients flowing between you and the baby. Though your breasts will continue to grow throughout the next 9 months, they should be noticeably less sore and uncomfortable by the end of the first trimester.

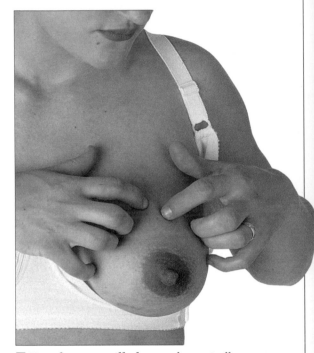

■ **Your breasts will change** *dramatically during your pregnancy, not only in shape and size but also in the way they feel.*

Wearing a sports bra to sleep may help alleviate discomfort from your sore breasts during the first 3 months.

Veins, veins everywhere

Veins carry blood back to the heart. The network of veins all over your body has expanded to handle the increased volume of blood necessary during pregnancy. Depending on your skin type, you may notice more blue lines under your skin, especially on your breasts and abdomen. Women with light complexions are more apt to notice this than others, especially early in pregnancy. These prominent blue lines are a good sign that your body is doing its job.

Much of the time veins work against gravity, especially in the extremities. Veins have a series of valves that are designed to prevent back flow. But if some valves are missing or faulty, blood can pool in the veins. Where gravity's pull is greatest, in the legs in particular, the pooling results in bulging veins, called varicose veins. In women who are susceptible to this condition, varicose veins sometimes occur for the first time in pregnancy and can get worse with each succeeding pregnancy.

VARICOSE VEINS

To help prevent varicose veins in pregnancy:

1. Try to avoid heavy lifting

2. Don't wear tight clothing

3. Try to elevate your legs when sitting

4. Don't stand or sit for long periods

5. Exercise every day

KEEP YOUR LEGS UP!

Why do I feel this way?

SOME OF THE CHANGES occurring inside your body are manifesting themselves in visible signs on the outside of your body, notably in your swelling breasts and belly and on your skin. Other changes affect the way you behave and feel.

Feeling fatigued

If you are in your fifth week, you might not be able to stop yawning long enough to read this. If you are lucky enough not to be sick and nauseous, your chief complaint of early pregnancy is probably an amazingly strong sense of fatigue. It was all I could do to hold my head up until 2 p.m. before giving in to my need for an afternoon siesta.

■ **Get your head down:** *As a general rule of thumb, if you feel tired have a rest. If you are at home there is no excuse not to, and if you are at work try to take regular breaks – even in the toilets!*

If you are feeling fatigued, the best thing you can do is rest. Take naps when you can during the day. At work, finding time to rest comfortably with your feet up can renew your energy. If you can't nap during the day, maybe you can do so right after work, before dinner or evening activities. If you have a partner or older children, get them to help as much as possible. Also, cut down on social events if they're wearing you out. Those who care about you will understand and will be more than happy to make allowances for you. Ask for the support and understanding that you need during this time, keeping in mind that you will almost certainly have more stamina in later pregnancy. If you need to go to bed at 6.30 or 7 p.m. to feel rested, just do it.

If you are waking up frequently during the night to empty your bladder and this is interfering with a good night's rest, it may help if you avoid drinking fluids for a few hours before bedtime. It's not a good idea, though, to restrict your fluid intake at any other times of the day during pregnancy. You should be drinking 8 to 12 glasses of fluid a day – just not at night.

Frequent urination

The increasing size of your uterus in the first 3 months, along with more efficient functioning of your kidneys, may cause you to feel the need to urinate more often. Your growing uterus presses against your bladder, which lies directly in front of and slightly under the uterus during the first few months of pregnancy. By the fourth month, your uterus will have expanded up out of the pelvic cavity so that the pressure on your bladder is not as great.

What can you do? Urinate as often as you feel the need to. Holding in your urine can result in incomplete emptying of the bladder, which may in turn lead to a urinary tract infection. Leaning forwards while you urinate will help to empty your bladder more fully. Completely emptying the bladder may also have the added benefit of cutting down on how often you need to urinate. If you leak urine throughout the day, wearing panty liners will make you more comfortable. And don't forget to do your pelvic floor exercises! They can also help you control leakage.

Headaches and dizziness

Occasional headaches trouble many women in early pregnancy. The cause is uncertain, but like so many other discomforts of the first trimester, changes in your hormone levels and increased blood circulation may be factors. Other possible causes are the stress and fatigue that often accompany the emotional and physical adjustments to pregnancy. If you were a regular coffee drinker who suddenly eliminated or cut down on caffeine once you learned you were pregnant, this change may also cause headaches for a few days.

■ **Changing positions:** *To prevent mild, occasional dizziness, move slowly as you get up from lying or sitting down.*

Try to keep your blood-sugar level on an even keel by munching occasionally on snacks such as dried or fresh fruit, whole-wheat bread, crackers, or low-fat yoghurt.

Dizziness is common in pregnant women and can result from circulatory changes during pregnancy. Stress, fatigue, and hunger can also be causes of dizziness or faintness.

A more serious but much rarer cause of dizziness in early pregnancy may be an *ectopic pregnancy*, especially if dizziness is severe and occurs with abdominal pain or vaginal bleeding. For this reason, it's always a good idea to tell your doctor about this symptom.

DEFINITION

An **ectopic pregnancy** is a pregnancy in which the fertilized egg develops outside the womb, most often in one of the Fallopian tubes. An ectopic pregnancy cannot proceed; there is no source of nourishment for the embryo.

If the misplaced growing embryo is not diagnosed and removed immediately, it may rupture the Fallopian tube or the ovary and cause internal bleeding, a serious threat to the woman's health or life.

Although headaches and dizziness at this point in your pregnancy may be nothing to be concerned about, call your doctor right away if these symptoms are persistent or severe. If you experience migraine-like, throbbing headaches or fainting spells in your last trimester you should call your doctor immediately.

Talk to your doctor or midwife before using pain relievers for headaches in the first trimester.

Even though over-the-counter medications that contain aspirin, ibuprofen, or naproxen sodium may help you, they could harm your developing baby. If you must take something, drugs that contain paracetamol are a better choice during pregnancy. However, it's best to avoid any medication during pregnancy unless absolutely necessary, and then only when prescribed or advised by your doctor or midwife, so be sure to seek his or her advice first.

■ **Headache pills** *may shift pain fast, but try a non-medicinal course of action first.*

Relaxation exercises can help alleviate headaches as well as give you a greater overall sense of well-being. These exercises may consist of simply closing your eyes and imagining a calm, peaceful scene. You can soothe sinus headaches by applying warm compresses to the front and sides of your face, around your nose, eyes, and temples, while a cold compress to the back of your neck may relieve a tension headache. Eating well and getting enough rest and exercise are important too. It's easier said than done, but minimizing stress in your life will help you get through the first trimester, as well as the rest of pregnancy. Some sources of stress, of course, can't be avoided. The key, then, is to improve your coping skills. If you are under more stress than you feel you can handle, helpful advice and ideas might be gained from a one-off trip to a therapist or counsellor.

I don't feel anything

MANY WOMEN SUFFER NONE of the problems or have just a few symptoms of early pregnancy. Are they human, you may well ask? These types sail through early pregnancy without vomiting or being light-headed. Do not panic if you do not have pregnancy symptoms. You are one of the lucky ones. And in many women who do have pregnancy symptoms, they disappear over a couple of days around week 12 without being abnormal. On the other hand, you should contact your care provider if you suddenly lose all your pregnancy symptoms.

POSSIBLE SIGNS OF MISCARRIAGE

If you notice any of the following symptoms during pregnancy, call your doctor or midwife immediately.

1. Pregnancy symptoms that disappear without explanation

2. Breasts that enlarged early in pregnancy suddenly diminish in size

3. Bleeding

4. Blacking out or fainting (if accompanied by bleeding)

5. Severe abdominal pain without bleeding

6. Crampy pain

Hey baby, what are you doing in there?

WE KNOW MANY THINGS *about life in the womb before birth. Thanks to ultrasound, doctors and researchers can actually "watch" human development unfold over 40 weeks.*

For the first 8 weeks, your developing baby is called an "embryo". Tiny limb buds, which will grow into arms and legs, appear. The embryo looks like a tadpole. Heart and lungs are beginning to form. By day 25 the heart starts to beat. The neural tube, which becomes the brain and spinal cord, begins to form. At the end of the first month, the embryo is about 1¼ cm (½ in) long and weighs only a few grams (a fraction of an ounce).

The way of all things

The development and growth of the embryo and fetus closely resemble the development of the species as described in evolutionary theory. First comes the single cell, which divides into a cluster of many cells. The cells then differentiate. Originally, the developing creature resembles a tadpole, breathing through gill-like structures and moving about by swimming. Later, limbs develop, organs take a recognizable form, and the creature breathes through lungs and

INTERNET

www.visembryo.com

Visit this web site to preview the development of the embryo and fetus – complete with amazing colour pictures.

moves by crawling. The human embryo, as it grows into a person, reaches the highest development with a sophisticated brain, speech and understanding, and walking upright. If you are interested, the technical term describing how development of the individual approximates development of the species is "ontogeny imitates phylogeny".

Here comes the brain

During the second month, the embryo is inside a sac formed by a thin membrane. This is the amniotic sac, which will fill with fluid for your baby to float in and be cushioned from jolts and from the organs around it. The embryo is now shaped like a C, because its back is growing faster than its front. At this stage, your baby is about 0.6 cm (¼ in) long. Much of it is the head, which is forming the beginnings of its brain. In the last half of the second month, the tiny buds of arms and legs begin to grow, and the lenses of the eyes begin to form. By about week eight, the baby is more human-like. All the major body organs and systems are formed, but they're not yet fully developed. Still, from head to buttocks the embryo is only 3.2 cm (1¼ in) long and weighs about 8.25 g (⅓ oz). Ears, ankles, and wrists are formed. Eyelids have formed but are sealed shut. Fingers and toes are developed.

Feel the beat

After 8 weeks as an embryo, the baby in the third month of development is now called a "fetus". The fingers and toes have soft nails. The mouth has 20 buds that will become baby teeth. You can hear your baby's heartbeat for the first time (at 10 to 12 weeks) using a special instrument called a "doppler ultrasound". Your baby is beginning to release urine into the amniotic sac for removal through the mother's circulation. Bones and muscles have begun to grow to support the tiny organs. The bones are very soft

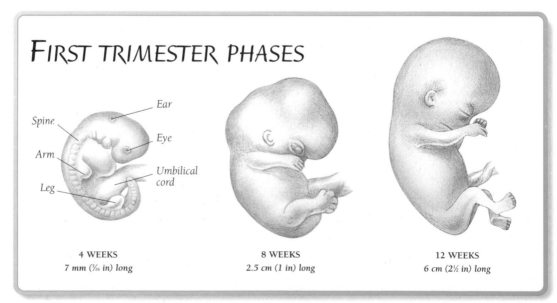

FIRST TRIMESTER PHASES

Spine

Arm

Leg

Ear

Eye

Umbilical cord

4 WEEKS
7 mm (⁹⁄₁₆ in) long

8 WEEKS
2.5 cm (1 in) long

12 WEEKS
6 cm (2½ in) long

now; they will begin to harden later. Your baby's reproductive organs are formed during the eleventh or thirteenth week. The umbilical cord is in place, and the placenta is well formed and doing its job of carrying nutrients to the baby while carrying waste away to the mother. Your baby's back is beginning to straighten, and its arms and legs are long enough to bend at tiny elbows and knees. By the end of this month, your fetus will be clearly recognizable as human. For the rest of the pregnancy, all the baby's organs will mature, and the fetus will gain weight. By the end of the third month, the fetus is 10 cm (4 in) long and weighs a little over 25 g (1 oz). The first trimester is now over.

A simple summary

✔ A pregnancy is divided into three equal parts, called trimesters. Counting from the first day of the last menstrual period, the first trimester lasts 12 weeks, the second from 13 to the end of 27 weeks, and the third from 28 to 40 weeks.

✔ Many changes occur in the body during the first trimester. By understanding the changes taking place in your body and how the embryo is developing during this time, you can be prepared as to what to expect in the weeks to come. You must know what is normal and how to recognize signs of trouble, if they should occur.

✔ Changes you don't notice include: new and increased hormone production; thickening of uterine muscle fibres along with softening and growth of the uterus itself; increased blood volume; and growth of a placenta to nourish the developing embryo.

✔ Normal first trimester changes that you may notice include: breast swelling and soreness; increased urination; visible blue veins on breasts and varicose veins in legs; fatigue; increased breathing rate and pulse rate; and headaches and dizziness.

✔ Causes for concern include: disappearance of pregnancy symptoms (except at the end of the first trimester); migraine or blinding headaches; blacking out or fainting if accompanied by bleeding; and severe abdominal pain, with or without bleeding.

Chapter 11

Second Trimester

BY NOW YOU'RE PROBABLY feeling pretty good about yourself and your pregnancy. The second trimester, which begins on week 13 and lasts until the end of week 27, is sometimes referred to as the "golden period" of pregnancy. Many women report a surge of energy and emotional boost. Your hormones have begun to level off, and the nausea, fatigue, and other challenges of early pregnancy have gone. You're "showing", and the whole world begins to know that you are pregnant. These weeks are a great time to really learn about having a baby and a wonderful time to enjoy your changing body.

In this chapter...

✔ Months four, five, and six

✔ May I do anything I want?

✔ Breaking the news at work

✔ What's that baby up to now?

✔ Baby's sensory world

Months four, five, and six

UNDERSTANDING THE CHANGES *taking place in your body and the development of your fetus during months four, five, and six of pregnancy will help prepare you for what to expect in the weeks to come. You must know what is normal and also how to recognize signs of trouble, if they should occur.*

You feel pregnant, that's for sure. In every sense of the term, you are now "with child". Your waistline is expanding. Your appetite is increasing as morning sickness goes away. You begin to feel more energetic. Don't be surprised if around month five you feel a good kick in your belly. Most first-time mothers notice their babies move for the first time between weeks 20 and 23. This is sometimes known as quickening. Quickening is an exciting, if somewhat bizarre sensation, and the first couple of times you might just think that this subtle movement is not the baby but the hamburger you ate for lunch. By the end of month six, your belly is beginning to feel like party central as the baby's movements progress from gentle jabs to somersaults that can keep you awake at night.

I'm starting to grow!

The second trimester is the beginning of real expansion. Stretch marks begin, sometimes invisibly. Everything grows: moles get bigger; skin tags get bigger; even warts can get bigger. Thanks to oestrogen, everything has a better blood supply. This also explains why your gums may bleed after brushing your teeth. Your uterus will grow to the height of your belly button. The skin on your growing belly may start to itch. The placenta has usually picked a permanent spot during the second trimester, and the rest of the uterus is expanding away from its site of implantation. You may feel pain down the side of your belly as your uterus stretches. Your heart beats faster. You may need 8 hours of sleep each night. Take rest breaks during the day if you feel tired; don't push yourself. You may get leg cramps, especially at night, if you're not getting enough calcium. At the end of the second trimester, it may come as a shock that you are now sporting an extra 8–9 kg (18–20 lb). There may be a stripe running down your abdomen. You are on the downhill side of the rollercoaster now. It may be time to start making a list of names and focus on preparing your nest.

■ **Here comes the bump:** *Up until now you probably haven't gained much weight, but that's all about to change!*

INTERNET

www.maxpages.com/ babynames

This site is one of the most complete sources for baby names on the Web.

Round ligament pains

The menstrual-like cramps, the growing pains, of the first trimester are replaced by the second trimester's "round ligament" pains. The round ligaments are supports that originate on the sides of the uterus. During the second trimester the uterus gets so big that it can no longer sit in the pelvis but pops up into the abdominal cavity. Since the round ligaments are a pretty lousy support even when the uterus is only the size of a pear, they're a real nuisance when the uterus gets considerably larger in the second and third trimesters. The uterus can actually flop from side to side, twanging the round ligaments so that you may feel discomfort on one or both sides of your abdomen. This is a completely harmless pain, but it really knocks some women for six and can stop you dead in your tracks. Usually, changing position will relieve this strain on the ligaments, lessening the discomfort, but the only real cure comes with delivery several months later.

You may be tempted to leave off your seat belt in the car because you find it uncomfortable on your belly. Don't fall for the temptation.

Surprisingly, the most common way for women of childbearing age to lose their lives is in car accidents. The best way to avoid becoming a statistic is to buckle up. For safety and minimum discomfort when you are pregnant, fasten the belt below your belly with the shoulder harness across your chest. Don't worry about the baby; he or she has the extra cushion of amniotic fluid to protect against the pressure of a secured seat belt.

Constipation

This is not a usual topic of conversation, but constipation is a real cause of discomfort. Hormonal changes actually slow the digestive tract, and iron-loaded prenatal vitamins and pressure from your enlarging uterus contribute to constipation as well. The best and simplest remedy includes drinking at least eight glasses of water a day and eating high-fibre foods such as raw fruits, vegetables, bran cereal, and whole-grain bread. Exercise contributes greatly to the cure.

Trivia...

Surely it's an old wives' tale, but supposedly the mother with bad heartburn will give birth to a baby with a full head of hair. Don't take this wisdom too seriously, but if your baby does emerge ready for its first haircut, expect to hear lots of pity for the heartburn you must have suffered.

Heartburn

The burning sensation in my upper abdomen and chest following eating in my middle, as well as my last, months of pregnancy drove me batty. No amount of Tums or antacids seemed to work for me. Basically, heartburn strikes when digested food is pushed back up past the oesophagus by your expanding uterus. Avoiding spicy, greasy, and acidic foods may help, as does eating small meals. The only cure I found was delivery, after which I could enjoy eating again. Ask your doctor or midwife about acceptable over-the-counter remedies.

Forgetfulness

My friend Barbara refers to this time as pregnancy amnesia – when you can't remember your own phone number. Apparently losing brain cells and your capability for dealing with complicated situations – when you were great just a few months ago – seems to be a condition of pregnancy. No one knows for certain what the cause is, and we can only make wild guesses blaming hormones. It may be that preoccupation with the pregnancy overrides other mental functions. Whatever the reason, I can assure you that this scatterbrain syndrome is temporary and will disappear.

Weight gain

The second trimester is the time during which all your pent-up anxiety over gaining weight gets its true test. Some women get depressed and anxious as they stand in profile and gaze at their ever-expanding waistlines. Remember that weight, like forgetfulness, is only a temporary situation as long as you are taking good care of yourself and eating healthily. (Take another look at Chapter 5.)

Trouble finding a comfortable sleeping position

Clothes aren't the only challenge you face with your burgeoning growth. During the latter part of the second trimester, and even more so in the third, lying comfortably in bed becomes a battle that distracts many women. Needless to say, sleeping on your belly is nearly impossible. And, as you learned in chapter 6, lying on your back rests the entire weight of your belly on your intestines and also constricts blood and oxygen circulation in the major vein supplying nutrients to your baby. If sleeping on your back was your preferred position, giving it up can be traumatic. Losing sleep while tossing and turning trying to adjust to your new shape is very common.

I found the best position for sleep during pregnancy was lying on my side (the left was ultimately preferred, but either side is fine) with a pillow between my legs and one under my head. Some women find comfort in using a long body-pillow that helps take some of the pressure off joints and bones. Curling up or stretching out on your left side with the top leg crossed over and in front of the bottom one helps promote blood flow and nutrients to the placenta while also enhancing kidney function. Not surprisingly, this position is also super-comfortable, and that's what really counts.

■ **Be prepared** *to experiment with myriad sleeping positions before finding the one that is most comfortable for you.*

Back pain

Many women experience lower back pain starting in the second trimester of pregnancy. Wearing flat shoes and adopting a correct posture are the simplest and most effective solutions, but you might try wearing a pregnancy support girdle – it helped me. These gadgets feature abdominal support straps that help support the pregnant uterus and help you move more freely. Also, if you have access to a swimming pool, go for it – swimming is wonderful exercise for pregnancy, and water will also help support your pregnant uterus.

Do strengthening exercises. Pelvic-tilt exercises help strengthen the back, relieving pain. And just putting yourself into the knee-chest position to get the baby out of the pelvis and off your pelvic nerves may make you more comfortable.

May I do anything I want?

THE SECOND TRIMESTER *is the most stable time of your pregnancy. You are feeling well, despite some minor discomforts, and are ready to conquer the world. Slow down. You are still pregnant. There are some activities about which you must think twice, and some that you had best avoid altogether.*

Carrying heavy loads

Whether it's moving boxes, picking up armloads of heavy shopping bags, or carrying an older child, none of this is a good idea during pregnancy. The strain of your growing belly is already stretching your muscles and ligaments to their limits. Adding a few extra or many extra pounds on top of what you are already carrying is asking for trouble. If you've got to move house, this is the time to play the queen and hire an army of hunks. Or at least ask for the assistance of one he-man to help you carry the shopping. It is also a good time to ease your older child out of the habit of being carried for lengthy periods of time. Of course there will be times when he or she just has to be held, and this is a good time to learn to lift wisely, i.e., bending at the knees and rising slowly with your added load.

■ **STOP!** *Do you really need to lift that box? Is there nobody else around who could do it for you? Lifting while pregnant should be avoided.*

■ Unborn babies fly for free: *If you are planning on an aeroplane trip during your pregnancy, the second trimester is the time to do it. But check with your doctor for safety and with your airline for restrictions.*

Travel

Travelling is best during the second trimester of pregnancy. You've passed the first trimester, which is not a well-advised time for travel. In the first 3 months, your body is just adjusting to pregnancy, and there is the very real possibility of upsetting this delicate state and causing miscarriage. And during the third trimester, travel is pretty uncomfortable for you personally. Travel of any great distance is usually not advised after a certain point in the pregnancy because of the possibility of early labour. During the second trimester, you are feeling energetic, and, when you have to consider the children, holidaying will probably never be this easy again.

Check with your doctor if you have any health conditions that may preclude travel or if you are planning a trip to some remote destination or country.

Your doctor might advise special precautions. If you are planning to travel by air at any time, check with the airline to see if it has any restrictions regarding pregnant women. Also, when travelling by plane, request an aisle seat in a bulkhead where there is lots of legroom. You will tend to get leg cramps if you sit in one position too long, and, of course, there are those frequent trips to the toilet to consider. Drink lots of water, bring food and healthy snacks, and be sure to move around as much as you need to.

What about radiation?

The question arises: should I microwave my food? And the jury is still out on this one. Current research implies that the type of radiation emitted by microwave ovens, TVs, and computer monitors – called non-ionizing radiation – isn't harmful. However, you may feel happier taking preventive steps.

Sit at least 1.25 metres (4 ft) from the rear of your computer monitor, don't stand in front of the microwave when heating food, and sit at least 3 metres (10 ft) from the front of the TV screen. This is good advice even if you are not pregnant.

Household hazards

As for cleaning the house, use common sense when employing cleaning solvents. Always wear gloves, try using non-toxic cleaners found in health food stores, open windows for ventilation, opt for spray bottles over aerosols, avoid products with toxicity warnings like oven cleaners, and never mix products that may create dangerous gases. And, by the way, check with your doctor before painting the nursery or touching up the kitchen walls. Some paint fumes and chemical solvents in paints should be avoided during pregnancy.

Sleep with an electric blanket? Try cuddling up to a warm body instead. Electric blankets can raise your core body temperature too much, and they also create strange electromagnetic fields that are the subject of some controversy.

Breaking the news at work

NOW THAT YOU ARE SHOWING, *it may be time to break the news of your pregnancy at work. Most women choose to keep pregnancy private until the second trimester. This approach gives you time to plan your announcement, negotiate the best maternity leave, and protect your job. It's shocking to think that pregnancy discrimination still exists, but it does. In the UK it is illegal to sack or refuse to promote someone simply because she is pregnant. Employers must treat pregnancy like any other medical condition.*

It's good politics, when you finally decide to spill the beans, to tell your boss about your pregnancy before you tell your co-workers.

Don't make the mistake of agreeing immediately to a maternity leave that's too brief. If you're fortunate enough to work in a place that supports families, great. Otherwise you may have to downplay your pregnancy and highlight your work commitment.

Trivia...

One of my friends in Europe told me that during a job interview she was informed by a prospective employer that because she was in the prime of her childbearing years (which I thought was 20 to 40) she did not qualify for the position. Although this type of discrimination is not legal in the UK, it still exists in subtle and not-so-subtle ways. That is why it's still a good idea to use your common sense when discussing your family plans with employers.

Maternity leave is very well defined in Britain – Northern Ireland has similar laws – and the following information should only be used as a rough guide in conjunction with your employment contract. After giving 3 weeks' notice, you can usually start maternity leave any time after the beginning of the eleventh week before the week the baby is due. Under the terms of ordinary maternity leave, you need not return to work until 18 weeks after the date of commencement. If you have been with your employer for over a year, leave can be extended until 29 weeks after the date of birth. Bottom line: determine what you are entitled and go for it. Babies only stay babies for a very short time.

On-the-job hazards

Airline personnel, bakers, dry cleaners, artists, dental care workers, farmers, and even secretaries, among many others, face an amazing array of workplace hazards that can have troubling effects on your pregnancy. In addition to physical stressors such as long hours, standing on your feet, or sitting in front of a computer, there is the potential exposure to hazards or chemicals that have been associated with dangers to both mother and fetus. If your job exposes you to toxic chemicals or requires a lot of physical effort, you may need to cut back on your hours, talk to your supervisor about a reassignment, or consider taking an early maternity leave.

Many workplace chemicals can affect your pregnancy. Watch out for anaesthetic gases, dibromochloropropane, ethylene oxide, lead, methyl mercury, organic chemical solvents, vinyl chloride, industrial dusts, and radiation.

What's that baby up to now?

DURING WEEKS 13 TO 26, the fetus moves, kicks, swallows, and can hear your voice. Throughout the fourth month, the umbilical cord continues to grow and thicken in order to carry enough nourishment from mother to fetus. The placenta is now fully formed. By the end of month four, the fetus is up to 18 cm (7 in) long and weighs about 140 g (5 oz). Your baby looks fully formed, although its head is quite out of proportion and has an ET, alien-like, quality. Its parchment-thin skin is covered with an ultrafine layer of hair called lanugo. Eyebrows and hair have begun to grow. The baby's heartbeat is getting stronger.

I've said it before, and I'll say it again: exercise! Exercise is one of the best ways to increase your energy level. The more you exercise, the more energy you seem to have to continue exercising, as well as to perform your daily tasks. Even moderate exercise, such as walking for 30 minutes each day, can really help you feel energized. What's good for you is good for the baby too, and baby is exercising these days.

Oh, how my baby grows

Starting in month five, the fetus becomes more active, turning from side to side and sometimes head over heels, giving mum a few good kicks in her belly. The fingernails have grown to the tips of the fingers. The fetus now sleeps and wakes at regular

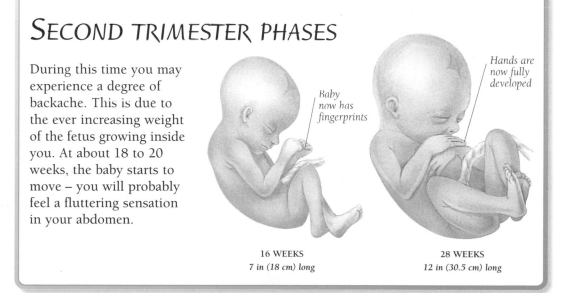

SECOND TRIMESTER PHASES

During this time you may experience a degree of backache. This is due to the ever increasing weight of the fetus growing inside you. At about 18 to 20 weeks, the baby starts to move – you will probably feel a fluttering sensation in your abdomen.

Baby now has fingerprints

Hands are now fully developed

16 WEEKS
7 in (18 cm) long

28 WEEKS
12 in (30.5 cm) long

intervals. This is a month of rapid growth; at the end of the fifth month the fetus is 20–30 cm (8–12 in) long and weighs around 225–450 g (½–1 lb). Your baby has begun to practise breathing now and may even be sucking its thumb. Your baby can hear at this time, too.

In month six, your baby's skin is red and wrinkled. At this stage the fetus is usually too small to be born; its lungs are not ready for life outside its mother. The eyelids begin to part, and the eyes open this month. The fetus continues its rapid growth. At the end of the sixth month, the fetus is 28–35 cm (11–14 in) long and weighs 680 g (1½ lb).

The peaceful womb experience

In the past 20 years, new and exciting discoveries have been made about the fetus' sensory and emotional awareness *in utero*. Mother and her unborn baby share emotions. When you are upset, your baby may be upset. If your pregnancy is cluttered with emotional stress (especially the last 3 months), you have a higher risk of having a child who is anxious, and an anxious child has a high risk of being a difficult sleeper. By creating a peaceful pregnancy, you begin creating harmony with your baby. This prenatal harmony may well carry over into the baby's personality, waking behaviour, and sleep patterns.

Baby's sensory world

YOUR WOMB IS AN OPTIMAL, *stimulating, interactive environment for a baby's development. Activity never ceases, and your baby is never isolated. Touch, taste, smell, hearing, and seeing – the cornerstones of human experience and communication – all begin in the womb.*

Touch in the womb

According to current research, the first sensitivity to touch manifests itself just before 8 weeks gestational age. Experiments with a hair stroke on various parts of the embryonic body show that skin sensitivity quickly extends to the genital area (10 weeks), palms (11 weeks), and soles of the feet (12 weeks). By 17 weeks, all parts of the abdomen and buttocks are sensitive. The skin of a fetus is marvellously complex, containing a hundred varieties of cells that seem especially sensitive to heat, cold, pressure, and pain. By 32 weeks, nearly every part of the baby's body is sensitive to the light stroke of a single hair.

Taste and smell in the womb

The structures for tasting are developed at about 14 weeks, and experts believe that tasting begins at that time. Tests show that swallowing increases with sweet tastes and decreases with bitter and sour tastes. A range of tastes is presented in the liquid womb space. These include lactic, pyruvic, and citric acids, creatinine, urea, amino acids, proteins, and salts. Tests made at birth reveal that babies have exquisite taste discrimination and definite preferences.

Until recently, no serious consideration was given to the possibilities for smell in the womb, since researchers assumed that human sensation through the nose depended on air and breathing. However, the latest research has opened up a new world of possibilities, and it is now believed that your baby at 11 to 15 weeks receives complex olfactory input. Many chemical compounds cross the placenta to join the amniotic fluid, providing the fetus with tastes and odours. The amniotic fluid surrounding the fetus bathes the oral, nasal, and throat cavities, and the fetus breathes it and swallows it, permitting direct access to receptors of several sensory systems.

■ **You are not the only one** *enjoying your favorite foods and drinks while pregnant. In the second trimester your baby starts to taste and smell what you ingest.*

Learning likes and dislikes

Associations with the senses formed in utero are thought to alter subsequent behaviour and are retained into postnatal life. There is evidence for direct and indirect learning of odours in utero. Researchers point to an extraordinary range of smells in the womb. In addition, products of the mother's diet reach the baby via the placenta and the blood flowing in the capillaries of the nose. In one experiment, fetuses registered changes in fetal breathing and heart rate when mothers drank coffee, reflecting whether it was caffeinated or decaffeinated. Newborns are drawn to the odour of breastmilk, although they have had no previous experience with it. Researchers think this may come from cues they have learned in prenatal life.

INTERNET

onhealth.webmd.com/
baby/y2k/story/
item%2C45520.asp

This page of OnHealth.com's "9 Months" site contains some interesting details about likes and dislikes learned in the womb. But hunt around — there's other good stuff, too.

Listening and hearing in the womb

Although a series of barriers buffers the fetus from the outside world – amniotic fluid, embryonic membranes, uterus, and the maternal abdomen – the fetus lives in a stimulating matrix of sound, vibration, and motion. Many studies now confirm that voices reach the womb and are not overwhelmed by the background noise created by the mother and placenta. Intonation, patterns of pitch, stress, and rhythm, as well as music, reach the fetus without significant distortion. Your voice is particularly powerful because it is transmitted to the womb through your body, reaching the fetus in a stronger form than outside sounds.

Researchers in Belfast have demonstrated that fetal listening begins at 16 weeks. This is especially significant because fetal listening begins 8 weeks before the ear is structurally complete, which is at about 24 weeks.

Hearing is clearly a major information channel for your baby, operating for about 24 weeks before birth.

Trivia...

Sounds have a surprising impact upon the fetal heart rate: a 5-second stimulus can cause changes in heart rate and movement that last up to an hour. Some musical sounds can cause changes in metabolism. Brahms' Lullaby, for example, played six times a day for 5 minutes in a premature baby nursery produced faster weight gain than voice sounds played on the same schedule.

Vision in the womb

Vision is probably our most dominant sense after birth. It evolves steadily during gestation but in ways that are difficult to study. At the time of birth, vision is perfectly focused from 20 to 30 cm (8–12 in), the distance to a mother's face when feeding at the breast. Studies have shown how extraordinary vision is in the first few months of life. Although testing eyesight in the womb has not been feasible, researchers have learned a lot from testing premature babies.

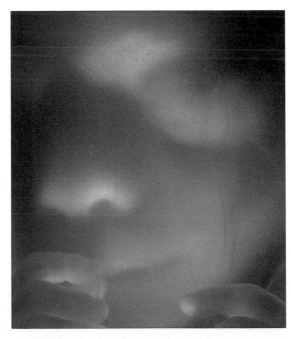

■ **There's not much space** *in the womb, so the baby does not need to see very far. Indeed the eyes don't even open until the end of the second trimester.*

Although the eyelids remain closed until about week 26, the fetus is sensitive to light in utero, responding to it with heart rate accelerations following projections of light on the mother's abdomen. Babies have been known to react to the experience of amniocentesis (usually done at around 16 weeks) by shrinking away from the needle, or, if a needle nicks them, they may turn and attack it. Mothers and doctors who have watched this under ultrasound have been unnerved. Similarly, at 20 weeks, twins in utero have no trouble locating each other and touching faces or holding hands.

A simple summary

✔ In the second trimester, you should feel well and energetic and should be eager to enjoy your pregnancy. This is a good time to take a holiday.

✔ Towards the middle or end of this trimester, you will feel the baby's movements. You will also feel some pains related to the growth of your uterus and your entire mid-portion. Heartburn, constipation, back pain, forgetfulness, and difficulty finding a comfortable sleeping position are all annoyances that will pass.

✔ Try to negotiate the longest feasible maternity leave. You'll need it for recuperation, and you'll want it to spend time with your new baby.

✔ During the second trimester the fetus is growing rapidly and appears to be fully formed.

✔ At this time, the fetus has rudimentary use of all its senses: touch, taste, smell, hearing, and vision.

✔ If you can avoid excess stress during pregnancy, you are more likely to give birth to an easy-going baby and a good sleeper.

Chapter 12

Third Trimester

A S THE THIRD TRIMESTER ARRIVES, you are well on your way to the finish line. Weeks 28 to 40 mark a period of rapid fetal growth: your baby will gain nearly half its birth weight and cause your uterus to expand to more than a thousand times its original size. If you had a window on your womb, you'd be astounded at all the activity in there. Your baby is making faces, kicking, hiccuping, and even crying (but we hope not too much). You may vacillate between excited anticipation of your baby's arrival and panic about labour and delivery. Both ends of the emotional spectrum are to be expected. Taking the time to understand the birth process can help alleviate some of the anxiety you feel as you approach your due date.

In this chapter...

✓ I don't feel so great

✓ What if my baby comes late or early?

✓ Medical visits now

✓ And what's the baby doing?

THE BIG DAY APPROACHES

I don't feel so great

UNDERSTANDING THE CHANGES *taking place in your body and the development of the fetus during months seven, eight, and nine of pregnancy will help prepare you for what to expect in the weeks to come, what is normal, and also how to recognize signs of trouble, if they should occur.*

You are most certainly uncomfortable, uncommonly tired, and probably pretty nervous. The looming question as you peer at your belly button is, "How is this watermelon-like creature ever going to get out of there?" At this point your body may be warming up with Braxton-Hicks contractions, causing you some discomfort as your uterus contracts and tightens.

While these contractions are not exactly painful, they can be distractingly irritating, causing you to stop whatever activity you are engaged in and take a seat.

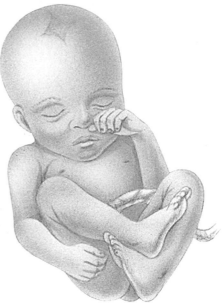

36 WEEKS
50 cm (20 in) long

I'm sorry to report that discomforts are all but a fact of life during the last 3 months of pregnancy. This is the point when many of us are ready to throw up our hands. But hold on – you're almost there.

Tired belly muscles and itchy skin

Abdominal aches continue in the third three months. They are usually related to your stretching tummy and the ligaments in the abdomen. The growing uterus and baby are also causing crowding in the abdominal area, and itchiness can result from the stretching of the skin. A good moisturizer can sometimes relieve this itch problem.

If you're thinking about a soak in a very hot bath or sauna, don't do it! High temperatures are potentially hazardous to your baby all throughout pregnancy.

HEADACHES AND BACKACHES

Headaches may also occur more frequently in the third trimester. Try to get enough rest and relaxation, especially if you are feeling tense and emotional. Backaches can occur as your growing belly affects your posture. Wear flat shoes, and try to be aware of sitting and standing with good posture. In addition, don't stand or sit for extended periods of time. Exercises to improve muscle tone and posture during pregnancy can also help resolve nagging backaches.

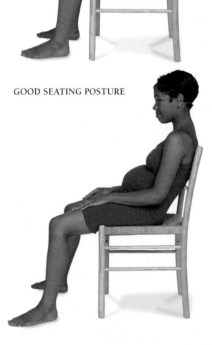

GOOD SEATING POSTURE

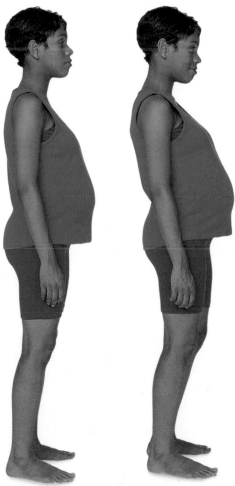

GOOD STANDING POSTURE   BAD STANDING POSTURE

BAD SEATING POSTURE

I feel like a fireball

Feeling hotter than usual during the last 3 months of pregnancy is a normal metabolic response. Your body is working hard to support your baby. You may be sweating when everyone else around you is shivering. If you are pregnant during the hot summer months, don't overexert yourself and try to stay cool. I found floating like a hippo in a cool, clean, freshwater lake to be absolutely divine heat relief.

Leaky bosoms

Colostrum may begin to leak from your nipples during the last months of pregnancy. Colostrum is the yellow, nutrient-rich liquid your baby will nurse on in the first couple of days after delivery before your milk comes in on the second or third day after delivery.

I can't get a wink of sleep

Difficulty sleeping and fatigue are common complaints at this time. Frequent nocturnal urination and discomfort because of the size of the growing belly usually make getting a good night's sleep difficult. Rest, and nap when you can. (Reread Chapter 11 on suggestions for comfortable sleeping positions.)

Trivia...

A friend tells me of a most embarrassing incident. She was in her sixth month of pregnancy with her third child when her very beloved father-in-law suddenly passed away. Standing at the graveside at this emotional moment, she felt her breasts engorging and beginning to leak profusely. Within minutes, the whole front of her dress was soaked.

■ **You will probably find** it hard to stick to your usual sleep patterns. That's okay – just be sure to sleep any time you can.

Leg and foot cramps may be bothersome in the third trimester, especially at night when you desperately want uninterrupted sleep. Avoid pointing your toes down when you stretch; keep your feet flexed to reduce cramping.

Nasal congestion

Hormonal changes can cause swelling of mucous membranes, a stuffy nose, postnasal drip, and occasional nosebleeds. Allergies may seem worse. Be sure to check with your doctor before taking any medications to treat this problem.

Breathlessness

Slight shortness of breath is a result of hormonal changes that affect the blood flow and muscles in the lungs. In the third trimester, shortness of breath can also be attributed to the enlarged uterus pressing up against the diaphragm, making breathing more difficult. Avoid overexertion. Some women with no history of asthma develop symptoms of asthma in late pregnancy. If this happens to you, be sure to consult your doctor or midwife. There is asthma medication that is safe in pregnancy.

Fluid retention

Swelling of the legs and feet in pregnancy is caused by fluid retention. This problem stems in part from the sheer volume of liquid – water, blood and amniotic fluid – present in your body right now. The remedy, and don't laugh, is actually drinking more water. Swelling can be most extreme during the hot days of summer and also in the weeks just before your due date. Elevate your legs as much as possible and don't sit cross-legged. Sometimes support hose can help bring relief. If you are experiencing more than mild swelling in your hands and face, get in touch with your doctor or midwife. Sometimes swelling can be a warning sign of high blood pressure or pre-eclampsia.

Haemorrhoids

Technically, haemorrhoids are varicose veins in your rectal area. Hormones and pressure on your intestines, as well as straining during bowel movements, can cause or aggravate an existing condition. Sometimes haemorrhoids can also develop following delivery thanks to the pressure exerted on the rectal area. Warm baths and witch hazel compresses are the most commonly suggested treatments. Sitting on a doughnut cushion can also relieve pressure to this area.

To help prevent varicose veins (swollen/bluish veins, usually in the legs), avoid sitting or standing for long periods of time, don't put on excess weight, be sure to walk or do other regular exercise, try wearing supportive pantyhose, and – do I have to say it? – don't smoke.

Swollen gums

Hormonal changes lead to swollen gums, too. You may even have some bleeding from the gums when you brush your teeth. Use a soft toothbrush and continue to brush and floss regularly.

Clumsiness

As you get bigger, it does get more difficult to manoeuvre. Step cautiously. Don't be afraid to ask for assistance when you need it. Wear comfortable shoes and try not to tread across precarious terrain where losing your balance is likely.

Leaking urine

Have you been doing your pelvic floor exercises? As your heavy uterus presses down on your bladder, a small amount of urine may be released during a laugh, cough, or sneeze. This leakage of urine is known as stress incontinence, and it can be a good wake-up call reminding you to do your pelvic floor exercises (see Chapter 6) and to practise contraction of the muscles surrounding your vagina and anus. These are the same muscles you would use to stop urinating in midstream.

You will have frequent urges to urinate during the last 3 months of pregnancy. Don't hold back; if you make a habit of not urinating when the call comes in, you can irritate your bladder and set off contractions.

Travel

You should stay closer to home toward the end of your pregnancy, or at least be near a medical facility. Most doctors and midwives discourage travel in the eighth and ninth months and many airlines have restrictions. Be sure to get the go-ahead from them all when planning a holiday or a visit to a distant destination. Even driving on car trips that last more than 1 hour can be too exhausting and uncomfortable during the last months of pregnancy.

Do not drive yourself to the hospital if you are experiencing contractions or going into labour. Call a friend or even 999 if no one is around.

LEAKY WATERWORKS?

What if my baby comes late or early?

IT IS THE RARE WOMAN who gives birth exactly on her due date. Most women give birth either a bit earlier or a few days late. But this is an important time to stay positive, get enough rest, and even do some moderate exercise, all of which will help stimulate labour.

To decrease the risk of premature labour, avoid heavy physical labour or lifting, be sure to drink plenty of fluids and to eat properly, and of course, avoid use of alcohol, drugs, and cigarettes.

DEFINITION

Going into labor before 37 weeks' gestation constitutes **premature labour**.

Discuss your personal risk of premature labour with your doctor or midwife. Regardless of medical advances on behalf of premature infants, the ideal is a full-term baby.

It used to be that 28 weeks was considered the "time of viability", i.e., that gestational milestone after which a premature baby could survive. With the advent of special care baby units (SCBUs), however, this time has been whittled down. Currently, 25-weekers are entertained as survivable. Less than that would put a baby into second trimester territory, but this is a zone that is hard to cross when talking about a baby's survival in the outside world.

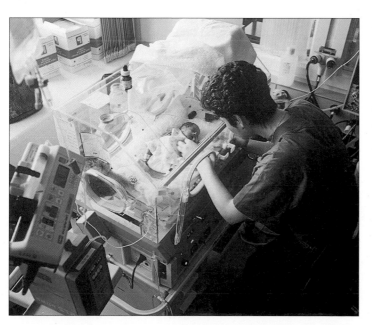

■ **Today's medical advances** *mean that premature births need not cause panic. Special care baby units give even babies born barely out of the second trimester a fair chance of surviving.*

Medical visits now

BY THE MIDDLE OF MONTH 7, or about week 32, your doctor or midwife may want to see you every 2 weeks. As you get very near delivery, they will probably want to see you weekly.

During your weekly visits you will have your weight and blood pressure checked, and you'll have lots of target practice peeing into cups so that your urine can be tested for sugar and protein at each visit. The baby's heartbeat will be monitored, and the doctor or midwife will evaluate the size and shape of your uterus by pressing on your abdomen. They will also try to feel which position the baby is in, head up or head down. Your doctor or midwife may also take a measurement of the **height of the fundus.**

Your doctor or midwife may ask you to pay attention to and record the frequency of your baby's kicks (called kick counts). When you are within a couple of weeks of your due date, your doctor may give you a pelvic exam to evaluate the condition of your cervix and determine whether or not it has begun to dilate or efface. These final visits are good times to discuss your concerns and thoughts regarding labour and delivery as well as to ask any questions.

> **DEFINITION**
>
> *The* **height of the fundus** *is the measurement of the growth of the uterus and where it is situated in your abdomen. Your doctor or midwife will use a tape measure to measure your belly from the top of the pubic bone to the fundus, or top of the uterus. At 12 weeks, the fundus should be just above the pubic bone. At 36 weeks it's usually just below the breast line.*

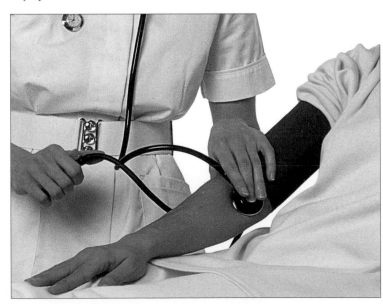

■ **One of the checks** *that will be carried out on you regularly at this time will be for blood pressure. It's quick and easy and doesn't even involve any needles!*

And what's the baby doing?

YOUR BABY IS BUSY getting ready for the big birthday. The fetus is beginning to regulate its own temperature and the bone marrow is completely in charge of production of the red blood cells. The fetus is even urinating about half a litre of urine into the amniotic fluid every day. Weight gain during the last 3 months is fairly incredible, with most babies gaining up to 3 or more pounds of weight, mostly fat and muscle tissue

The baby's irises can now dilate and contract in response to light. By virtue of the deposits of white fat underneath the skin, the skin is no longer red, but pink. The fingernails may reach the ends of the fingers, and there may be a lot of hair on the head. Movements of the fetus during the third trimester begin to change.

You once were the home of wild gymnastic parties; now, as the space becomes cramped, you will notice smaller movements, such as pokes by elbows and knees.

Medical tests

There is a range of tests that your doctor or midwife can perform to check on the baby's well-being at this time. The most commonly performed tests are an ultrasound, and a nonstress test in which the mother is hooked up to a fetal monitor. Other tests, usually reserved for special high-risk situations, include a fetal acoustical stimulation in which the fetus is stimulated with light and vibration, and a stress test to evaluate reactivity of the fetal heart to uterine contractions that have been stimulated artificially by oxytocin.

Is my baby okay?

One of the most frequently asked questions is that of the baby's health and well-being. Since we don't have a glass window on our wombs, fetal kick counts are becoming very popular. They are simple, free, and anyone can do them. While each fetus has its own movement patterns and rhythms, most healthy babies will move frequently in the uterus.

INTERNET

www.babybulletin.com

Visit this web site for a week-by-week illustrated update on your baby's growth and development.

Counting kicks

Here is how to do a fetal kick count. First pick the time of day at which your baby is generally the most active. This is the time to begin your count. Do not set yourself up for panic by waiting until the quiet times. Take a piece of paper and write down the time you start paying attention.

Recording your baby's movements at the same time every day will help with the accuracy of the test.

Put a tick on the paper every time you feel movement (kick, twist, punch, or turn). Do not count hiccups. When you have felt ten movements, write that time down as well.

If your baby is having a slow day, try walking for 5 minutes, eating, or drinking juice, and then go and lie down on your left side to see if that will perk up your sleepy little one.

Keep in mind that we do not feel all the movements of the baby. We are actually too busy most of the time to notice the majority of movements.

■ **Fetal kick counts** *are a great, easy, and free way of monitoring your baby's progress. At approximately the same time each day, count how many times you feel your baby move and keep a record of the number for comparisons.*

Also, a placenta that is anterior (located along the front portion of the uterus, directly under your belly button), or a mother with some extra weight may provide yet another barrier to feeling all the movements. Your baby should move ten times in 4 hours. If this does not happen, call your doctor or midwife for advice on what to do next.

A simple summary

✔ The third trimester is by far the most uncomfortable, but, fortunately, you can see the light at the end of the tunnel.

✔ Discomforts of the third trimester include: aches and pains in your abdomen, head, back, legs, and feet; Braxton-Hicks contractions; leaking of colostrum from your breasts and leaking of urine; itchy skin; swelling; and sleeplessness.

✔ Third trimester prohibitions are few, but you must not lift heavy objects, and you should check with your doctor or midwife before undertaking travel.

✔ As your due date approaches, you'll see more and more of your doctor or midwife, and you'll get frequent updates on your progress toward delivery.

✔ In this period the fetus grows to birthweight and size and continues developing. Its movements may be hampered by constricted space in the uterus.

✔ You may be unaware of most of your baby's movements because you are getting on with your own life. You can reassure yourself of the baby's well-being by taking fetal kick counts. These involve paying specific attention to fetal movements and keeping a written record for movements at the same time of day over a period of days.

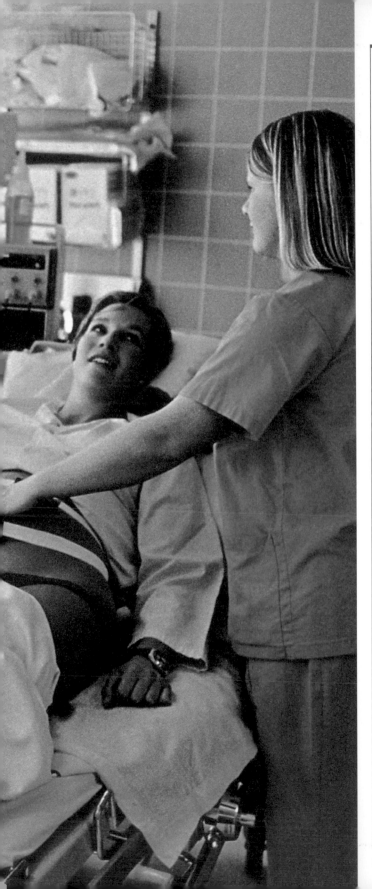

PART
FOUR

STAGES OF CHILDBIRTH

EW BIRTHS ARE HOLLYWOOD PERFECT with a mother labouring serenely in a rocking chair and then strolling over to the hospital where she lets out a groan and the baby is born. Labour for most normal mortals is *hard work* and full of *surprises*.

Although every woman describes her experience differently, three very specific stages always occur. Knowing what they are and how to recognize them is important for you and your partner. While no one can orchestrate the perfect birth, childbirth is easiest and most satisfying when you are *informed*.

Chapter 13

Is It Really Happening?

BIRTH TYPICALLY OCCURS 270 days after conception. However, there is no way to predict exactly when it will all start. Labour is different for every woman, and pinpointing when or how it will begin is not really possible. Some women don't even realize they are in the first stage of labour, mistaking it for wind, heartburn, backache, or indigestion. In this chapter we will help you recognize pre-labour, the common signs that labour is beginning, a false start, when to call the doctor or midwife, and what to take with you to the hospital.

In this chapter...

✓ The first signs

✓ A false alarm

✓ When should I call the doctor or midwife?

✓ The impending birth

✓ Packing your birth bag

183

The first signs

WHEN YOU'VE JUST *about had it with feeling huge and uncomfortable, you may notice some simple signs that tell you that labour may be approaching.*

The "drop"

For first-time mothers, a feeling as if the baby has dropped, also known as engagement, is one of the very first signs that labour is approaching. During engagement, the baby usually rotates into a downward position with its head settling into the bony part of your pelvis. When the baby engages, you'll probably feel a release of pressure on your abdomen. People may even comment that it looks as though your baby has "dropped". Sometimes this happens quickly, and you may find it suddenly easier to breathe. Engagement can take place 2 to 4 weeks before delivery in some first-time mothers. For others, engagement does not happen until after labour begins. It rarely occurs before labour in women who have given birth previously.

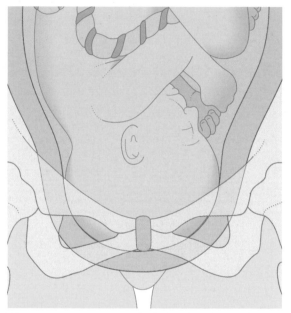

■ **During engagement,** *the baby's head drops down into the mother's pelvis, where it fits snugly until labour begins 2 to 4 weeks later.*

More frequent urination and bowel movements

If you didn't think you could fit any more trips to the toilet into your day, I have bad news. When the baby drops, it presses directly on your bladder, and so you can expect even more frequent urges to urinate. Also, a kind of natural cleansing of the bowels can occur at this time in preparation for delivery. The hormones acting on your intestines cause some women to have diarrhoea or even abdominal cramps.

To cut down on trips to the toilet when you're trying to sleep at night, try this exercise. As you get into bed, assume a cat-like position using your knees and hands for support. Now do 35 pelvic tuck-ins (see Chapter 6). These should help get the baby slightly off your bladder. The secret is then to lie right down. If you stand upright, you'll have to do the whole exercise over again.

Lower backache

This is a different backache from the familiar sort that has been grating at you through much of your pregnancy. Once the baby drops, there is increased pressure and stretching of the *sacroiliac joint* in your pelvic region. You may now find it hard to get comfortable in any position, standing or sitting, and it is likely to be much more difficult to find a comfortable position for sleeping at this time.

> **DEFINITION**
>
> *The **sacroiliac joint** is a slightly movable joint between your sacrum, which forms the back of the pelvis, and the ilium, the flat part of your hip-bones. For the baby to pass through your pelvis, hormones cause these joints and the ligaments that reinforce your pelvic girdle to relax.*

Braxton-Hicks contractions

In the weeks leading up to delivery, your uterus may begin warm-up exercises to help get your delivery system into good working order. These pre-labour contractions, known formally as Braxton-Hicks, may begin in the middle of your pregnancy and can go on for weeks until real labour contractions begin. You may notice the muscles of your uterus tightening for anywhere from 30 to 60 seconds. Not all women feel these random, usually painless contractions, which get their quirky name from John Braxton-Hicks, an English doctor who first described them in 1872.

■ **Back pain** *may start to feel slightly different, and become more difficult to relieve, once your baby has dropped.*

It is thought that Braxton-Hicks contractions may be brought on by dehydration, so drinking a couple of glasses of water often helps.

In general, a lack of adequate fluids can make your uterus more irritable – another of the many reasons to drink plenty of fluids while you're pregnant and even during early labour.

> **DEFINITION**
>
> **Effacement** *of the cervix is the thinning out and relaxing of the cervical canal in preparation for delivery.* **Dilation** *is the widening of the entry to the cervix.*

Braxton-Hicks contractions are normal during the last month of pregnancy. These contractions help tone the muscles of the uterus. They can also help adjust the baby's position and start the process of *effacement* and *dilation* of the cervix. Braxton-Hicks contractions can be annoying, even painful, and can rob you of needed rest, but they do much to prepare your body for labour. They also offer you a good opportunity to practise the breathing exercises you learned in your antenatal class.

The simple question, "How can you tell the difference between Braxton-Hicks and true labour contractions?" tops the most-frequent-question list for first-time pregnant women. Your friends will tell you not to worry – "You'll know real labour when it begins". And they're right. Real labour contractions are longer, more intense, and more painful than Braxton-Hicks contractions. They won't go away when you sit or lie down, change position, or just relax, all of which can help eliminate or, at least, ease the discomfort of Braxton-Hicks contractions. Braxton-Hicks contractions can increase in intensity, especially when your due date is approaching, and they may also appear to be rhythmic, like real contractions. However, they generally taper off or disappear altogether, unlike the real thing.

Do not self-medicate regardless of how harmless the remedy appears to be.

Herbal teas, such as black haw, black cohosh, and cramp bark, can help to relax the uterus and relieve the discomfort of Braxton-Hicks contractions, and magnesium supplements are sometimes prescribed by doctors or midwives, but please do not self-prescribe. Herbal and mineral sound healthy and natural, but they may not be right for you. Ask first!

Bursts of energy

Some people think a sudden burst of energy or "the nesting instinct" is Mother Nature's way of making sure you will be ready for the new baby. If you suddenly have the urge to put your underwear drawer in order, wash all the skirting boards, and polish the silver, this may be a sign that labour is approaching. Some women inexplicably start cooking meals for twenty or even cutting the grass. (Does a new baby really require a freshly-mown lawn?) As you can see, much of this nesting instinct gets expressed in what appears to be irrational behaviour, another sign that you're at the end of your rope or, more likely, the baby is coming. We all express our nesting instinct differently, and some of us, of course, simply never feel these urges at all.

■ **Bursting with energy:** *as labour approaches, you may experience an overpowering urge to get your house in perfect shape for your baby's arrival.*

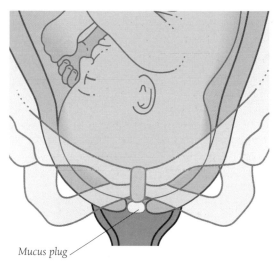

Mucus plug

■ **This cross-section** *shows a fetus at full term: the head is positioned over the pelvis with the mucus plug still in place to protect the fetus from any infection.*

Vaginal discharge or bloody show

As the baby's head descends and pushes down on your cervix – causing it to start opening – the mucus plug that had "corked" your cervix and uterus may discharge. The appearance of brownish or blood-tinged mucus, known as show, is a sign that the baby is on its way or will soon be coming out. The amount of blood should only be a spot or at most a teaspoon. In most cases labour begins within 3 days of passing the mucus plug. But sometimes it is possible that the baby will hang in there for as much as 2 more weeks. Still, this is a good sign that things are moving along.

A false alarm

YOU ARE IN FALSE LABOUR IF: your cervix isn't dilating even though you are having contractions (your doctor or midwife can confirm this during an examination); your contractions are erratic and don't feel increasingly intense; and a warm bath or massage relieves any pain you may feel in your abdomen or back.

False labour may feel just like the real thing. Unless you're a pro to the subtleties of labour, you probably won't be able to determine if you're experiencing false labour until it's over. But false labour can progress into true labour, and therefore it's good to keep in touch with your doctor or midwife as often as you feel the need. The truth is, your doctor or midwife can tell a lot by the tone and tenor of your voice, so verbal communication helps. He or she will also want to know how close together your contractions are, whether you can talk through a contraction, and what other symptoms you may have.

Trivia...

A report from a friend: "My first labour began at noon, a week before my predicted due date, and I called my doctor in great excitement. He calmly said, 'Stay at home as long as you can.' I called again at 3, 6, and 9 p.m. and got the same response. By midnight I hurt too much to call, so my husband phoned the doctor, who responded, 'Come now'. The baby was born at 6 a.m."

When should I call the doctor or midwife?

CALL YOUR DOCTOR *or midwife any time contractions are accompanied by watery or bloody vaginal discharge. If you have not reached 37 weeks gestation, call if contractions are accompanied by lower back pain, if you feel more than four contractions an hour, or contractions are coming at regular intervals. This could be a sign of premature labour, and your doctor or midwife may want to intervene. If you're past 37 weeks, there's no need to call your doctor or midwife unless your contractions last as long as 60 seconds each and are as close as 5 minutes apart.*

■ **Don't hesitate to phone** *your midwife once your contractions start coming at regular intervals and last for 60 seconds.*

Call your doctor or midwife immediately if you suspect a decrease in foetal activity or if you have any vaginal bleeding (unless it's just some bloody show), fever, severe headaches, changes in your vision, or abdominal pain.

The impending birth

BY THE TIME TRUE LABOUR BEGINS, *your cervix will probably have already started to dilate and thin. Your doctor or midwife will have given you this news at a recent visit, so you are alert to the possibility of impending labour. The best sign of real labour is contractions that occur at regular and increasingly shorter intervals, for a longer duration, and with increasing intensity. Other reliable signs of real labour include: persistent lower back pain, especially if it's accompanied by a crampy, premenstrual feeling; the shakes; diarrhoea; breakage of the water bag; and the appearance of a bloody show.*

Contractions

A good first indication that labour is occurring is the beginning of regular contractions. These contractions usually begin in your lower back and then travel to the front of your abdomen. Contractions are the tightening and relaxing of your uterus. Contractions help to open the cervix and push the baby out through your birth canal. During this stage, the cervix continues to open, thin out, and soften. This process is called cervical ripening.

Contractions of true labour occur regularly, follow a pattern, and with time become more regular, stronger, longer, and more frequent. Walking intensifies them, and they don't stop when you're lying down or changing activities. They usually start about 15 to 20 minutes apart and last 30 to 45 seconds. As your labour proceeds, the contractions become more frequent and last about 60 seconds. If you walk around or lie down they will not go away as do Braxton-Hicks contractions.

It's very important to drink plenty of fluids during early labour. You may not feel like eating, but you do not want to become dehydrated. Alternate between walking and resting, or try taking a warm bath or shower to ease any aches and pains. And, if you can, try to get some rest to prepare you for the work ahead.

The rest times between contractions are the clue as to how labour is progressing. This is the reason your doctor or midwife has probably instructed you to call when your contractions are regular and 15 minutes apart. For your first child, you will probably be instructed to come to the hospital or birth centre when the contractions are 5 minutes apart. Don't worry that you may deliver in the car; the first stage of labour lasts about 8 to 12 hours for a first baby. Generally speaking, if you have had at least one baby, your labour will be shorter than with the first.

When your waters break

A gush or trickle of water from your vagina indicates the breaking of the membrane or "bag of waters". The bag of waters is your baby's protective swimming pool of amniotic fluid, which is held intact by the amniotic membrane. Most often this membrane remains intact in early labour and helps cushion the baby's head as it pushes on your cervix. Later in labour, the membrane normally ruptures on its own. There is no pain; it just feels like a flow of warm water, but the amount depends on where the sac breaks. You can lose about a 0.9 litre (1½ pints) of amniotic fluid even as your body continues making it. If the membrane ruptures close to the cervix, you my feel a pop followed by a gush of water. Amniotic fluid, unlike urine, is normally clear and odourless. If your bag of waters breaks during the course of labour, be assured that birth is imminent.

INTERNET

www.babycentre.co.uk

This is a good general web site for all your pregnancy and parenting issues.

If, however, your bag of water breaks early in labour or if you suspect you're leaking amniotic fluid even before contractions begin, you should call your doctor or midwife immediately. Once your waters break, refrain from sexual activity and stay out of the bath at home.

Occasionally a woman's waters break long before contractions begin. Loss of the protective membrane and the protective fluid may open the fetus to infection. Often a doctor or midwife will choose to induce labour if contractions have not begun within 48 hours of the breakage.

Packing your birth bag

MOST EXPECTANT MOTHERS find comfort in meticulously packing their bags for the birth well in advance. Others choose to just rush out the door when the time comes and to send their partners home if they really need something. Some people suggest packing two bags: one for labour and one for you and the baby after the birth. If organization is your style, be sure to pack early, around your 34th week, so as not to get too caught up in the moment and flustered by forgetting.

Opposite is a list of suggested items you should think about packing, but you will undoubtedly want to personalize it with anything special you feel you might need and want. But do keep it simple; don't pack up the whole car. There are many things that can help make you feel more comfortable during labour but remember, you're only packing for a few hours of labour. And do leave valuables and jewellery at home – you have no use for them, and items do get lost.

■ **Plan and pack** *your overnight bag in the days, or even weeks, leading up to the birth, so that you're not caught unprepared.*

WHAT TO TAKE WITH YOU TO THE BIRTH

1. Two copies of your birth plan, if you wrote one

2. Toothbrush and toothpaste

3. Dressing gown

4. Comfortable clothes that you won't mind getting stains on

5. Comfortable shoes or slippers for walking during labour

6. A pair of thick socks

7. A picture or some other focal point for use during contractions

8. Your own favourite pillow(s)

9. Music, if it's allowed, and batteries

10. Coins or a phone card, and a list of important phone numbers

11. Camera or camcorder, if they're allowed

12. Lip salve

13. Massage oil and a rolling pin (or back massager) to ease strong back pains during labour

14. Extra clothes for your partner if he plans to stay around for a long while

15. Shampoo and toilet articles

Presents for brother or sister top the list for mothers on their second round. Buy and pack early. Shopping from your hospital bed is limited, and your partner will be much too busy with you and childcare at home. You might also buy and put aside something for the children to bring when they visit you and the baby.

Packing for after the birth is a little more straightforward. The hospital may provide you with most of what you need for baby's first hours. You will want to supply nappies, a bonnet or cap, an undershirt, and an all-in-one stretch suit, or Babygro. If the weather requires, bring some warm blankets to wrap your baby in. Most important: come prepared with an approved car seat. You will not be allowed to leave hospital without one.

What you'll need for you

For yourself, bring a dressing gown and nightdress that are not too precious. They will get stained, so save the fancy ones for home. For the same reason, you may want to include several pairs of well-worn, comfortable knickers (maternity size, since you will not be back to normal size for a while). I made the

DRESSING GOWN AND NIGHTIE

mistake of making a trip to the lingerie store before giving birth and securing a lovely ensemble fit for a bride. Luckily I kept the new undies safely tucked away in my suitcase for the duration of my hospital stay. While we're on the subject of bodily fluids and what they may do to your clothes after birth, you may want to include your own sanitary towels in that bag. Your own are usually more comfortable than the overstuffed hospital variety. If you plan to breastfeed, you'll need a comfortable nursing bra and breast pads.

If you are not planning to breastfeed, your maternity bra will do for a while, but you'll still need pads because you will leak until your milk dries up. You'll also need a roomy going-home outfit because you will still be looking about 6 months pregnant.

Trivia...

A friend who lived directly across the street from the hospital in which she gave birth had a dreadful time getting her baby released. Even though her husband planned to carry the baby home in his arms, the hospital stuck stubbornly to its rule that newborns be discharged into car seats.

BREAST PADS

The maternity wardrobe will serve until you shrink back into shape. Being fashionable at this time will be the last thing to cross your mind. And finally, a book on the care of newborns and breastfeeding can be useful, especially if you end up staying in the hospital for a few days.

A simple summary

✔ As labour approaches, you may feel some, all, or possibly none of the following symptoms: lightening or dropping of the baby into your lower pelvis; lower backache; more frequent urination and bowel movements; Braxton-Hicks contractions; a burst of energy; or a small bloody show.

✔ You'll know it's false labour if your contractions are erratic and don't feel increasingly intense, if a warm bath or massage relieves pain, or if the contractions stop altogether.

✔ Call your doctor or midwife at once if you feel real contractions before 37 weeks of gestation; this may be a sign of premature labour. Also call if you sense a decrease in fetal activity or if you have vaginal bleeding, fever, severe headaches, changes in vision, or abdominal pain.

✔ In true labour, contractions become more regular, stronger, longer, and more frequent as labour progresses. Other signs of labour include breakage of the bag of waters, the shakes, and diarrhoea.

✔ When you pack, pack simply and sparsely. Leave valuables at home and carry only the essentials. Bring comfortable clothing that you don't mind getting stained, and don't forget the car seat for taking your baby home.

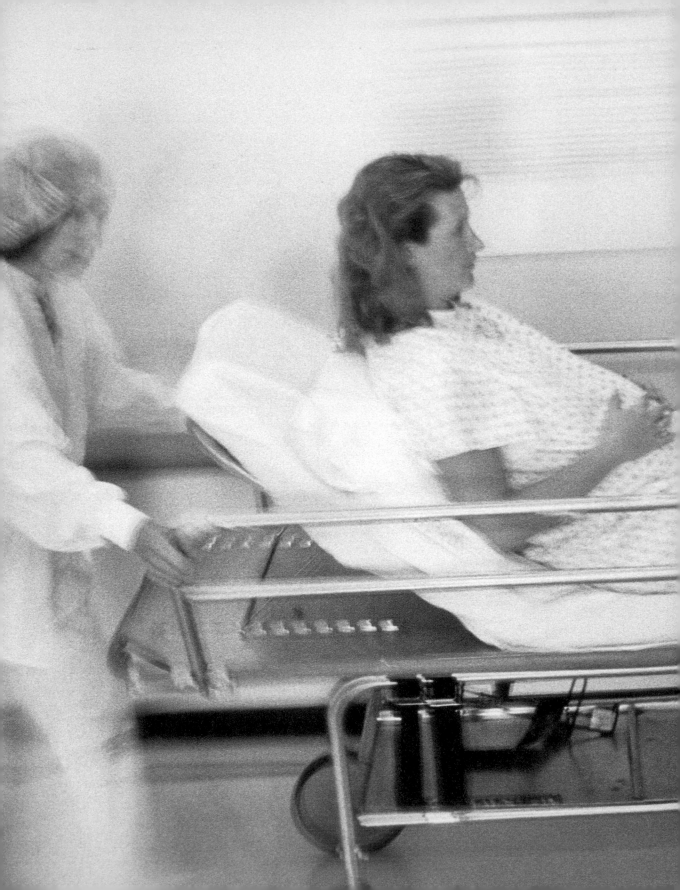

Chapter 14

Countdown to Delivery

THE ANTICIPATION OF LABOUR causes mothers-to-be a great deal of anxiety. Worrying about labour and wondering how you are going to survive it is normal. Nobody likes pain, and nearly everyone is terrified at the thought of losing control. Millions and millions of women have been pregnant, and you will not find one who wasn't scared. The fact is, however, that most of these same women have gone on to have more children. So, hey, it can't be all that bad. Memory of the pain dims, but the joy of the child endures. In this chapter you will learn what goes on during labour and the many methods of dealing with pain.

In this chapter...

✔ Working your body to the birth

✔ The first stage

✔ The active phase

✔ Best birth positions

✔ Medicated pain relief

Working your body to the birth

IN SIMPLEST TERMS, *the dictionary defines labour as "work". During birthing labour it is your job to move the baby from your uterus into the world, and this is indeed work. Throughout pregnancy, your cervix, which is made up of firm tissue shaped like a small doughnut with a tiny hole in the centre, has been tightly closed. As your due date has come closer and closer, the cervix has been* **ripening**. *During labour it must stretch wide enough for your baby to pass through. To accomplish this mind-boggling task, your uterus will tighten or contract repeatedly to force the opening wider. This happens little by little, over a period of several hours.*

DEFINITION

Ripening *refers to the softening of the tissues of the cervix as the due date approaches. Once the cervix is ripe, it is able to start effacing (thinning) and dilating.*

To put it simply, labour is broken up into three stages that typically overlap each other. During the first and longest stage, your cervix must dilate completely to 10 centimetres (4 inches) to allow the baby passage through. Initially the contractions are gentle, but they tend to become more powerful and more uncomfortable. The second stage begins when you start to push the baby out of the uterus and into the birth canal. This stage concludes when the baby is born. The third stage consists of delivery of the placenta or afterbirth, which must be expelled from the uterus. The whole process of labour generally lasts about 12 to 14 hours for a first baby and about 7 hours for subsequent babies.

The first stage

AS YOU LEARNED *in Chapter 13, the first stage of labour is the longest. It starts with mild contractions that may be 15 minutes or as much as 30 minutes apart and that last 60 to 90 seconds. During this time, the cervix opens to 4 or 5 centimetres.*

Current wisdom is that once your contractions start you should stay at home as long as possible or at least until your contractions are 5 minutes apart, unless your bag of waters has ruptured. At home you can walk around, distract yourself with friends, activities, and baths. Most important, at home you can rest to help preserve your strength for the more demanding later events.

■ **You'll know it's not a false alarm**
*when your contractions become more
painful, and occur at regular intervals.*

Time for the medics

Gradually, your contractions will become more regular, until they are less than 5 minutes apart. You will probably go to the hospital or birthing centre at this point. As described earlier, a small amount of pink liquid, or blood-tinged show, may appear during this phase. When the cervix begins to open wider, a thick plug of mucus or show may be discharged from the vagina.

Contractions feel different to different women. Some describe them as a wave that builds to a peak and then recedes. The best thing about the pain of contractions, unlike most pain, is that it doesn't linger. Once the contraction stops, the pain stops. There is no aftermath, no pain, until the next one comes along.

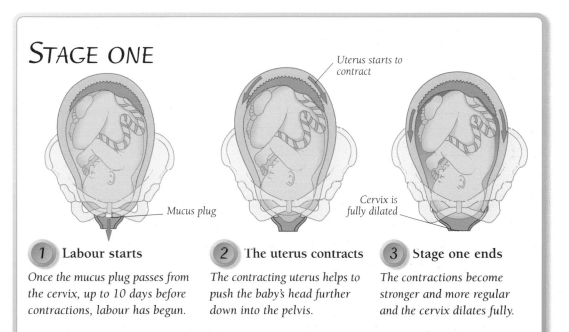

STAGE ONE

Uterus starts to contract

Mucus plug

Cervix is fully dilated

1 **Labour starts**
Once the mucus plug passes from the cervix, up to 10 days before contractions, labour has begun.

2 **The uterus contracts**
The contracting uterus helps to push the baby's head further down into the pelvis.

3 **Stage one ends**
The contractions become stronger and more regular and the cervix dilates fully.

The active phase

WHEN YOU HAVE REACHED the active phase, you should be under the care of your birth team either at the hospital, at home, or at another chosen birthing centre. In this phase of labour, your cervix will dilate from 4 to 8 centimetres, and contractions will become more intense. Contractions will progress to an average of 3 minutes apart and may last about 45 seconds. The active phase concludes with the transition phase during which the cervix dilates from 8 to 10 centimetres, and contractions that last 60 seconds are 2 to 3 minutes apart. On average, this phase lasts from 15 minutes to an hour.

The first stage of labour ends and the second begins when your cervix is completely opened. At this point your cervix will be dilated to about 10 centimetres. If your bag of waters has not already broken, it surely will when the cervix has opened wide enough for the baby's head to begin to pass through causing a gush of fluid to flow from your vagina.

All eyes on your cervix

During the first stage of labour, you will be examined regularly to ascertain the progress of your labour and how fast your cervix is opening (dilating). This is done by a vaginal examination. A midwife or doctor will measure your cervical opening in centimetres. When the cervix is open to its fullest, 9 to 10 centimetres, the opening is large enough for the baby to pass through.

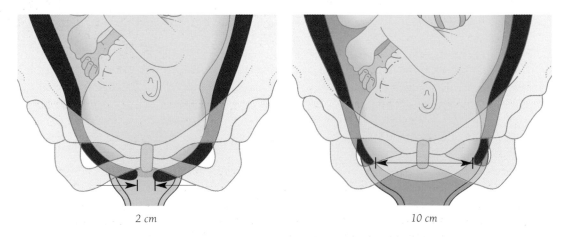

2 cm

10 cm

■ **From the start of labour to the end of stage one** *the cervix softens and thins, stretching to a diameter of about 10 centimetres and creating an open channel through which your baby can emerge.*

What is progress?

The progress of labour is expressed as a measurement of how much your cervix has dilated and how far the baby has descended. The generally accepted rate is 1 centimetre per hour of dilation and 1 centimetre per hour of descent following the beginning of active labour. Your body, however, may not be in such a great hurry and may be operating under a different set of principles. You are an individual, and your body follows its own rhythms. Just because your labour is diverging from that described in the rulebook doesn't mean that things are going badly or that the baby is in trouble. You should keep a positive attitude and not watch the clock. Perhaps your cervix is taking longer to efface and therefore is not dilating as rapidly. And even in active labour, part of the time, your uterus may be working on turning the baby rather than on its descent. All of the above is positive progress; it just means that it may take you a little longer to get the baby out.

If your labour stalls

If you've been labouring for hours and all of a sudden hear a pronouncement that your labour is not progressing, you may well become discouraged or frightened. This is not the time to give up or to panic. Think positively, and ask questions. Make sure you understand just what your doctor or midwife means with this statement and review the progress you have already made. Ask what you can do to help. Perhaps you should think about changing positions or walking. Maybe some nipple stimulation by your partner will help get your body to release more oxytocin, which will help encourage your contractions to become more effective. Feeling stressed or anxious can also slow labour, so you need to relax. Maybe a shower or warm bath or back rub can help. Being hungry or thirsty might also stall your labour. Maybe your energy reserves have just run out and you need to refuel. Even a little nap can help you regain your energy and get labour moving. Give it a try, if you can.

■ **Use your partner** *as a support and reassurance if your contractions start to tail off. Try to relax your body so as not to stall contractions any further.*

If none of the above helps to move your labour along, your doctor or midwife may suggest some medical remedies. Prostaglandin gel applied to your cervix can help encourage it to soften and dilate. If you are exhausted or uncomfortable, some pain relief may be in order. On the other hand, if you have already begun an epidural, it may in fact be stalling contractions. If pain relief, such as an epidural, stalls contractions in a previously progressing labour, the medication may have to be decreased or turned off.

ELECTRONIC MONITORING OF YOUR BABY

To make sure the baby is in good condition during labour, a nurse or midwife will check the baby's heartbeat by listening with either a stethoscope or an electronic fetal monitoring device.

An electronic fetal monitor (EFM) is a small box that sits next to your labour bed. It spits out graph paper with needle marks that show a pattern of the baby's heartbeat and your uterine contractions. You are connected to the EFM by two external belts that wrap around your abdomen. One belt holds an ultrasound sensor in place to detect your baby's heartbeat, and the other belt secures a sensor gauge that reflects your contractions. Two ink-filled needles then record the information on the paper flowing out of the EFM for your doctor or midwife to read.

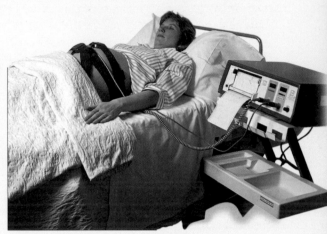

■ **Electronic fetal monitoring** *checks the baby's progress by tracking its heartbeat, which provides early warning of any fetal distress.*

An average fetal heart rate varies between 110 and 160 beats per minute. This is much faster than your own heart rate, which is about 60 to 100 beats per minute.

Internal monitoring

Changes in the fetal heart rate that occur along with contractions form a pattern. Certain changes in this pattern may suggest a problem. One such problem could be that the umbilical cord, which connects the mother and baby, is being pinched or squeezed. In some instances, an internal fetal monitor (IFM) device may be attached directly to the baby's scalp through the vagina after the bag of waters has ruptured naturally or has been broken by the doctor. This method is more accurate than external monitoring, but it is also more invasive and risky. For this reason it is not used routinely.

Early warning signs

Fetal monitoring is considered important during labour because labour is a stressful time for both mother and baby. Most babies will have heart rate changes at some point during labour and delivery. Normally a baby's heart rate accelerates with movement and stays stable or goes down slightly with contractions. The heart rate recovers quickly if the baby is tolerating labour well and is getting enough oxygen. If the baby's heart rate does not recover normally, this can signal a problem. Fetal monitoring cannot prevent a problem from occurring, but it can alert your doctor or midwife to warning signs.

During contractions, there is a temporary decrease in blood flow through the placenta, and therefore in the flow of oxygen, but there is also enough reserve oxygen from your healthy placenta for the baby to manage through a contraction.

The pros and cons

Fetal heart rate monitoring, either continuous or intermittent, is now part of routine care by most obstetricians and midwives during labour. However, use of electronic fetal monitor devices is not without controversy. Advocates argue that these devices have reduced the number of stillborn and brain damaged babies by alerting doctors to early signs of trouble. This is undoubtedly true. Opponents argue that the use of EFMs has led to the high rate of caesarean births. Also true. When a suspicious pattern is traced over a period of time, it alerts the doctor to the possibility that the baby is not tolerating labour well or is not getting sufficient oxygen.

Doctors tend to err on the side of caution and perform emergency deliveries rather than risk an unwanted outcome. But opponents of EFM argue that abnormal fetal heart rate patterns do not always mean that there is a serious problem, nor does the device tell you what the exact problem is. Other tests may be used to get a better idea of what is happening with your baby.

In general, women who are at high risk for problems during labour and delivery will most likely have electronic fetal monitoring. If you do not fall into that category, you should discuss your questions about fetal monitoring with your doctor or midwife when preparing for the birth of your baby.

Best birth positions

DESPITE THE MANY YEARS *that lying on your back has been advocated by doctors and hospitals, this is not the best position for birthing. Before the 18th century, women laboured vertically, using birthing stools and holding on to bars and squatting to cope with labour pain. Today these homespun tools are back in vogue and many women are choosing to use them during delivery.*

15TH-CENTURY BIRTHING STOOL

Keeping your baby on course

Walking, standing, showering, or even dancing during labour are also great ways to cope with labour pain. In addition to minimizing your discomfort, vertical movement helps the baby make his or her way out. Gravity, as you may well discover, is a great ally in helping to get the baby out. When the baby descends into the birth canal, it does not find a straight shot out into the world. Instead, the birth canal is a twisty passage. The baby has to navigate among the pubic bones and the sacrum in order to traverse a long tunnel and come out. Nature has made the journey somewhat easier on the baby by giving it a soft head that moulds to the different contours of the birth canal. But nature could use some help. That's where standing and walking during labour and birth come in.

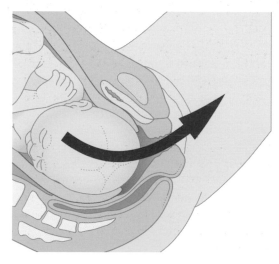

Being "on your back" is the worst position for birthing a child as it tends to compress the vagina and make contractions weaker and less effective. A woman who is standing during labour and birth can help shrink the distance the baby has to travel (especially when squatting or using a birthing stool), thereby making the journey a little easier on herself and her baby.

■ **Your baby must navigate its path** *out into the world. Assuming an upright position allows gravity – one of Mother Nature's finest birthing tools – to help the baby make its way out of your body.*

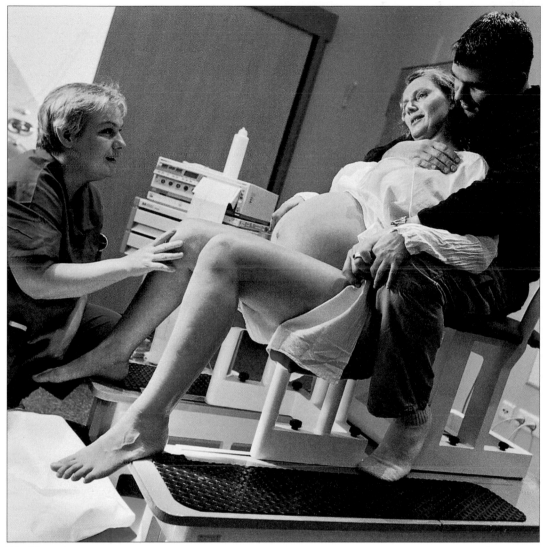

■ **Although many women** *choose to give birth on their back, you don't have to – some progressive hospitals even have specially designed birthing chairs to help you maintain a more upright position more comfortably.*

If you are in the hospital, tied up with all those wires and tubes, there are some things to try when you are confined to a bed. Try getting on all fours on the bed, or squat on the bed when possible. Discuss other birth positions with your birth attendants, and, by all means, read up and gather information and more ideas. This is one way to work with your body and aid your labour. If you are having your baby in a hospital, you will discover that some nowadays offer birthing chairs that can be adjusted to many angles and positions even while you are hooked up to monitors.

Dealing with pain

We all deal with pain in different ways, and when your contractions begin, you will quickly discover your very own coping style. Some of us do great without medications and interventions, and others really do need pain relief. You are the best judge of your pain thresholds and coping ability, especially if you have prepared yourself. Contractions of your uterus are involuntary muscle contractions. You cannot control these contractions, but relaxation helps cope with the pain.

There is no doubt that deep breathing is a great tool to help you relax during the 60 seconds or so when the contraction is working. But don't limit yourself to one technique. Many women concentrate on counting, focusing, and breathing, and come through the contractions feeling capable and in control. Maybe a good primeval scream, a moan, squeezing a pillow, walking, dancing, swaying, or even visualizing a chosen image will help you manage your labour experience. Perhaps you just can't cope and want some pain medication. Listen to your body, and follow your body's cue. It will guide you if you let it.

Natural pain relief

In Western cultures, many women ultimately opt for medicated pain relief. The truth is, though, that most anaesthesia, particularly an epidural, may not be delivered until far along into the transitional stage when the worst of your contractions are usually over. In the early stages of labour, you will indeed need to utilize all your personal coping resources. In general, if you can handle it, you and your baby might do better without anaesthesia. So don't forgo practising techniques for relaxation and natural pain relief. You may still need these tools, even if an epidural is the first item on your birth plan.

Don't stick slavishly to any one preconceived plan. If you had chosen anaesthesia, don't insist on it from the outset. Try going it alone first; you can always ask for relief if and when the pain becomes unbearable for you. On the other hand, even if you were dead set against anything "artificial", don't be a hero and continue suffering if you find the pain excruciating. Be flexible.

> ### Trivia...
> *If your mother, or most certainly your grandmother, gave birth in a hospital in the Western world, she may well have slept through the entire experience. In the late 1950s and early 1960s childbirth education was in its infancy, and anaesthetics that blocked pain in a portion of the body had been only recently developed. Some progressive doctors were using spinals, caudals, and saddle blocks, but most knocked out their patients with intravenous sleeping potions or inhaled gas.*

Keeping your options open

Even if you are adamantly for or against the use of pain relief medications, remember the old adage: "It's a woman's privilege to change her mind!" No two women experience childbirth in quite the same way, so it is important to keep your options open. You should be prepared for the possibility of not needing or, on the other hand, of eventually wanting an anaesthetic. As with any drug or procedure, once you understand the benefits and risks you will feel more confident when the nurse asks you to sign off on the dotted line before administering the medication.

■ **Before crying out** *for an epidural try to focus on the relaxation and breathing techniques you and your partner learned at your antenatal classes.*

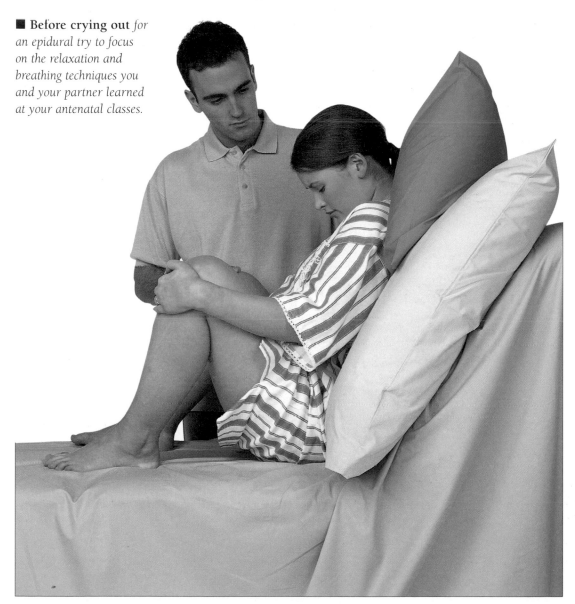

Medicated pain relief

ANAESTHETICS ARE MEDICINES *that completely deaden feeling in part or all of your body. However, the use of anaesthetics for obstetrical purposes differs from all other anaesthesia use in that there are two patients involved – you and your baby. The object of pain relief during labour is to allow you to deliver your baby with minimal pain and anxiety while, hopefully, still allowing you to fully participate in the birth experience. Ideally the anaesthetic should not stop contractions or make your baby sleepy.*

Since no two women experience pain or react to drugs in quite the same way, and because different anaesthetic techniques have different effects, there is no ideal anaesthesia for everyone. For example, while the anaesthetic may relieve pain, it may also weaken the contractions and thus slow labour. Also, some anaesthetic may reach the baby. You should also be aware that once pain medication or anaesthesia is administered, most hospitals require that you be confined to your bed or birthing chair with an electronic fetal monitor strapped around your belly. This means you will spend more time in bed, and you will not be free to move about.

Local anaesthesia

Local anaesthesia is exactly that: local, or in one narrowly defined spot. The injection that your dentist gives you to deaden only the specific nerve of the specific tooth under the drill is an example of local anaesthesia. So is the surface anaesthetic with which he or she anaesthetizes the gum where the needle goes in. Sometimes a local anaesthetic or a series of local injections are sufficient to numb the skin for an episiotomy and for putting in stitches if you need them.

■ **Don't be afraid** *to ask for pain relief if you feel you can no longer cope: excessive tension and anxiety can slow down labour.*

Regional anaesthesia

Regional anaesthesia is the most common form of pain control offered during labour and delivery. This method of anaesthesia deadens pain in limited areas of your body but allows you to remain awake to help your baby come into the world. By far the most popular form of regional anaesthesia at this time is the epidural. An epidural is delivered through a tiny tube called a catheter placed in the small of the back, just outside the spinal canal. The medication is then injected in small amounts near the spinal nerves several times during labour. Simultaneously, the patient is hooked up to an intravenous drip. This keeps the mother's body hydrated, which, in turn helps keep blood pressure from falling. When you receive an epidural, you will be told to lie on your left side and will be assisted when moving. A catheter may also be inserted in your urethra to help empty your bladder.

Epidurals, which are strong medicine, are not without side effects. The most common of these are shivering and itching.

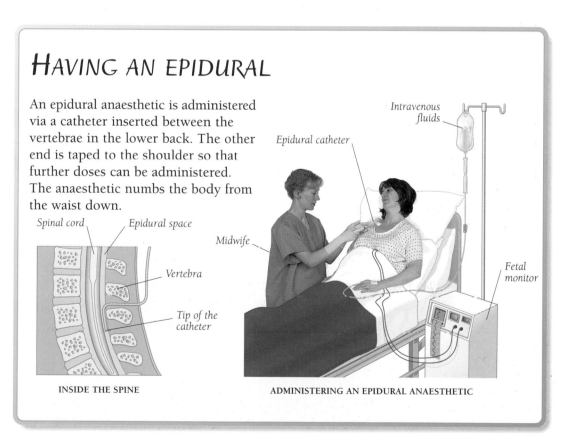

HAVING AN EPIDURAL

An epidural anaesthetic is administered via a catheter inserted between the vertebrae in the lower back. The other end is taped to the shoulder so that further doses can be administered. The anaesthetic numbs the body from the waist down.

Intravenous fluids

Epidural catheter

Spinal cord

Epidural space

Midwife

Vertebra

Fetal monitor

Tip of the catheter

INSIDE THE SPINE

ADMINISTERING AN EPIDURAL ANAESTHETIC

Other more serious, but less common, side effects are falling blood pressure, long-term backaches, and spinal headaches. Nerve injuries occur in only one in every 10,000 epidurals so are really not a factor to worry about. An advantage of the epidural is that it allows you to fully participate in the birth experience (you continue to feel touch and pressure) while relieving most, if not all, of the pain of labour. An epidural can actually help enhance labour if the doctor determines you are exhausted and not doing your share.

Although many women want the epidural started the moment they enter the labour ward, in most cases a doctor will not order an epidural until your cervix has dilated at least 4 to 5 centimetres. Under certain circumstances, epidurals may begin earlier, especially if labour has been induced. The medication for induction brings on much stronger contractions than those experienced during natural labours. Epidurals are also commonly used during caesarean deliveries, allowing the mother to be awake during the surgery. Generally, babies of mothers who choose epidurals show no adverse effects following delivery.

Spinal anaesthesia

Spinal anaesthesia is another form of regional anaesthesia. It is similar to an epidural, but it is administered with a needle directly into the spinal canal, and so its effects are felt much faster. A "saddle block" is a spinal injection that is given in the back to anaesthetize a smaller area. With spinal anaesthesia, you may feel numb and need assistance in moving during the delivery. Spinal anaesthetics are sometimes used for delivery by caesarean section or when the use of forceps is indicated.

Other regional anaesthetics

There are two other regional anaesthetics sometimes used during labour and delivery. Caudal anaesthesia consists of one or more injections near the tailbone. Pudendal and paracervical blocks consist of injections through the walls of the vagina and near the cervix, respectively. These are sometimes used during the last stage of labour if the mother is having trouble pushing the baby out.

General anaesthesia is rarely used during labour and delivery today except in the case of a medical emergency.

General anaesthetics are administered quickly, so they're considered the best choice when time is of the essence.

Are anaesthetics safe?

Anaesthesiologists and obstetricians regard the medications currently used in labour and delivery as totally safe for you and your baby, and most of the research seems to back up their claim. But some argue that no one really knows the truth, and suggest that before signing up for powerful pain relievers, you at least give your body a chance to deal with labour naturally.

We do know that once you receive a drug intravenously, the drug enters the baby's bloodstream at 70 per cent of its concentration in your blood.

In some cases large doses of sedatives like pethidine and diamorphine can affect your baby so that he or she is sleepy at birth and for the first few days of its life, making it harder for him or her to breastfeed. However, drugs used in epidural anaesthesia cannot enter your baby's blood, and so a baby born after an epidural stands a very good chance of being wide awake and alert.

A simple summary

✔ Birthing labour is hard work, and it is painful.

✔ The first stage of labour is the longest. In this stage, contractions begin gently and rhythmically far apart. As labour progresses and the cervix dilates, contractions become closer together, more regular, stronger, and more painful. And the baby moves along the birth canal.

✔ In the active phase of labour, the cervix dilates completely. Unless it has already broken the bag of waters breaks, and the baby is born.

✔ During labour, the baby's condition is monitored either by stethoscope or electronic fetal monitor (EFM). If fetal distress is indicated, medical or surgical measures may be taken.

✔ Anaesthesia can relieve some pain of childbirth. Most anaesthesia is entirely safe and allows the mother to experience and help out in the process of delivering her child. While doing without anaesthesia is admirable and "most natural", there is no shame to using pain relief.

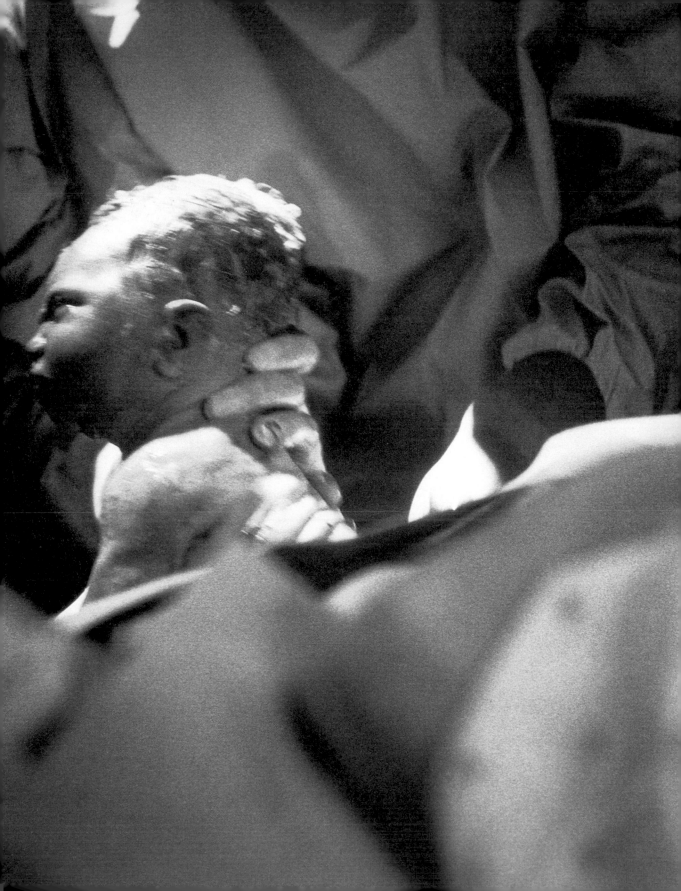

Chapter 15

Here Comes the Baby

"ALL BABIES COME OUT ONE WAY OR ANOTHER", a wise midwife informed me when I was having my doubts. And in the second stage of labour, I began to believe her. In this chapter we'll help you understand the moment when you finally, truly, give birth.

In this chapter...

✔ Transition

✔ The second stage

✔ When is induction necessary?

✔ The baby is born

✔ Unusual positions of baby

✔ Instruments to aid delivery

✔ The third and final stage

211

THE MOMENT YOU'VE BEEN WAITING FOR

Transition

THE TRANSITION PHASE *marks the point between the first and second stages of labour, and it is perhaps the most demanding part of labour. During transition your cervix is dilating to the final few centimetres, and the baby is beginning its* **descent** *into the vagina. This is the part of labour that many of us would rather skip over. This is a time when we want to quit. Plenty of my friends have told me that during the transitional stage they became incredibly irritable towards their husbands, threatening divorce or proclaiming that they would never, ever give birth again. These decisions were, I'm happy to report, reversed immediately after the baby was born.*

DEFINITION

Descent *is the term used by doctors and midwives when the baby is dropping down into the vagina.*

Both the length of the transitional phase and the intensity of contractions vary widely among individual women. Some women experience a particularly intense transition and others a mellow one. If your transitional contractions are intense, don't feel put upon. Intense transitional contractions may serve to get the baby out more quickly. Nice strong contractions tend to speed the process, whereas mellower ones can act to slow progress down.

Transitional contractions

Transitional contractions are definitely the most demanding. At this point maximum pressure is being put on the muscles surrounding the cervix. For this reason you may find it much harder to relax, and you may find this to be the time of maximum pain. During the earlier phases, your contractions may have felt like waves you could float on. During transition they may feel like King Kong gripping you with all his might before dropping you to the floor. Sometimes the contractions come every 2 minutes and last up to 90 seconds. You may barely have time to recover from one before the next one begins.

Fear actually tightens the cervix, slows down contractions, and interferes with the work of the uterus during labour. Relaxation techniques help labour in many ways. Relaxation untenses birthing muscles, raises your pain threshold, releases natural pain-killing hormones, enhances your ability to think clearly, and conserves your energy, thereby lessening exhaustion.

The second stage

THE SECOND STAGE OF LABOUR is gratifyingly the finish line of the long marathon that has been your pregnancy. In transition, a few moments ago, you may have felt as if you couldn't go any further. Now the pain of cervical dilation has mercifully passed and so has the hardest part of labour, but there is still work to do. In the second stage of labour, your energy may be renewed as you push the baby through the open cervix, through the birth canal (vagina), and give birth.

For many women, a water birth is the simplest method for a comfortable labour. Submerging in special birthing baths relieves pain thanks to the laws of buoyancy. Weightlessness in water helps support muscles and bones and helps muscles relax, sparing muscles for birth.

This second stage is much shorter than the first, about 90 minutes for first babies and 30 minutes or less with later children. Your contractions during this part of labour feel less intense than during transition but are actually much stronger. They tend to be about 2 to 3 minutes apart and last about a minute.

RELIEVING PAIN IN A BIRTHING POOL

Avoid hyperventilation during labour. Breathing too fast or too heavily can cause imbalances in blood chemistry, which may compromise the oxygen supply to you and the baby.

The more relaxed you are at this point, the better you may handle the task at hand, pushing. As the baby moves, little by little, through the birth canal, it puts pressure on the rectum, and you should feel an urge to "bear down" as though having a bowel movement.

When do I begin pushing?

Your doctor or midwife will tell you when to begin pushing; it's important to listen to instructions. You may find that pushing comes as a great relief, or you may think of it as the final great challenge – not unlike that faced by a mountain climber in the last few moments before reaching the summit. The pushing phase of labour, despite the accompanying elation, may be the hardest work you've ever done. When the job is over though, a tiny warm baby will be resting outside your belly.

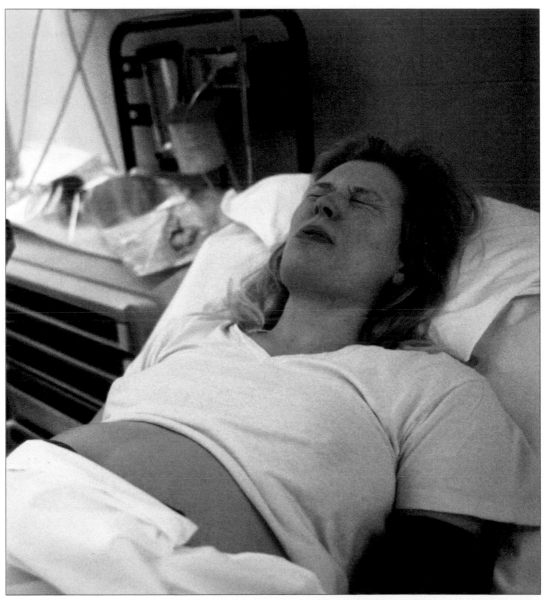

■ **As you push** *try to keep the muscular effort as smooth and slow as possible; remember to take long, deep breaths to control the pushing so that you don't cause damage to the cervix and perineal tissues.*

Pushing usually relieves some discomfort. Believe it or not, pushing is actually an involuntary movement, and you may find yourself doing it during a contraction without even realizing it.

Some women also describe this point as a fine line between pain and pleasure. Your doctor or midwife may ask you to use special breathing techniques while pushing.

How to push

There are basically two schools of thought about how you should push your baby out. The "big push" school argues that it is best to get the baby out as speedily as possible. Practitioners subscribing to this school might want you to push harder and longer. A doctor or nurse will grab your legs and pull them back and, when the contraction starts, will yell "push" while you take a deep breath and push to the count of 10. With eyes bulging and a red face, this is an exhausting form of pushing. With this method you are physically straining and can tear your perineal tissues (area between the vagina and the anus), among other undesirable effects. This method of pushing probably dates back to the days when mothers were so medicated they were completely out of touch with their bodies and couldn't feel or push properly.

Don't hold your breath during pushing. Deep long breaths help keep a good supply of oxygen to the baby during the crucial descent down the birth canal.

Listening to your body

INTERNET

www.childbirth.org/ articles/labor.html

Learn more about the processes of labour, pain-relief options, and pick up great advice on when and how to push.

A more natural method of pushing is simply listening to your body and doing what comes naturally. This usually results in short, frequent, instinctive pushing. You don't hold your breath or strain. This method spares your energy, won't burst blood vessels, and, best of all, helps to gently stretch your perineal tissues, preventing painful tearing. Basically your body knows how to push, and a good birth team will take the cues from you unless there is some complication. The process may take a little longer, but not much.

Possible perineal problems

While you are pushing, you may experience a kind of burning sensation when the baby's head is crowning at the opening of your vagina. This results from stress on the tissues in the area. In order to prevent tearing of the perineum, and to avoid an *episiotomy* or the use of forceps, some doctors and most midwives will perform a perineal massage to help relax and stretch these tissues.

DEFINITION

An **episiotomy** is a surgical cut to the perineum, the muscular area between the vagina and the anus. Episiotomy, often done with a local anaesthetic, is made in order to increase the size of the vaginal outlet and to allow more room for the baby to be delivered. Making this cut prevents possible tearing of your tissue. Episiotomy should be done only when necessary, though the old school of medical practice performed an episiotomy as a matter of routine. A few stitches are used to close the cut.

PERINEAL MASSAGE

Perineal massage is simple to do; ask your midwife for a demonstration. The first thing you need is clean hands, of course. It would also be a good idea to give your nails a good trim. A long thumbnail poked into the perineum tissue will give you a good idea of what real pain is. After scrubbing and trimming, find a petroleum-free oil to massage with. (KY jelly or any vegetable or olive oil is great.) You may also find a mirror handy so you can get a good look at what you're doing.

You stretch your perineum in two ways: by widening and lengthening.

The widening stretch

1. Place your thumbs deep into the vagina while spreading your legs.

2. Press the tissue down towards the rectum gently until you feel a burning or tingling sensation. Hold the stretch until the sensation subsides, then release.

The lengthening stretch

1. Using a little lubricant, pull your vaginal tissues forward with your thumbs.

2. Now perform the widening massage. This stretch will mimic the stretching your baby's head will do as it begins to crown.

Be careful to be gentle on yourself and not to overdo it or be too brutal. You could cause irritation or infection to the urethra if you apply too much pressure. A daily gentle perineal massage can be a great help in preparing you for birth.

DADS IN THE DELIVERY ROOM

If your partner is participating in the birth, as I hope he is, he may be offered a chance by your doctor or midwife to catch the baby as it is emerging from the birth canal. Of course, not all dads are up to this honour; some prefer a view from the side of the bed.

The best contribution a partner can make during labour is to share the experience in whatever way is comfortable for him and, of course, to be there for encouragement, love, and support. Some men have been known to faint in the delivery room. A lot of men have told me it was hard to watch their partners in so much pain, but nevertheless they carried on. Assuming that a man wants to be there at all, he should feel free to concentrate on being there for you and providing comfort. There are plenty of experts who can concentrate on the business at hand without his assistance.

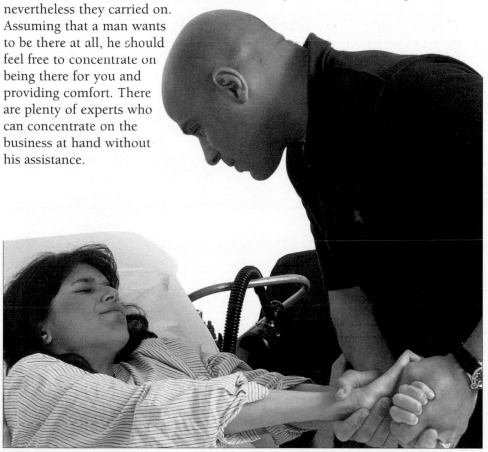

■ **Having your partner by your side** *can be the best pain relief there is. If he's willing to be at the birth he can help you relax, as well as offer support to help you through the pushing stage.*

When is induction necessary?

ONLY 5 PER CENT OF BABIES *are born on their actual due dates. Generally, once you pass your due date, you will have a 10-day grace period in which to wait for labour to occur naturally. After that, your placenta begins to be less efficient each day beyond your due date. The longer you wait beyond the grace period, the more risks to the baby. Amniotic fluid can become compromised, at which time the baby's whole support system in the womb is not at its best.*

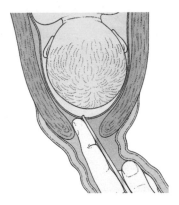

■ **The doctor can induce** *labour by rupturing the amniotic sac using an amniotomy hook; this procedure causes the uterus to contract within a few hours.*

Means of induction

Your doctor may decide to induce labour if you or your baby, or both, are at risk. Some high-risk situations may include a pregnancy that lasts past your due date, or medical problems such as high blood pressure or diabetes. If the cervix is not dilated, your doctor may need to use a cervical ripener before labour can be induced. Your doctor may also determine that inducing or augmenting labour is necessary if the cervix is open and contractions have not begun or are not strong enough. Labour induction can start contractions and augmentation can strengthen contractions so as to assist labour and delivery. There are several ways to induce labour.

One of the ways of inducing labour is to break the fluid-filled sac that surrounds the baby. This is done during a vaginal examination. Most women go into labour within 12 hours after their membranes are broken.

INTERNET

www.pregnancy.about.
com/health/pregnancy/
library/stories

Click here to get an inside view of other women's birth experiences, including induced labour and caesareans.

Another method for beginning labour is treatment with a drug called Oxytocin. The drug helps start contractions or makes them stronger. The medication is given by an IV (intravenous) pump, which measures the amount of the drug being delivered.

The baby is born

DURING THE SECOND STAGE of labour, your baby is forced out through your birth canal under extreme pressure and is intermittently deprived of oxygen. During this time the baby secretes the hormones adrenaline and noradrenaline, collectively classified as catecholamines, at levels that are higher than they are likely to be at any other time throughout his or her life. Adrenaline helps open up the lungs and dry out the bronchi, thereby achieving the switch from a liquid to an air environment. Noradrenaline, which is especially prevalent, slows the heartbeat, enabling the fetus to withstand fairly lengthy oxygen deprivation.

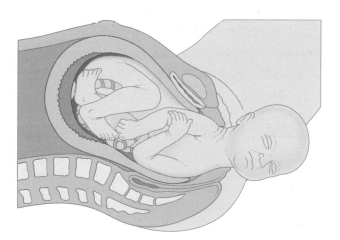

THE BABY'S HEAD EMERGES

First contact

Immediately after birth, depending on the policies of your hospital or birthing centre, your baby may be suctioned to assist in the drainage of amniotic fluid, mucus, and blood. A small bulb syringe may be used to suction the mouth and nose. The cord is then clamped and the baby is dried and its warmth is assured with blankets, heat lamps, or a heated bassinet. Often the baby is placed on your chest immediately after birth to establish skin-to-skin contact.

Both you and the baby will have identification bands placed on you before leaving the delivery room. The baby may also have its hand and foot prints taken.

Trivia...
A recent survey showed Chloe to be the most popular choice of name for girls, followed by Emily and then Megan. For boys Jack was the number one choice, second was Thomas, and the third most popular was James.

Unusual positions of baby

ABOUT 97 PER CENT *of babies are born in the head-first position. The fetus' skull is soft and pliable, which helps the head to pass through the birth canal. Rarely, a baby may enter the birth canal in another position. But this does happen. These complicating presentations are breech, footling breech, and shoulder.*

Breech

A breech baby is one whose feet or buttocks enter the birth canal first. Only 2.4 per cent of babies are born rump first; this is called a breech birth. During a breech birth, great care must be taken to avoid damage to the baby's head, which is the most difficult part of the infant's body to pass through the birth canal. This usually makes labour longer and more difficult for the baby, so nearly all breech babies are delivered by a caesarean section. However there is a movement afoot among some obstetricians who have recommended that caesarean sections are not used routinely in a breech birth. They argue that breech births for low-weight babies, especially if the obstetrician is skilled, may present no difficulty. Some midwives have received training and have practised techniques to help turn the baby and will deliver a breech baby vaginally.

External version or the "bottoms up" procedure is the term used to describe the turning of the baby from breech to head down. This technique, exercised close to your due date, involves manipulating your abdomen to turn the baby.

There is some risk that this exercise can cause the cord to become entangled and/or the placenta to separate from the uterine wall. For this reason, the procedure usually takes place in a hospital in case an emergency caesarean section becomes necessary.

■ **The breech position** *is when the baby settles bottom- or breech-down in your uterus; often the midwife will attempt to shift its position manually before delivery.*

Footling breech

Even rarer than the rump first breech is the footling breech in which the baby presents both or, more commonly, one foot. Vaginal delivery of the footling breech is extremely difficult and risky.

A footling breech should be delivered by caesarean section.

Most babies assume the breech position in the weeks before delivery, but some babies do the flip at the beginning of labour. Your doctor or midwife will let you know if your baby is in a breech position and will tell you what to expect.

Shoulder presentation

An even rarer occurrence is the shoulder presentation. This occurs in only one birth out of 200. The shoulder presentation is extremely dangerous because the baby must be forced by the attendants into a breech position. This forcing can rupture the uterus, which may cause the death of the infant and severe haemorrhaging in the mother. To be on the safe side, most babies who are not presenting head first will be delivered by caesarean section.

When is surgery necessary?

If there is a problem during labour, the baby may be removed from the uterus by caesarean section. The caesarean is commonly used when vaginal delivery might threaten the life or safety of the mother or infant or in the presence of certain diseases and conditions.

Caesarean section, or surgical delivery, is the name of the operation in which the baby is delivered through an incision in your abdomen rather than through the vagina.

Even though a caesarean delivery is considered major surgery, the risks are considered relatively small. When it is truly necessary, a caesarean section can be a lifesaver for both infant and mother. If a caesarean is not mandated by a mid-delivery crisis, the mother usually is awake, anaesthetized with an epidural, and the father may be present throughout. This should help you all feel better about the birth and makes bonding with the baby easier for both parents.

INTERNET

www.babycentre.co.uk /expert

Get answers to any worries or queries you may have about giving birth to a baby that's not in the head-first position.

Reasons for a surgical delivery

In the UK the rates for caesarean delivery vary from area to area, and hospital to hospital. In some districts the rate is as low as 13 per cent, while in others it is as high as 25 per cent. There are many reasons why a caesarean birth may be suggested, among them: the baby is too large to pass safely through the pelvis, also known as CPD (cephalopelvic disproportion); the baby may not be in the head-first position or be exhibiting signs of fetal distress; this is a closely spaced repeat caesarean; the mother may have a medical illness or condition that renders vaginal delivery unsafe. A caesarean delivery is also mandated when the mother has severe toxaemia, uncontrolled diabetes, active genital herpes, placenta praevia, abruption of the placenta, prolapsed cord, or a fetus lying transverse (sideways).

Interestingly infants born by caesarean section often have respiratory problems and may require special attention. One reason for such problems might be that the baby has not benefited from the compression of the lungs during descent through the birth canal. Also the baby has missed out on the rush of adrenaline and noradrenaline and the usual stresses of birth. Generally, however, caesarean section babies are healthy and happy.

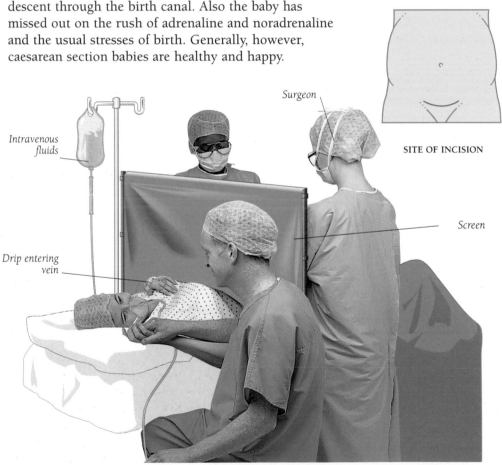

Intravenous fluids

Surgeon

SITE OF INCISION

Screen

Drip entering vein

■ **Caesarean delivery** *is usually performed under epidural anaesthesia to allow you to remain awake and share in the first moments of your baby's delivery. Your partner can be with you throughout the operation.*

Instruments to aid delivery

INSTRUMENTS SUCH AS FORCEPS *and a vacuum extractor are used to assist in bringing the baby down and out of the birth canal. Sometimes anaesthetics and other pain medications make it difficult for a woman to feel or control her muscles and participate in pushing the baby out. Or perhaps the mother is just too exhausted to push at a crucial moment. Indications of fetal distress once the baby has descended into the birth canal also dictate a need for instrument assistance and a more rapid completion of delivery.*

What about forceps?

Forceps look like a bigger, single-handle version of the metal tongs you might use for cooking. Forceps are used in delivery when a doctor feels that pressure on the baby's head must be relieved, or if the birth of the baby is not progressing. But the baby must be at least in the middle of the mother's pelvis or very low in order to qualify for forceps delivery. If the baby is higher, a caesarean delivery is favoured over forceps. The baby's welfare is always foremost. If a forceps delivery is performed it should be no more harmful than a caesarean delivery, neither to the baby nor to you.

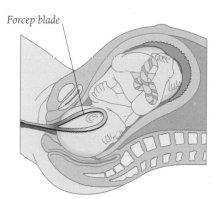

Forcep blade

■ **The forceps blades** *help to draw the baby out with a few gentle pulls.*

Forceps are attached at either side of the baby's head around the ear area, when the head is well down into the mother's pelvis.

Because this procedure can be painful for the mother, the doctor generally orders anaesthesia. In order to make room for the instrument, the doctor must perform an episiotomy. The rules of informed consent require that you understand that if an attempt to deliver the baby with forceps fails, a caesarean section may be required.

Historically, forceps came into vogue before caesareans became widely available and safe. Forceps were the only alternative available when the baby got stuck in the birth canal. In the last 100 years, forceps were often used when mothers laboured on their backs and were over-medicated during birth. Both situations made it difficult for women to push and fully participate in birthing their babies. Today, as women have been assuming more favourable positions for birthing and have been rejecting high-dose regional anaesthesia, the need for forceps has almost disappeared.

What is vacuum suction?

A vacuum extractor is an alternative to forceps, although unlike forceps, it can be used when the cervix is not fully dilated. With this instrument, a soft silicone cup is attached to the baby's head in the birth canal, and gentle traction is applied to help bring the baby down and out for delivery when assistance is required. Anaesthesia is not necessary, and the discomfort is not dissimilar to regular old pushing. There is a possibility that the baby's head may swell at the site at which the cup was attached, but this should disappear after 24 hours. Generally there are no other risks to vacuum suction. If you have any concerns, you should talk to your doctor, and he or she should put your fears to rest.

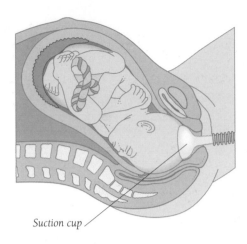

Suction cup

■ **Vacuum extraction** *is an alternative to forceps delivery; this process requires less pain medication and there is less risk of the mother needing an episiotomy.*

The third and final stage

WHEN THE PUSHING IS OVER, *the job is done, and the baby has arrived, the final phase of your birth experience must be the expulsion of the placenta, which has been your baby's life-support system inside the womb.*

After all the work of getting that baby out, this is a simple but important exercise for you. The placenta will separate from the uterine wall and you will feel some more contractions, close together but less painful, for about 15 to 20 minutes. Then you will push the placenta out without too much trouble. It is very important that the placenta be whole and intact. Your doctor or midwife will examine the placenta carefully to make sure. As long as no one has tugged too hard on the umbilical cord, while it's still attached to the placenta, all should be well.

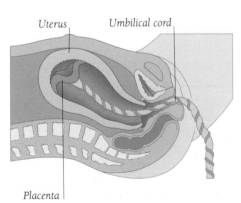

Uterus   *Umbilical cord*

Placenta

■ **Further contractions** *help push the placenta out through the birth canal once it has separated from the uterine wall.*

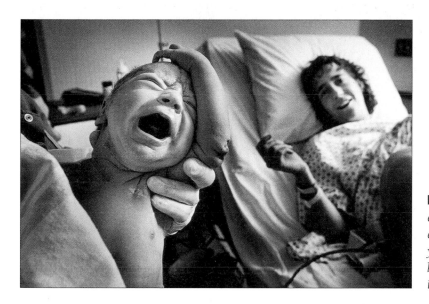

■ **After the pain:** *Relief, excitement, joy, and exhaustion. The sight of your baby taking its first breath will make you feel it was all worth it.*

A simple summary

✓ The transition phase occurs between the first and second stages of labour. Transition is the most demanding and the most painful part of labour.

✓ The second stage is the pushing stage. It culminates with the baby's birth.

✓ An episiotomy is a controlled cut in the perineal area, which must be stitched shut after the birth. Small tears are thought to be better for the mother because they usually heal more quickly.

✓ The great majority of babies are born in the head-first position. The fetus' skull is soft and pliable, helping the head to pass through the birth canal. Some babies enter the birth canal in another position – breech, footling, or shoulder presentation.

✓ Caesarean section, or surgical delivery, generally requires a longer recovery period.

✓ The third stage of labour is the easiest. It consists of pushing out the placenta.

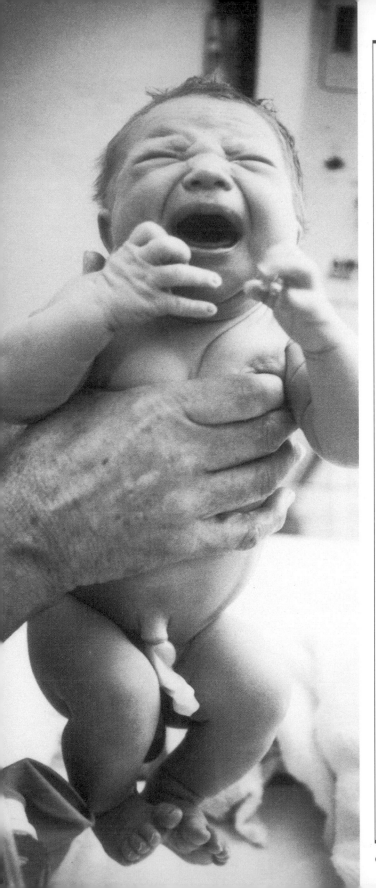

PART FIVE

CONGRATULATIONS, NOW YOU'RE A PARENT!

THE EARLY DAYS AND WEEKS

WITH THAT FINAL PUSH and the arrival of a slippery baby, you are treated to one of life's most *joyous* moments. Gazing into the eyes of your newborn sets you off on the trail of a love like you've never known before and your new role as a *parent*.

Caring for and feeding a newborn is not as instinctive as you may think. Motherhood is a constant on-the-job *learning experience*, so in these early days it's important to take it one day at a time, and deal with the daily challenge of your new relationship with your child.

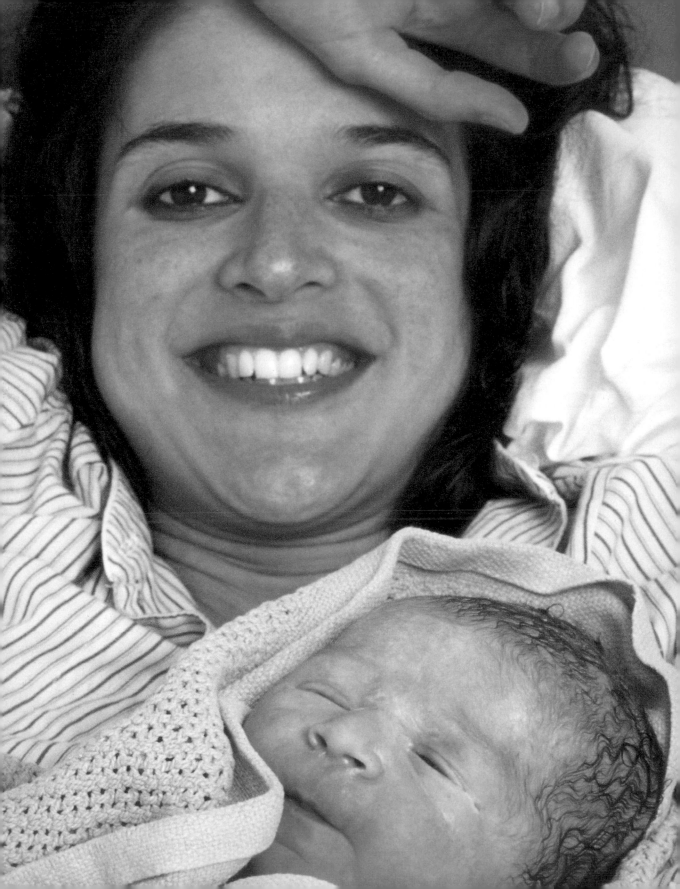

Chapter 16

The First Day of a New Life

THE BABY HAS ARRIVED; what a thrill! Nobody can describe for you exactly how you will feel when you first lay eyes on your newborn. Your baby may look purple and wrinkled, but to you this is beauty realized. In this chapter we will review what you can expect during the baby's first hours following delivery.

In this chapter...

✓ Love at first sight

✓ Immediate care

✓ Taking stock

✓ What a newborn can do

✓ Care after the birth

✓ Your body after the birth

✓ Nursery or rooming-in

Love at first sight

YOUR FIRST MEETING *with your baby is overwhelming. You may not know what to look at first. Maybe you will feel the need to count fingers and toes. Then you may notice a funny dimple. You may already try to decide if the baby looks more like mum or dad. You may be worried by red or bruised birthmarks. Most of these will disappear within days; one may be your child's special lifetime identification mark.*

You may be surprised to see how alert a newborn really is. Its eyes are open. It appears to be taking in the new environment and especially studying its parents' faces. Newborns often react to the sound of your voices, which they have been hearing in the womb. All of the baby's senses are turned on now, including smell and touch with which it will shortly identify you. He or she is bonding and falling in love too.

For now, savour the momentous occasion of meeting your child in person. A big adventure is beginning. However your baby looks, your heart stirs. Chances are you have never before experienced such a powerful feeling of love at first sight.

■ **Establishing a relationship with your baby** *starts from the moment you first hold your child in your arms: he or she may be screaming or crying but it'll be an emotional experience you'll never forget.*

Immediate care

YOU MAY HAVE BEEN EXPECTING the midwife or nurse to turn the baby upside down and slap him or her on the bottom to get the breathing going as soon as the baby appeared. Sorry to disappoint, but they do that only in movies. Rather, you may hear strange vacuum-like gurgling noises as the doctors or midwives suction the baby's nose and mouth clear of pinkish amniotic fluid that is often swallowed during the passage down the birth canal. Some babies need extra suctioning to breathe more easily even if they were born via caesarean section.

Warmed, weighed, and tagged

Newborns get cold easily, so after a cosy moment naked on your belly, your newborn may be wrapped in a receiving blanket or put on a warmer in the birthing room. A warmer is a specially built infant-sized bed with a heat lamp that radiates down from the top. Your newborn will go through a few other quick procedures, in accordance with the policies of your hospital. The baby will be weighed and its length and head circumference will be measured. While doing this the midwife or paediatrician will also assess the baby's well-being by carrying out five simple tests, known as the Apgar score or test (see overleaf).

If you are in the hospital, the baby will be issued with two identification bands: one for the wrist and another for the ankle. The identification details will include the baby's name, hospital number, and the date and time of the birth. Many of these routines happen very quickly, some even before your baby arrives in your arms.

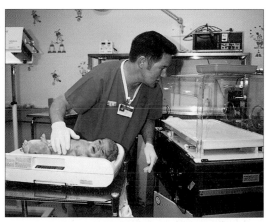

■ **Your baby is weighed** *and its body length and head circumference measured immediately after the birth, or once mother and baby have had time to bond.*

Sometimes the weighing and measuring of your baby is delayed until you have enjoyed a long and relaxed bonding period with your child immediately following birth. Discuss the options with your doctor or midwife before labour begins.

Cutting the cord

In some hospitals and birth centres, you can request that your partner participate in the cutting of the cord, which your doctor or midwife may then clamp with a special plastic device. Or, instead of a clamp, some hospitals use a new "triple-dye" technique. This triple dye is a chemical that dries up the cord, causing it to look as if it had been dyed purple.

If a plastic clamp was put on the cord, it may be removed before the baby goes home. The dry, twisted 1-inch stump that remains will fall off in a couple of weeks.

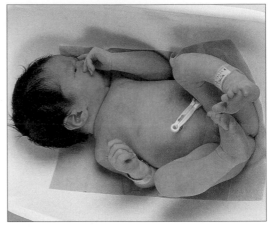

■ **Once the umbilical cord** *is cut, it is usually clamped with a plastic device and removed 4 or 5 days later when the stump has shrivelled up.*

Caring for your baby's cord is important so that the site does not become infected. To enhance the healing and shrivelling up process, go around the site a few times a day with a cotton bud dipped in alcohol.

The Apgar score

The Apgar score is a rating of a newborn's condition 1, 5, and sometimes 10 minutes after birth. This quick and easy test is given mainly to see if the baby needs help breathing.

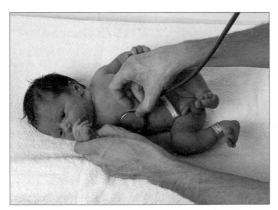

■ **As part of the Apgar test** *the doctor or midwife will listen to your baby's heart to measure the strength and regularity of the beat.*

This universal test, developed in 1952 by anaesthesiologist Virginia Apgar, measures a baby's responsiveness and vital signs. It checks five factors: heart rate, breathing, colour, muscle tone, and reflex response. If you see the pediatrician or a nurse with a stethoscope listening intently to the baby's chest, flicking the baby's heels, and picking up its arms and letting them drop in what appears to you to be a rather abrupt manner, you will know that your baby is taking its Apgar test.

The baby receives a score of 0 to 2 in each category, and the resulting five numbers are added together. As an ideal, the total score would be 10. (Yes, there are lots of applications for the expression "a perfect 10".) Rarely, if ever, can a baby get a 10 in the first minute of life because babies are "less than pink" at birth. (Variations in colour from slightly pale to rosy are perfectly normal.) A score of 7 to 10 is generally considered normal, and if your baby receives this score, no special actions need to be taken. A lower score indicates that some extra measures, perhaps giving the baby oxygen, may be needed. Generally speaking, you are not told the score, unless you ask. Caesarean section babies tend to have slightly higher Apgar scores because they don't have much difficulty coming out and their colour is usually better.

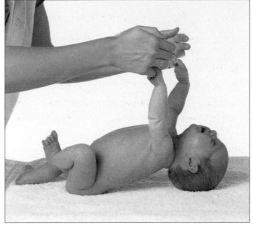

■ **The grasp reflex** *is one of the reflexes checked by the doctor or midwife soon after birth; the baby should be able to grasp any object that is put in the palm of its hand.*

APGAR TABLE

Sign	Points		
	0	1	2
Appearance (colour)*	Pale or blue	Body and lips pink, hands and feet blue	Completely pink
Heart rate	Absent	Below 100	Over 100
Grimace (reflex irritability)	No response to stimulation	Grimace	Lusty cry
Activity (muscle tone)	Flaccid, limp	Some movement of extremities	A lot of activity
Respiration (breathing)	Absent	Slow, irregular	Good, strong (crying)

*In black and Asian children, the colour of the membranes of the mouth, of the whites of the eyes, of the lips, palms, hands, and of the soles of the feet will be examined.

Vitamin K for the newborn

Immediately following birth, your newborn may receive an injection of vitamin K. Babies are sometimes temporarily deficient in this important nutrient, which helps promote normal blood clotting and lessens the risk of abnormal bleeding into tissues. A vitamin K supplement administered at birth prevents a now rare, but often fatal, bleeding disorder called haemorrhagic disease of the newborn (HDN). HDN can cause bleeding into the brain, which may result in brain damage.

Babies do not have enough of their own vitamin K until they are a few months old, and they often need extra vitamin K until they build up their own supplies. If your baby needs to have vitamin K but you want to avoid an injection, it may be given by mouth. This is more complicated. Because oral vitamin K is not absorbed as well and the effect does not last as long, several doses of oral vitamin K are essential as opposed to just one injection. If given orally you will need to make sure that your baby gets all the doses: one at birth, another between 3 and 5 days later, and the last in the fourth week.

If your baby boy is to be circumcised, he will need vitamin K. Vitamin K helps protect your baby against the rare possibility of excess bleeding at circumcision.

Ask your doctor or midwife if you have any queries about vitamin K for your baby. There are no known risks or adverse effects.

Eye ointment

In some birthplaces, an ointment is routinely placed in the eyes of newborns to protect them from a variety of infections that could occur during the birth process. Although this ointment is put in the eyes at birth to prevent infection, it can cause the lids to become puffy, and the baby may even develop an eye discharge. So special attention is warranted to keep the eyes clean and clear.

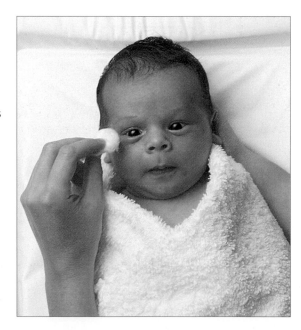

■ **Keep your newborn's eyes** *clean and free from infection by regular wiping, making sure you use a different cotton wool ball for each eye.*

Penicillin

In some countries the baby is given a shot of penicillin to prevent a specific type of infection caused by vaginal bacteria. However in the UK antibiotics are only administered in cases of premature birth.

Other tests

Other newborn tests vary from one birthplace or hospital to another. A sample of your baby's umbilical cord blood may be taken to determine blood type. Your newborn may be given a blood test to check blood sugar levels. If the level is too low or other imbalances are discovered, the baby will receive immediate medical attention to manage the problem. Also, a newborn screening blood test sample will be drawn to look for phenylketonuria (PKU), a rare metabolic disease that need to be diagnosed early in infancy to ensure successful treatment.

Another test may be performed to measure the bilirubin level, which, if elevated, is a sign of jaundice. Bilirubin is a yellow substance produced by the body when breaking down red blood cells. A nurse or technician draws blood from the baby's heel to do most of these tests. This explains the band-aid on your baby's foot.

Some hospitals in the UK will also give your baby an additional vaccine against tuberculosis. Known as a BCG, it will be administered in the form of an injection.

Taking stock

SOME INFANTS come out yelling at the top of their lungs; some even come ready to suckle; still others seem prepared for a nap. Regardless of first impressions, your newborn will be in a state of rapid change during the first hours and days of his or her life, and this change is a wonderful thing to watch unfolding before you.

A newborn will look directly into your eyes. Although its vision is blurry, it can see you and any other person or object that's up to about 30 centimetres (2 feet) away. Many will grab onto a finger that is placed in its palm. Some exhibit a voracious sucking reflex and will suck your finger but, of course, would rather eat. While most newborns are alert, others who have gone through a tougher than normal birth may be rather sleepy and prefer to cuddle up on your chest for a nice rest with the sound of your familiar heartbeat still close by.

Skin

Skin colour and tone varies greatly from one baby to the next. Regardless of ethnic background, some look red, pink, or purple at first. A lot of babies arrive with their white, waxy *vernix* coating still covering their bodies. Some babies are born very wrinkled. Some have a soft, furry appearance because of *lanugo*. Rashes, blotches, or tiny white spots are also not unusual on newborns. These generally clear up over the first few days or weeks after birth. No matter how your baby's skin appears following delivery, it will change dramatically in the coming weeks, even hours.

> **DEFINITION**
>
> The **vernix** is the protective coating that protects the skin in the womb from its constant exposure to amniotic fluid. **Lanugo** is a fine hair that develops while in the womb. Lanugo falls out after a week or two.

When to give a newborn its first bath is the subject of some debate. Generally a sponge bath is sufficient until the cord falls off. Newborns don't really get very dirty, and numerous bathings tend to dry out their sensitive skin. But be sure to keep the nappy area clean.

Birthmarks

You may notice lots of little marks and blemishes. Some newborns have pimples covering their bodies. Birth marks and blotches are a common occurrence following delivery. There are many reasons why these marks appear, but almost universally they fade by the time the baby celebrates his or her first birthday. At the base of your baby's neck you may see red "stork bites", so named because that is supposedly where the stork carries the baby with its beak. The official name of this collection of tiny blood vessels under the skin is *naevus flameus*, which simply means "red mark". *Naevus flameus* may also be present between the eyebrows, under the nostrils, or on the eyelids. You may also see a bluish discolouration at the base of the spine or over the buttocks.

Head

A newborn's head seems huge in comparison to the rest of its body. The forehead may seem large as well, but this is just an optical illusion because the infant has so little hair. All babies have two "soft" spots or fontanelles. One is at the top of the head, and a second, smaller one, is slightly towards the back. The head is actually made of six overlapping flat bones that are not fused at birth, allowing the skull to be moulded during delivery as well as to accommodate the baby's brain as it grows. These bones slide apart to give the growing brain more room, and the soft spots are the areas between some of these plates. The smaller, posterior fontanelle closes soon after birth while the anterior one is open into the second year of life.

Hair

Many babies are born bald. Others arrive with full heads of hair. Babies who have dark hair on their heads tend to have body hair as well, covering the shoulders, the small of the back, and maybe even the forehead and tips of the ears. Don't worry; your baby will not turn into a monkey, and most of this primary hair will fall off in the coming weeks and months as it is replaced by more permanent hair.

Genitals

You may notice that your baby's genitalia are enlarged following birth. Enlargement stems from the pressure put on the genital area during a vaginal birth and also from the large quantity of hormones transferred from the mother. The vulva and labia in girls and the scrotum in boys will all appear quite large in comparison to the rest of the body. Newborn girls may have a vaginal discharge; this is quite normal. In most boys, when the scrotum is relaxed, you can see and feel two marble-sized testicles. Some boys are born with one or both testicles not yet in the scrotum. This should resolve within a year.

Limbs

Your baby may look scrunched up because its legs and arms have been kept bent at the knees and elbows for many months of growing in ever-tightening close quarters. This is quite normal. Some newborns stay in the fetal position for many weeks after birth. This helps them keep warm and keeps heat closer to their bodies. Sometimes shoulders are hunched up, arms are flexed, and hands are fisted. If your baby was born in a breech position, you may find it sucking on its toes for a few days.

Some newborns enter the world with very long fingernails. These should be cut right away to prevent scratching.

Use a miniature clipper designed especially for babies. Even the youngest of babies dislikes being constricted and will squirm if you try cutting its fingernails. Avoid this interference by doing the deed while the baby sleeps.

Bodily functions

Babies are unfinished works in progress from their gastrointestinal, or GI, tracts to the muscular system. Few of the many functions of the body are working at capacity yet. There is a lot of fine-tuning that will develop with usage. Signals from the brain for eye control and breathing are not evenly coordinated at first. Control of body temperature is in flux, so newborns can easily overheat or chill. Everything inside your baby is still adjusting and will slowly come together into perfect operating mode.

YOUR NEWBORN BABY

Although the vision is that babies look like little cherubs, the reality is that newborns are tiny, wet, usually red creatures when they first emerge. Babies delivered via caesarean section don't differ all that much from those born vaginally, but they seem to look a little better because their heads are nice and round, since they haven't been squeezed down the narrow passage of the pelvis .

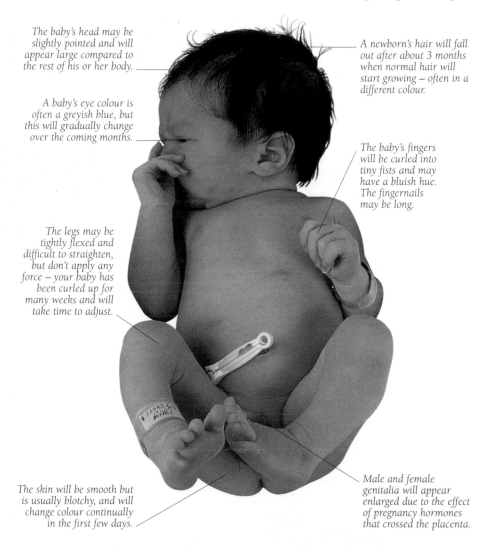

The baby's head may be slightly pointed and will appear large compared to the rest of his or her body.

A baby's eye colour is often a greyish blue, but this will gradually change over the coming months.

The legs may be tightly flexed and difficult to straighten, but don't apply any force – your baby has been curled up for many weeks and will take time to adjust.

A newborn's hair will fall out after about 3 months when normal hair will start growing – often in a different colour.

The baby's fingers will be curled into tiny fists and may have a bluish hue. The fingernails may be long.

The skin will be smooth but is usually blotchy, and will change colour continually in the first few days.

Male and female genitalia will appear enlarged due to the effect of pregnancy hormones that crossed the placenta.

What a newborn can do

A NEWBORN is definitely not a blank slate. It has a large repertoire of movements, reflexes, and other abilities. At birth all of our human senses are operating. Newborns can smell, taste, and feel. They can also hear and see.

Communicate

Newborns are surprisingly good communicators at birth, and if you are paying close attention to the subtleties, as you will over the coming weeks, you will soon understand your own baby. Researchers have noted that a newborn baby will try to catch your eye and, when you smile, will reward you with a subtle smile in return. Newborns can see best at a distance of about 30 centimetres (2 feet) – the rest is fuzzy. Often they blink their eyes and flutter their eyelids when you withdraw.

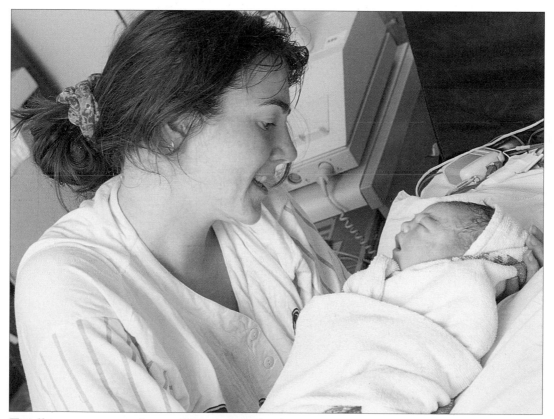

■ **Talking to your newborn** *will help with the bonding process, as your baby will find the recognizable sound of your voice both soothing and comforting.*

It is important to talk to your newborn during the first hours and days following birth. A newborn can make sounds other than its high- and low-pitched cries. The other sounds you will notice most often are soft squeaks, tweaks, and grunts coming from deep within the chest.

Hearing

Babies can hear at birth, but they don't always respond to sounds. Babies seem to have the ability to selectively close out noises. Sometimes they respond, even in their sleep, to soft noises, and sometimes they don't respond to loud sounds even when they are awake. Infants do seem to have a preference for soft and repetitive sounds, like the sound of your heartbeat. A very loud noise, such as a slamming door, will produce a startle reflex in which the baby may cry out and exhibit jerky flinging of its arms and legs. The startle may be caused by the noise itself or by vibrations.

Motor skills

In terms of motor skills, newborns can move their arms, kick their feet, cry, blink their eyes, open and close their mouths, suck, grasp, and even tug on your hair or your finger. They can move their heads around but do not yet have neck-muscle control, so the head really just twists from side to side.

Natural reflexes dominate most of a newborn's movements, and the "rooting reflex" ranks as most important if you wish to breastfeed. To test your baby's rooting reflex, stroke the side of its face near its mouth; hopefully the baby will turn towards your finger and open its mouth. This rooting reflex is helpful in getting baby to latch on to the nipple for breastfeeding. Other reflexes include the "Moro reflex" or the "startle reflex", which is noted when the arms and fingers flail outwards and then return towards the body and relax. The "tonic neck reflex" is easy to recognize. When the baby turns its head to the left, the left arm extends and the right arm flexes up to its head. Gradually all movements will become more deliberate as the baby matures.

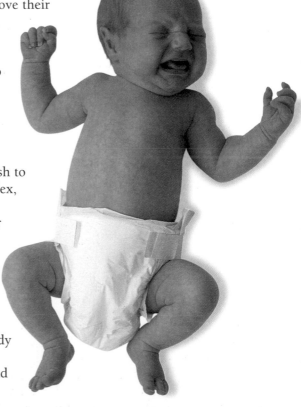

■ **In terms of motor skills,** *there'll be no mistaking your newborn's ability to cry.*

Breathe

You may think this is obvious, but, remember, newborns do not use their lungs for breathing until they exit the womb. So breathing is very new stuff for them in the first hours following birth. You may notice that your baby breathes irregularly; this gives some new mothers cause for worry. Quick and then shallow breaths is a normal breathing pattern for newborns in the first 24 hours following delivery. Also a newborn's heart rate is almost twice yours. It will slow down in about 2 months. Newborns sometimes periodically cough and sneeze in order to keep their breathing passages clear.

Care after the birth

FOR ABOUT AN HOUR AFTER DELIVERY, you will be watched closely by a nurse or midwife and will be checked frequently for any excessive bleeding or unusual change in blood pressure. Hopefully your baby is wrapped up in a blanket and in your arms. Your partner is probably right beside you as well.

If you've had anaesthesia, it's beginning to wear off, so you are probably experiencing some pain. You may start to feel pain around the incision area if you had a caesarean section or at your vaginal opening, especially if you needed stitches. Ice packs are a good idea at this time to help stop both the pain and the bleeding. You may also be offered pain relief medication.

A nurse or midwife will come in and press on your abdomen to check that your uterus is contracting and to change the pads you are lying on, which may be blood soaked. Your vital signs (temperature, blood pressure, pulse rate, and respiration) will be closely monitored. If you feel you have to urinate, a nurse may bring you a bedpan; you will probably not be steady enough to walk to the toilet. Most women don't have a bowel movement for a couple of days following labour.

Your emotions

Don't be surprised to find that you go through a broad range of feelings following delivery. You may experience everything from elation and joy to feeling tired, in pain, and overwhelmed. Don't be too hard on yourself. Your body has been through a lot. You are probably exhausted and feeling some effects of sleep deprivation as well. I found just holding the baby on my chest and resting together, even sleeping, to be the best cure in the whole world. If you are in a birthing centre, you will probably have the option of resting and sleeping until you feel ready to make the journey home.

Positive breastfeeding

Breastfeeding immediately following delivery, if possible, promotes the healing process in your body and lessens postnatal bleeding. The release of oxytocin and prolactin hormones from nipple stimulation also helps your mothering instincts come up to speed.

Immediate breastfeeding may prove impossible. Some babies are just too exhausted from the delivery process. Others take a day or so to figure out how to latch on and suck. This is not unusual and does not constitute a problem.

When to eat

You may feel hungry in the hours following delivery; it probably has been a very long time since you've eaten. Usually you are free to eat whatever you want following delivery, but go slowly; your body has been through a lot. If you've had anaesthesia, you are probably feeling very dehydrated and thirsty. Start with sips of water and then work up to a glassful.

INTERNET

childbirth.org/articles/
postpartum.html

This site contains informative articles on how to deal with the physical and psychological changes of having given birth.

■ **Putting your child to your breast** *as soon as you can after the delivery will greatly increase your chances of breastfeeding successfully, as well as help in your body's healing process.*

Your body after the birth

NO, YOU HAVEN'T BEEN HIT by a truck; it just feels that way. Whether you gave birth vaginally or had a surgical delivery, you are going to need time to recover.

Your uterus

This incredibly elastic organ will shrink back to its normal size much more quickly than it expanded. In just under 2 months, your uterus will retract from 1.1 kg (2½ lb) to only 56 g (2 oz). But first, especially in the first few weeks, you may feel afterpains and cramping. When you breastfeed you may feel these sensations very strongly. Afterpains are less severe with first babies; with subsequent births you may feel as if you are in labour again, especially when the baby hooks on. This happens because the hormones for milk production also help the uterus shrink back down. Postpartum bleeding, known as lochia, is also normal during this time, beginning immediately following delivery and continuing sometimes for as long as 4 weeks.

You should use only sanitary towels to absorb any bleeding after delivery because your cervix is still closing down and tampons could encourage an infection.

This bleeding, by the way, is not your menstrual period, which probably won't resume for perhaps 7 to 9 weeks if you are not breastfeeding. If you choose to nurse, your period will be in hibernation for a longer stretch of time.

Your vagina and perineum

If you delivered vaginally, you may find that sitting down in the week after delivery is quite a challenge. This area is tender. You may also have developed haemorrhoids from the strain of pushing. Ice packs offer good relief, as does a donut cushion. Sex is usually discouraged until you have stopped bleeding to avoid infection, but check with your GP or midwife regarding this subject.

Your bowel and bladder

Labour and the hormones, even drugs used during delivery, slow down the bowel, so you may feel constipated for a few days following birth. Drink plenty of fluids. Go gently if you are experiencing haemorrhoids; you could aggravate the situation by trying to push a bowel movement out too strenuously. If you've had a caesarean, it may take a few extra days for your bowels to recover.

Your belly

You may be surprised to find that you still look pregnant after the baby arrives. But though everything is still big, it's usually very loose and squishy. You are going to have to be patient about losing that extra weight and tightening up your stomach muscles. Ask about specific exercises, but don't even think about doing sit-ups until you've passed your postnatal check-up.

RECOVERING FROM A SURGICAL BIRTH

Although your recovery from a surgical delivery will be longer than from a vaginal birth, you will most likely be awake during the surgery in which the baby is delivered and in the recovery room. Normally the baby is whisked quickly out of the theatre while the doctors are sewing you up. But your baby should be brought to you in the recovery room as long as you are up to it. While you may be unable to get out of bed for the first 24 hours after surgery, there is no reason you cannot breastfeed and no reason not to have the baby next to you with the assistance of your partner or the hospital nurses.

Following surgery, you will probably be offered morphine in a drip or strong analgesics to make you more comfortable. Don't turn them away, and don't worry about the effects of the medicines if you are breastfeeding. Your milk won't come in for a few days, and the pre-milk (colostrum) the baby is feeding on is not affected. The pain relief will help you enjoy the first days with your baby. Within a day you should be feeling less groggy and in less pain. The nurses will also be encouraging you to get out of bed and give walking a try. Though you may be bent over at first, the sooner you get moving, the faster you will heal. The little bundle of joy in the basket next to your bed will also make your recovery a bit easier.

Nursery or rooming-in

IF YOU HAVE GIVEN BIRTH in a hospital you and your newborn will stay together in the postnatal ward, unless either one of you is seriously ill. Gone are the days when babies were lined up in see-through bassinets behind a plate glass window. Today, there are very few hospitals that as a matter of policy keep babies and mothers apart. The trend is towards rooming-in or modified rooming-in, which helps get breastfeeding, bonding, and attachment off to a good start.

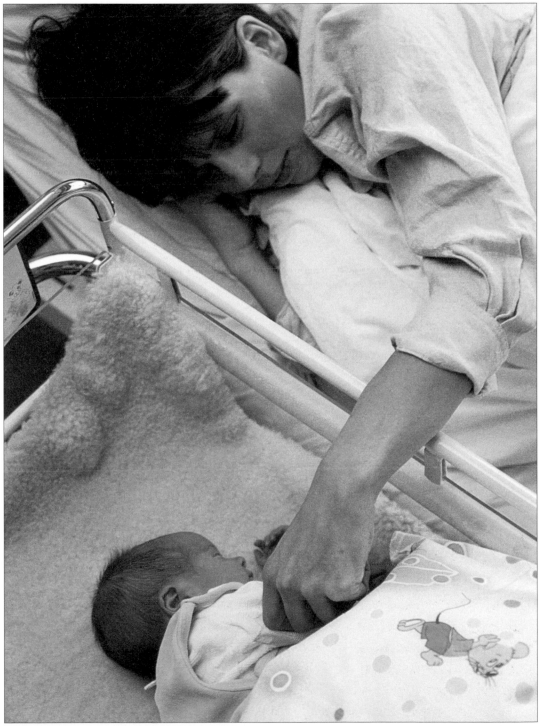

■ **Bonding with baby:** *After the delivery the hospital will make sure your newborn stays within your reach.*

Most healthcare professionals promote mothers and babies staying together at all times following delivery. However, if the mother is too exhausted from a difficult or drawn-out delivery, some hospitals will allow mothers to rest, especially at night, by putting the baby in a nursery where the infant will be carefully supervised. But some studies suggest that mothers who are separated from their babies do not sleep any better and that babies who are separated from their mothers sleep considerably less and have more trouble with breastfeeding.

In fact, most hospitals do not have staffing levels that allow babies who are separated to be closely monitored, so they are often left alone, their early cues for feeding ignored and signs of distress easily missed. Ironically, mothers are often unaware of this, believing that someone more "capable" than themselves is caring for their baby. Maybe, maybe not.

If you're a first-time mother don't worry if you feel inadequate to care for your newborn – this lack of confidence is understandable and even expected. Talk to the nurses and midwives on the ward; you should find them supportive rather than critical.

A hospital is a good place to begin to learn to cope with the demands of new motherhood. At least your meals are cooked and there's no washing or ironing to worry about. This leaves you time to learn how to care for a newborn, and the best way to do that is to have your child with you around the clock.

Keeping the baby with you

Having your baby with you, either in the postnatal or a private ward, allows you to begin learning your baby's feeding cues. By the time you go home, you will most likely be in tune with your baby's signs of hunger before he or she even starts to cry. If your baby is in a nursery full time, it may well be that by the time the baby is brought to you to feed it will be past the early feeding cues (rooting, opening mouth, sucking on tongue or lips). If there is a delay in bringing you the baby, the baby may even be past its initial attention-getting cries and well on the way to hysterical crying. This degree of chaos can make it difficult to get the baby nursing and be upsetting to the mother.

Rooming-in during your waking hours means more time to hold your baby, more time to look at your baby, more time to talk to your baby, more time to get to know your

Trivia...
In the United States, in response to the unfortunate rise in baby-snatching, many hospitals will not allow the baby to remain in its mother's room while the mother is sleeping, unless someone else – partner or grandparent – is in the room. Baby spends much time in mother's bed or at the bedside, but moves to the nursery to let mum sleep.

baby, and simply more time to form your initial mutual connection. Some studies show that babies who room in are generally more content, cry less, and seem to develop more regular sleep-wake cycles earlier. Despite what you may think, if your baby rooms in with you, you actually tend to get more rest. Newborn babies sleep so much, that you will have plenty of time to relax and read. Also, you won't be feeling anxious about the separation or wondering how your baby is. He or she will be right near you.

A simple summary

✔ A newborn baby does not look like a cherub. It is shiny and wet with red splotches, a misshapen head, and fuzz all over. But it is beautiful.

✔ The newborn can see, hear, smell, taste, and touch. It likes that which is familiar – your heartbeat, the sound of your and your partner's voices, and your body temperature. It also moves as programmed by its reflexes.

✔ Immediately after birth, the baby is weighed, measured, and footprinted. It also is subjected to the Apgar Test, which assesses its physical condition, and numerous blood tests to discover problems that must be corrected in the baby's first hours.

✔ After you give birth, expect to be sore and tired. By all means, give in and get some needed sleep. You may also find yourself feeling a full gamut of weird emotions, from giggly to weepy. This is a normal adjunct of tiredness and gushing hormones.

✔ Having your baby at your side most of the day is a good idea. You can learn to read its hunger signs and other messages and you can really bond. Newborns sleep a lot, so the baby won't wear you out and you won't feel so anxious.

✔ Don't try to leave the hospital before you're ready: your body needs time to recover, and life at home with baby will be busy and hectic right from the start.

Chapter 17

Feeding the Baby

THERE ARE TWO CHOICES when it comes to feeding your baby: your own breast milk or bottled formula. From the moment you became pregnant, you have been hearing that breast milk is best for your baby – from protection against allergies to increased intelligence. Breastfeeding is also a wonderful and fulfilling way to spend time close to your child. But this method of feeding is not for every mother. Only you can decide.

In this chapter...

✓ Is breastfeeding for me?

✓ The benefits of breastfeeding

✓ When to start breastfeeding

✓ Learning how to nurse

✓ Common breastfeeding problems and their solutions

✓ How long should I breastfeed?

Is breastfeeding for me?

INTELLECTUALLY, YOU KNOW THAT MOTHER'S MILK *is better than formula milk and that breastfeeding is better than bottle feeding. However, it is impossible to know before the baby arrives whether or not you will enjoy breastfeeding. The fair position is to at least give breastfeeding a try once the baby arrives.*

Not as easy as it looks!

Even though breastfeeding is very natural, be aware that it doesn't come naturally to all women. While you are pregnant, it may appear that all you need to do to breastfeed is pull up your shirt discreetly and put the baby to the breast. But in reality, it's not always so simple, and most babies and new mothers need help. Inexperienced mothers tend to give up very early in the breastfeeding game when they start having any sign of trouble. If you find yourself in trouble do seek out help. Breastfeeding, once established, should not be painful, and almost 99 per cent of mothers have more than adequate supplies to nourish their babies.

■ **Successful breastfeeding** *may not be easily established until a few weeks after delivery, but once you and your baby have got the hang of it, you'll find great benefits from this nurturing experience.*

Co-sleeping, that is, having the baby sleep in your bed with you, has been the subject of some controversy of late but it's really a judgment call on your part. For many mothers it is the easiest way to breastfeed and still get a good night's sleep.

Parents have been sleeping with their infants and children for centuries. Although there have been some cases of children being rolled over or smothered when sharing their parents' bed, these are usually exceptional cases. If it makes you feel more secure, you can choose to have your newborn sleep in a moses basket or cot right beside your bed. Otherwise if you choose to sleep with your infant, take some comfort in the fact that some of us – mothers and fathers both – have a sixth sense about where the baby is in our bed and thus naturally avoid causing any harm.

However, if all else fails, and you just don't like breastfeeding or can't seem to handle it physically, you should give yourself permission to stop. Despite what the politically correct propaganda machine may say about bottles, not breastfeeding is not a form of child abuse. Not breastfeeding also doesn't mean that you don't love your child, will not form a good attachment, or that he or she will fail at school. If in the end you've given it a good try, and you just can't hack it, do not feel guilty about your decision to stop.

The benefits of breastfeeding

THE BENEFITS of breastfeeding are many. The one that seems to push most women over the top is the selfish fact that it helps your body recover and, if you eat wisely, lose weight more quickly following pregnancy. It goes without saying that your baby also benefits enormously.

More and more research is showing that breastfeeding leads to optimal brain development. While there are behavioural aspects to this, the milk is important, too. Human milk has special ingredients like DHA (docosohexaenoic acid) and AA (arachidonic acid) that contribute to brain and retinal development.

■ **Mother's breast milk** *provides all the nourishment a baby needs to protect him or her against any infection or illness*

Benefits for baby

The list of benefits of breastfeeding your baby is very long. Human milk is the best food for babies. It contains the right amount of nutrients, in the right proportions, for your growing baby. Your milk is a living, biological fluid that contains many unique components. For example, lactoferrin provides optimal absorption of iron and protects the baby's digestive system from harmful bacteria; lipases assist in digestion of fats; and special growth factors and hormones contribute to your child's optimal growth and development. Your own milk changes during a feeding from thirst-quenching to hunger-satisfying and comes in a variety of flavours as your diet varies. As your baby grows, the composition of your milk changes to meet his or her changing nutritional needs.

The World Health Organization, UNICEF, the World Alliance for Breastfeeding Action, and a range of other worldwide health concerns all recommend that, barring illness or other negative factors, infants be given breast milk for up to a year or even more.

Breast milk contains your antibodies and passes these to the baby, helping to protect it against illness and allergies. Sucking at the breast is thought to help with good oral development. Breastfed babies have fewer speech impediments. Breastfed babies have good cheekbone development and jaw alignment; consequently, there is less chance of needing braces and other dental treatment. Breastfeeding also creates a very special and long-lasting bond between mother and baby. This list of benefits goes on and on.

New growth charts from the World Health Organization confirm that breastfed infants grow differently from formula-fed babies. Breastfed infants grow faster initially, then slow down as they approach their first birthday. (This can sometimes be interpreted as "dropping off the growth curve", but really represents normal growth.)

Benefits for mother

First of all, it almost goes without saying that what's good for babies is good for mothers. One of the best things about breastfeeding for mothers (as my mother, who bottle-fed three children, will tell you) is how easy it is. The milk is always available for your baby. No stress and no mess. You don't have to worry about running out of formula, or your local chemist being out of your specific formula. You don't have to pay for formulas – a big plus. You never have to worry about heating a bottle, sterilizing bottles, or mixing formula in the middle of the night when your baby is ready to eat. You don't have to worry about keeping breast milk warm or cold when going out. And best of all, you can feed your baby lying down in bed at night.

Breastfeeding is also good for you in other ways. The baby's sucking at the breast causes uterine contractions right after birth. These contractions, while initially painful, lead to less bleeding for the mother and return the uterus to its pre-pregnancy shape much faster.

■ **Worried about having** *to clean and sterilize bottles every time your baby is hungry? You don't have to be if you decide to breastfeed. Breast milk is readily available, sterile, and comes at the right temperature.*

More benefits for mother

Milk production uses up 200 to 500 calories a day. To burn off an equivalent number of calories, a bottle-feeding mother would need to swim 30 laps or ride a bicycle for over an hour. With a newborn on your hands, breastfeeding is simply and definitely easier. Of course, if nursing is your justification for overindulgence, you can counter the weight-reduction value of nursing. But if you eat judiciously, it goes without saying that you can lose much of your pregnancy weight faster than if you bottle-feed your baby.

Continued exclusive nursing (i.e., breastfeeding without added bottles of formula or solids) tends to delay the return of ovulation and menstruation. In fact, breastfeeding, or the lactational amenorrhea method (LAM), is a well-studied method of child spacing. It is 99 per cent effective in preventing pregnancy in the first 6 months following delivery provided that exclusive nursing is practised. However, since you have to be feeding many times a day for it to be effective, it should not be relied on.

Research first suggested by the high incidence of cancer in Roman Catholic nuns, has shown that mothers who breastfeed for at least 6 months during their lifetime have a decreased risk of breast cancer, and similar reduced rates have been shown for ovarian and uterine cancers.

By breastfeeding, a woman can reduce her risk of pre-menopausal breast cancer by up to 20 per cent.

Even being breastfed seems to be associated with decreased risk of breast cancer, over and above the fact that women who were breastfed themselves are more likely to breastfeed their own children.

■ **Not only is breastfeeding** *beneficial for both you and your baby, but the skin-to-skin contact helps in the bonding process.*

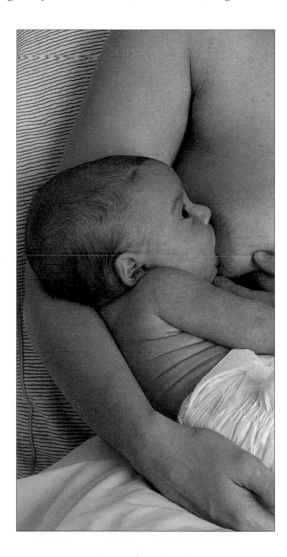

253

When to start breastfeeding

INITIATE BREASTFEEDING as soon as possible following your baby's birth. Research has shown that in the 2 hours following the birth, many infants are in a state of alertness, which is accompanied by a strong sucking reflex. It is at this time that your baby, eager for the comfort of your arms, will lick or nuzzle your nipple and may even decide to latch on and take its first taste of your **colostrum**.

These early feeds have an imprinting effect and help to get breastfeeding off to a good start. Although breastfeeding without delay is optimal, if circumstances don't allow it, or if you can't persuade your baby to take your breast, don't become discouraged. Many mothers whose babies had a delayed start at breastfeeding have gone on to establish a wonderful nursing relationship. Continue to give your baby many opportunities to learn this new skill.

> **DEFINITION**
>
> **Colostrum** *is the first milk, actually a pre-milk, that your breasts produce in the early days of breastfeeding. This special thick yellow "milk" is low in fat and high in carbohydrates, protein, and antibodies to help keep your baby healthy. It is extremely easy to digest and is therefore the perfect first food for your newborn.*

FEEDING POSITIONS

It's very important that you're in a comfortable position before you start breastfeeding, as this helps relax both you and the baby. Whether you are sitting or lying down, make sure your baby's body is angled towards you so that he or she is more likely to latch on the first time. Whichever position is right for you, make sure your baby is able to get a good mouthful of breast, with close to an inch of areola. If you start to feel uncomfortable, gently break the suction by inserting your finger into its mouth.

a **Sidelying**

Lie on your side with your head on a pillow. Nestle your baby up close to you with its head in the crook of your arm, its mouth level with your nipple, and its tummy against yours. This is a great middle-of-the-night position.

Learning how to nurse

TECHNIQUE IS EVERYTHING when it comes to breastfeeding. This is true for both baby and mother. First, it is important to find a comfortable position. The basic options include cradling your baby in your arm, tucking the baby under one arm, and reclining on your side with the baby lying next to you.

Once you're both in place, the next important step is latching on. One method is to tickle the baby's lips with your breast to stimulate the rooting reflex. This causes the baby to open its mouth wide. It can take several tries to get your baby on your breast just right. When properly latched on, your baby takes into its mouth all or part of the areola – the dark area surrounding the nipple – as well as the nipple itself.

When your baby sucks, its gums squeeze the milk ducts beneath the areola, and the milk comes out through multiple openings in the nipple. Sucking should be smooth and even. You need to hear the baby swallowing.

b **Football Hold**

Lay your baby along your side so that its back is supported by your forearm and its head is cradled in your hand. This is a good position if you're recovering from a caesarean section.

c **Cradle Hold**

Hold your baby in one arm and your breast in the other. Tickle your baby's lips with your nipple and allow the baby's mouth to open wide, as in a yawn, before bringing it quickly to your breast.

To make sure the baby is swallowing milk, observe the neck area around the Adam's apple. If your milk is flowing and going down the hatch, you will notice the Adam's apple moving up and down. Watch for signs that the baby is not latched on correctly, namely, if it has only taken the tip of your nipple, its lips are curled inwards, or you hear clicking noises. If your baby doesn't latch on properly, it won't get enough milk, you'll get sore nipples, and you'll both be frustrated.

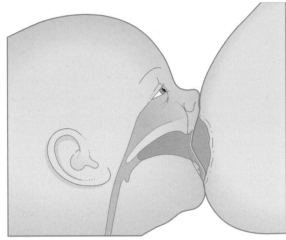

■ **Your baby is correctly latched on** *when its gums are firmly gripped around your breast tissue so that your entire nipple is deep inside its mouth.*

The role of colostrum

It is very worthwhile to start breastfeeding your baby very soon after delivery so that he or she can receive the benefits of colostrum. It provides not only perfect nutrition tailored to the needs of your newborn, but also large amounts of living cells that will defend your baby against many harmful agents.

The concentration of immune factors in colostrum is much higher than in mature milk. Colostrum actually works as a natural, 100-per-cent-safe vaccine.

It contains large quantities of an antibody called secretory immunoglobulin A (IgA), which is a new substance to the newborn. Before your baby was born, it received the benefit of another antibody, IgG, through your placenta. IgG works through the baby's circulatory system while IgA protects the baby in the places most likely to come under attack from external germs, namely the mucous membranes in the throat, lungs, and intestines.

Colostrum has an especially important role to play in the baby's gastrointestinal tract. A newborn's intestines are very permeable. Colostrum seals the holes by "painting" the gastrointestinal tract with a barrier that prevents foreign substances from penetrating and possibly sensitizing the baby to foods the mother has eaten. Colostrum also has a laxative effect on the baby, helping newborns pass their early stools. This aids the excretion of excess bilirubin and helps prevent jaundice.

Colostrum also contains high concentrations of leukocytes, protective white cells that can destroy disease-causing bacteria and viruses. Later, when you are producing mature milk for your baby, the concentrations of the antibodies in the milk will be lower, but your baby will be taking in much higher volumes of milk. The disease-fighting properties of human milk do not disappear with the colostrum. In fact, as long as your baby ingests your milk, it will receive immunological protection against many different viruses and bacteria.

When will my milk arrive?

If you breastfeed your newborn early and often, your breasts will begin producing mature milk around the third or fourth day after birth. Your milk will then increase in volume and will generally begin to appear thinner and lighter in colour. In those first few days, it is extremely important to breastfeed your newborn at least nine to 12 times in 24 hours – and more often is even better. From then on, you'll experience a letdown reflex when your baby begins to suck. After a few weeks, your milk will let down when it gets close to feeding time. Some women describe this letdown feeling as a sensation of pins and needles. Others never notice a thing.

Pick up a copy of The Womanly Art of Breastfeeding by the La Leche League (a worldwide breastfeeding advocacy group) for answers to all your breastfeeding questions.

Supply and demand

The science of making milk is simple: the more the baby drinks, the more your body will produce. If you are feeding often and on the baby's demand when he or she is hungry, or hopefully every 2 to 3 hours, your body will keep up a good milk supply. You really do not have to worry about making enough milk. The challenge of maintaining your supply sometimes arises with sleepy babies who breastfeed infrequently or with women who return to work. With sleepy babies, waking every 3 hours to eat is one good solution. Do not skip feedings. If you're away from your baby for extended periods, pump every 2 to 3 hours rather than waiting for your breasts to become uncomfortably full.

Trivia...

Breastfeeding creates a bond between you and your child, helping you learn your baby's cues and signals faster. This simply makes mothering a whole lot easier. Just as important, breastfeeding a second child can strengthen your bonds with your first. One nice part of breastfeeding is that it leaves at least one hand and arm free. So sit up against a big pillow on a couch or bed and put your arm around the toddler who is snuggling up beside you. This is a perfect time to read favourite books and to have friendly conversation. If feeding time is attention time for the older child, you will avoid jealousy and truly bond with the displaced prince or princess.

There are some women who really do not produce enough milk. If your baby cries often without pulling its knees up in pain or does not seem to be putting any weight on, do check with your GP. If your doctor senses that the baby is not getting enough to eat, you may have to supplement with formula or simply switch to bottle-feeding altogether.

If you're breastfeeding, throw those dummies away. Better still, specify "no dummy" at the hospital. Mothers who use dummies breastfeed less. A 1999 US study found that giving your baby a dummy was associated with significant declines in the duration of breastfeeding.

What about my diet?

Well, this does cause some new mothers concern. You may well have to modify your diet so as to keep your baby comfortable. Your basic diet is the same healthy one that you have been on throughout pregnancy: protein, fruits and vegetables, wholegrains, and a little bit of fat. However, your baby may dislike some foods that you love. Remember that your milk reflects your diet. Baby may hate garlic, for instance. Or, baby may get tummy aches from chocolate or from spicy foods. If your baby shows signs of gastric distress, you'll have to play trial and error to find out which foods give trouble and which do not.

You should drink plenty of fluids while breastfeeding so as to replenish your own supply, but you do not need to drink milk. Water will do just fine. For many years, mothers were plied with gallons of milk. As a wise doctor said to my editor, "There is no direct pipeline". Just keep up the liquids.

Don't make the liquid of choice cups of strong coffee. Caffeine does cross into the milk supply. I know a young mother, a coffee addict, who was unaware of this fact. She tanked up on over a dozen cups a day and created an insomniac infant.

■ **Don't subject your baby** *to spicy foods: chillies may be a favourite ingredient in your diet but your baby may not enjoy the results.*

How long should a feeding last?

Your baby best determines the length of a feeding. A newborn may nurse 12 or more times a day for 15 to 45 minutes each session. The most vigorous nursing often occurs on the first breast, so always start on the opposite side the next time.

Remembering what side to start nursing on is a common struggle for most mothers. I used a safety pin (not very glamorous, but useful none the less) on my nursing bra to mark the side my daughter finished on at her last feeding session, which was the side I was to begin on next time.

How do I know if my baby is getting enough to eat?

Apart from the obvious sign – weight gain – you know if your baby is getting enough to eat if your breasts feel softer after nursing and the baby wets at least six to eight nappies and passes several yellow stools a day. If you have any concerns about whether your baby is getting enough to eat, give your GP a call.

Asking for help and finding support

Most mothers face at least one challenge with breastfeeding; some face many. Some issues are just frustrating and a few are uncomfortable, but none are insurmountable. Whether you're having real troubles or just have a question or two about breastfeeding, don't feel shy about consulting with experienced mothers or finding a nurse or breastfeeding specialist (who may be available at your hospital). When seeking out help with breastfeeding questions, ask your GP, paediatrician, or midwife for references or contact the La Leche League. This organization has support groups led by trained volunteers in local communities around the globe, as well as a 24-hour hotline and web site for breastfeeding problems (see Appendices).

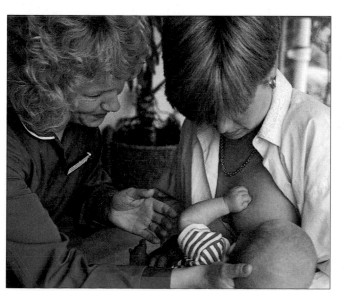

■ **Don't be afraid to seek** *advice from a midwife, nurse, or close friend if you're having trouble breastfeeding.*

REASONS NOT TO BREASTFEED

There are very few reasons not to breastfeed, particularly from the baby's point of view. The most compelling reason not to breastfeed is the mother's infection with the HIV virus. Very recent research has proven that the HIV virus is transmitted in breast milk. Also, if the mother is ill the baby may be lactose intolerant. Few other medical conditions preclude breastfeeding, as there are many appropriate medications that are suitable, if needed, for breastfeeding mothers. However, women who are susceptible to postnatal depression may be advised to bottle-feed. Some studies have shown increased rates of postnatal depression among breastfeeding mothers.

Unfortunately, some babies are unable to suckle normally. Among these are very premature infants, many infants with cerebral palsy, and infants with cleft palate. While many of the benefits of breastfeeding are denied to these unfortunate babies, they can still benefit greatly from mother's milk. Mothers of babies who cannot suck should purchase a good breast pump and provide their milk for administration in whatever form the baby can take.

Common breastfeeding problems and their solutions

WHEN YOUR MILK *first comes in, your breasts may be hard, swollen, and very tender to the touch. This is called engorgement. Feeding actually helps alleviate this problem, but sometimes the baby can have difficulty latching on. Engorgement and sore nipples are the issues that top the list in discouraging many well-intentioned mothers. Clogged ducts, mastitis, leaking, and maintaining your supply are some of the other hurdles you may or may not face.*

Sore nipples and engorgement

Tenderness should disappear once you get through the first week or two of breastfeeding. If pain persists, incorrect positioning and latching on is the most likely culprit. Expressing a little milk by hand or with a pump can make things a little more comfortable when your breasts are engorged. In Switzerland, the midwives offered me an old-fashioned clay poultice and suggested I take a warm shower, letting the water wash over my breasts. This helped immensely. Ice packs between feedings also work to ease pain and reduce swelling. The best cure is to get the milk flowing, feed frequently, and empty each breast as much as possible. Most important is not to ignore a sore nipple problem. Seek help. Sore nipples left unattended can become cracked and infected.

INTERNET

www.waba.org.br

The web site for the World Alliance for Breastfeeding Action, an organization dedicated to promoting the the breastfeeding rights of women all over the world.

Check with a breastfeeding specialist, doctor, or midwife before applying any creams, lotions, or medications to your sore nipples. Make sure they are safe for the baby to ingest.

Clogged ducts

The first sign of a clogged duct is tenderness or swelling around your armpit area. Or you may see tiny white spots on the nipple. If the swelling is red, you probably have mastitis.

Warm water compresses may help open up a duct. Applying gentle pressure in a downward direction from the breast to nipple may also help. It's important to keep breastfeeding frequently with the clogged breast as this may also get the milk flowing.

Mastitis

Fluid trapped anywhere in the body can become infected. This can happen if you do not empty your breasts often enough, you have a clogged duct, you don't feed your baby for long enough, or your body produces more milk than your baby consumes. Mastitis is a breast infection. It feels like the flu with fever, aches, chills, and fatigue. Your breasts may also be engorged or you may see or feel a tender, red, and warm area.

Contact your doctor if you have any signs of mastitis since you will require an antibiotic that is safe to take while breastfeeding. You can also try taking paracetamol for fever and pain. Try applying warm wet heat on the sore areas at least four times a day. If you have mastitis you can still continue to breastfeed. Recurring mastitis with more than one baby may be a reason to discontinue nursing or even to bottle-feed a subsequent baby.

Leaking

It's normal to leak. In fact, leaking is a sign that you are a good producer and have a generous supply. Sometimes leaking occurs when your baby cries or even when you are just thinking of him or her. Leaking is most likely to occur around feeding times or when you are away from the baby.

To keep your shirts dry and free from leaking milk stains, try using breast pads. Keep a jacket or sweater handy in case you want to cover up the wet spots. Leaking usually lessens when you and your baby get the supply and demand thing regulated.

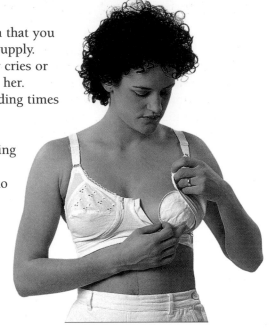

■ **Breast pads** *inserted inside your bra will soak up any leaking milk. The pads are easy to wear and will prevent any embarrassing staining.*

How long should I breastfeed?

HOW LONG you should breastfeed and when to wean depends on what theory you subscribe to and your own personal inclinations. Some mothers choose a time they think is best to wean their baby, and others prefer to leave that decision to the baby.

The La Leche League advocates breastfeeding toddlers and further advocates natural weaning for helping to strengthen a child's foundation of trust. I remember one La Leche League meeting where a 4-year-old pulled up her mother's dress and took a few sips. I was mortified, but I did nurse my daughter for 23 months, which some people in my inner circle thought was an absolute marathon. The length of time you nurse is a very personal decision and depends on your lifestyle, whether or not you work, and finally when you decide enough is enough.

Breastfeeding and working mothers

Mothers who need to return to work constitute a special situation. For some, breastfeeding seems simply too difficult and raises the question of whether to bother to breastfeed at all. Even if you need to return to work within weeks of giving birth, your baby can still benefit from colostrum and early breastfeeding. On your return to work, you have three options: continue to breastfeed exclusively by nursing while at home and leaving bottles of pumped milk for the baby while at work; continue to nurse while at home and feed formula while at work; or wean completely to formula.

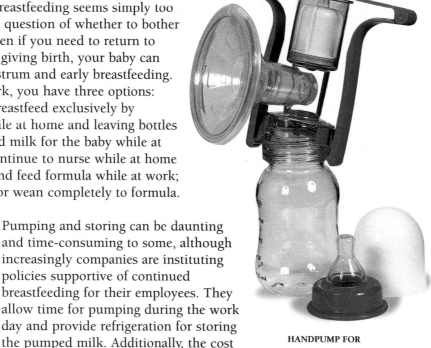

HANDPUMP FOR EXPRESSING MILK AND BOTTLE

INTERNET

www.stargate.co.uk/lllgb

The web site of the UK branch of the International La Leche League. You'll find a catalogue of information on breastfeeding, plus links to other useful sites.

Pumping and storing can be daunting and time-consuming to some, although increasingly companies are instituting policies supportive of continued breastfeeding for their employees. They allow time for pumping during the work day and provide refrigeration for storing the pumped milk. Additionally, the cost of renting or even purchasing a pump is much lower than the cost of formula.

Nursing is not for everyone

For many years we have lived in a bottle-feeding society, with little family or social support. Having grown up in a climate where bottle-feeding was the norm, where fathers-in-law and restaurants make breastfeeding women feel like pariah, many women simply do not find breastfeeding natural or enjoyable. They then make a very personal decision to bottle-feed because it fits their lifestyle best. While there are very few situations or medical conditions that preclude breastfeeding, there are some women who simply do not enjoy it.

Despite what the manufacturers say in the ads, commercial artificial baby formulas are far from perfect substitutes for human milk. Human breast milk does serve as the nutritional model for artificial baby milks, but none of these formulas can match it. For every "new" component that is added to commercial baby formulas to make them closer to human milk, several more components of human milk are discovered. You simply can't beat human milk. Having said that, many of us born in the 1950s and 60s were brought up on formula, and we're intelligent, alert, and often healthy individuals. So it can't be all that bad.

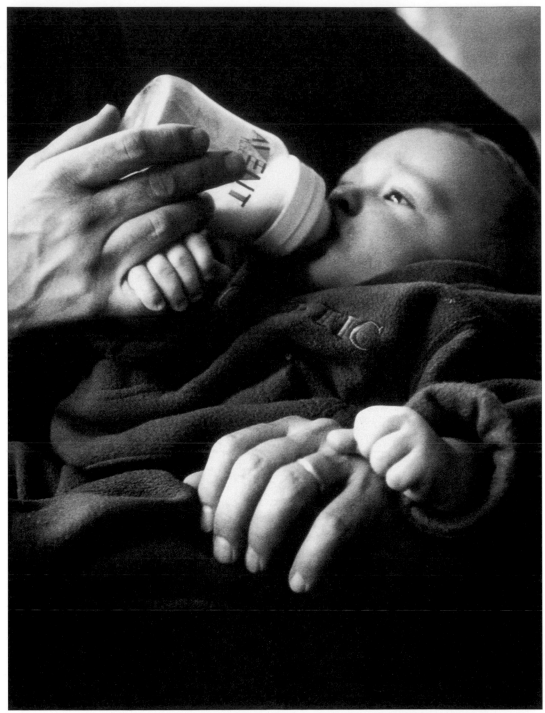

■ **Bottle-feeding with breast milk or formula** *has the great advantage of allowing both partners to share the feeding process; the father can cradle the baby in his arms and mimic the closeness of breastfeeding.*

Much is made about the way that breastfeeding facilitates the whole bonding process, but at the same time, it is clear that bottle-feeding mothers usually establish deep emotional bonds with their babies.

Make sure that guilt or anticipation of guilt is not be a factor in your decision to breastfeed your baby.

A simple summary

✓ You have two choices when it comes to feeding your baby: your own breast milk or bottled formula.

✓ Breast milk supplies the perfect combination of nutrients and antibodies to promote your baby's growth and to protect it from illness.

✓ Breastfeeding helps the mother's uterus shrink more rapidly and helps limit bleeding. It also greatly reduces the risk of breast cancer.

✓ Breastfeeding is natural, but you do have to learn how to do it. Proper technique is vital to success. A professional or volunteer coach or almost any woman who has successfully breastfed can easily teach you how. Take advantage of instruction and help, and you too can be successful.

✓ Some of the problems nursing mothers face are engorgement of the breasts, sore nipples, mastitis, clogged ducts, and leaking. All of these are surmountable. Some women have an inadequate milk supply and must supplement.

✓ Breastfeeding is best, but if you try to stop or if you just don't want to feed your baby in this way, you should not feel guilty. There is no shame to bottle-feeding.

Chapter 18

Getting Back in Shape

IMMEDIATELY AFTER CHILDBIRTH, you may feel as if you had just been hit by a train. This is not surprising. The energy you expended in giving birth is equivalent to that used in running a marathon. So exercise may not be the first thing on your mind right now. Yet exercise can be the best way to soothe your postnatal aches and pains and also to return to your pre-pregnancy figure. In this chapter, we will review safe and effective exercises for getting back in shape following birth.

In this chapter...

✓ The challenge: finding the time for exercise

✓ Why exercise?

✓ Will I ever return to my former shape?

✓ Simple exercise routines

The challenge: finding the time for exercise

JUGGLING HOUSEHOLD and family responsibilities, care of the new baby, and, perhaps, a job while trying to fit in time for yourself is one of the challenges of your new role as a mother. With all the demands of a new baby, it's understood that you don't have hours to lavish attention on yourself with an emphasis on getting back into shape and exercising. While it may be difficult to fit in a 2-hour stint at the gym, do try to be creative with your time and exercise routine.

Keep it short, simple, and fun

For many new mums, exercise takes a back seat to more pressing concerns – sleep, for instance. But you'll find you have renewed energy for yourself and your baby if you make time for even short bursts of exercise – 10 minutes here and there is better than nothing, and it will do you a world of good. The key is to find an activity that you enjoy and that meshes with your schedule and lifestyle. If you like your exercise of choice, you'll view it as a necessity, not an option.

GETTING STARTED

With the emphasis on little and often, here are some suggestions for getting out of the house to exercise:

a Go for a walk with your baby in a front pack or a backpack, whichever your neck and shoulders support best.

b Hand the baby off to dad when he returns from work and take a brisk walk around the neighbourhood.

c Ask around to locate and join a local health club or yoga studio that offers postnatal exercise classes at which babies are welcome.

■ **Tuck your newborn** *in a front pack as soon as you feel ready to get out and about – you'll be able to show off your beautiful baby as well as get some exercise.*

Why exercise?

YOU MAY FEEL DISCOURAGED and distressed because you seem to have no energy and are perpetually tired. Do not despair; exercise can be a surprising cure. Spending just half an hour a day exercising, walking, or even dancing around the house with your baby can make a world of difference to your energy level and can help you regain your health, your figure, and even your mental alertness.

How should I begin?

It's important that you find a routine or exercise programme that you enjoy. If you enjoy your exercise, it will become a positive part of your day rather than a chore. You should be able to rent or buy a postnatal exercise video and exercise with your baby watching or sleeping next to you on the floor or safely secured in a car seat. Or you might try *strollercising*, a new, popular pastime for mothers with infants who get a great workout pushing the baby around the park or on a shopping trip.

DEFINITION

Strollercising *is a means of using the stroller, or pushchair, with baby in it as a resistance tool for a programme of stretches, walks, and toning. Shops like Mothercare sell special three-wheel strollers or adaptive devices for this exercise. You can make this a social activity by joining with other new mothers.*

■ **Strollercising** *is a great way of getting back to your pre-pregnancy shape. You can work up a sweat while your baby goes for a fun ride!*

How soon after delivery can I start exercising?

Resume exercise following birth very gradually. If you've had a vaginal delivery with no complications, you can usually begin doing mild exercises as soon as the day after you've had your baby, with approval from your doctor or midwife. If you exercised right up until delivery, you can probably safely perform your pre-pregnancy workout – or at least light exercise such as modified sit-ups and stretching – right after delivery. If you stopped exercising during your pregnancy or are a newcomer to fitness, you must resume exercising more slowly. If you've never exercised or want to ease back into getting fit, go very gently and slowly the first month. The exercises outlined in this chapter can help you ease back into movement and retrain muscles that were stressed during childbirth. No matter how fit you were before the birth, you should ease your way in with a simple routine and continue gently until 6 weeks after the birth, or whenever you are cleared by your doctor or midwife. Only then can you gradually add more strenuous exercises. Should you suffer any discomfort during this time, you must stop and call your doctor or midwife.

What if I had a surgical delivery?

If your baby was delivered by caesarean section, you face different rules regarding exercise. Movement promotes the healing process, so get up out of bed and walk around. Slowly add daily household activities and move about more and more. But do not begin any sort of exercise regimen until you get the medical nod. At around 6 weeks after the birth it's usually okay to gradually resume your pre-pregnancy routine based on your personal physical capability. Check with your doctor or midwife for recommendations. And remember that your joints and ligaments will still be relatively loose for about 3 to 5 months, so watch your step to avoid spills (this is true for vaginal delivery too).

If you've had a caesarean or surgical delivery, do not begin exercise until your 6-week postnatal check-up.

Surgical delivery involves two incisions, the external one that you can see on your abdomen and the internal one on your uterus. You cannot watch the internal incision as it heals. You must wait to hear your doctor's or midwife's assessment of when healing has progressed to the point at which exercise can do no harm to the process.

Physical signs of trying to do too much too soon

Too much physical activity during the first few weeks after delivery can cause your vaginal flow, called lochia, to become pink or red and to flow more heavily – a signal to slow down. You should also allow time for your incisions to heal if you had a caesarean. Make an appointment to see your doctor if vaginal bleeding or lochia restarts after you thought it had stopped.

BREASTFEEDING AND EXERCISE

No doubt all your life you've heard that you should wait an hour after eating before swimming; now it turns out that you should also wait an hour after doing vigorous exercise before breastfeeding your baby. And if you overexercise, you can compromise the quality of your breast milk. Why? The amounts of antibody (immunoglobulin A) in breast milk decrease dramatically after hard workouts, and that antibody is precisely what your baby needs lots of to build up its immune system.

Recent research also suggests that if a mother attempts to breastfeed immediately after rigorous exercise, her baby may shun the breast completely or breastfeed less vigorously. Evidently, the toxins released into the bloodstream during rigorous exercise find their way into the milk and give it an unpleasant flavour. (This situation should pass within 60 minutes after the workout by which time the breast milk should be restored to the baby's satisfaction and taste.)

Words of advice

Avoid exercises that make your breasts sore or tender, and always try to exercise after feeding your baby. Your breasts won't feel uncomfortably full, and your baby will appreciate it, too.

Feed your little one before you work out and then make sure you wait an hour after finishing your workout before feeding again.

■ **It's a good idea to breastfeed** *before exercising so your milk remains free from any toxins and unpleasant tastes.*

Will I ever return to my former shape?

RETURNING TO YOUR PRE-PREGNANCY *shape is dependent upon two things: weight loss and exercise. But you need to be reasonable about your expectations. It took 9 months of weight gain to grow a healthy baby. You should give yourself at least that same amount of time to lose all your pregnancy weight. If you diet or exercise too fast or too soon, you can compromise your own long-term health. If you are breastfeeding your baby, you can compromise the nutritional adequacy of your breast milk as well. Overall, it is important to set realistic goals for yourself.*

Trivia...

One of the legacies of pregnancy may be bigger feet. You may very likely go up a half or even a full shoe size during pregnancy, and the new size may be permanent. Maybe it's all that extra weight pushing down on your arches. Continued bigger feet are not universal following pregnancy; you may be one of the lucky ones who returns to pre-pregnancy size in every way. Even if you remain at your new shoe size, chances are that in successive pregnancies you'll find that your feet have done all the growing they need to support and transport the next baby.

Some physical changes you see may be permanent. Many women find that the shape and contour of the breasts change, not only with pregnancy, but also with age. This does not mean you lose a cup size. Some women actually increase a cup size after pregnancy. All of these changes are individual and vary from one person to the next.

How long will it take me to lose weight?

Many new mothers are understandably eager to work off the excess weight as soon as the baby is born. The problem: your body needs time to recover from the beating it has taken during pregnancy and birth. A good goal for weight loss is to lose no more than 0.5 kg (about 1 lb) per week. This is a safe and realistic amount to lose. Weigh yourself only once a week to eliminate any stress you may feel in relation to weight loss.

The best way to lose weight is by some form of aerobic exercise, such as brisk walking, swimming, or cycling 3 to 5 days a week. However, you shouldn't do any of these until you have stopped bleeding. If you weren't active during your pregnancy, start gradually. If you tapered off on your fitness routine as your pregnancy progressed, begin at the modified level and increase the intensity or time as you feel ready.

Warning: dieting if you are breastfeeding can compromise the nutritional needs of your baby and yourself. Follow the good nutritional advice you adhered to during pregnancy. Cut down on fats and sugars, and avoid foods with empty calorie content.

You may find it difficult to lose those last few pounds as long as you're breastfeeding. Be assured though, that once baby's weaned, weight loss will follow – provided you keep up the exercise and eat the right foods.

Ten simple guidelines for getting back into shape

1. Get the okay from your doctor or midwife.

2. Take it easy and slow.

3. Exercise when your breasts are not full of milk. You will be more comfortable.

4. Drink lots of water. If you are breastfeeding, drinking water will help increase milk flow. Even if you are not breastfeeding, water is good for you, especially when exercising.

5. Go for walks whenever you can.

6. Listen to your body. Stop when you feel any pain or become winded.

7. Do pelvic tilts and pelvic floor exercises immediately following birth.

8. Choose exercises you enjoy.

9. Try yoga, which is great for rebuilding muscle flexibility and tone.

10. Eat healthily.

■ **Eat lots of fruit** *rather than snacking on foods with empty calorie content.*

Should I take an exercise class?

If you're inclined to take an exercise class, choose one taught by a specialist in the field of postnatal exercise or find a low-impact class with plenty of toning and stretching.

Be careful with high-impact leg and back exercises. Your joints and ligaments became relaxed during pregnancy in order to carry and deliver your bundle. It will take your pelvis, back, and legs time to realign and get back to normal.

A joint effort

Working out doesn't mean you have to part with your infant. You can enjoy exercise together. Here are some suggestions for exercising with your baby.

a Walk or hike with baby in a front pack or take walks around the neighbourhood with baby in the stroller.

b When your baby gets a bit older, you can take him or her cycling with a special bike trailer – but wait until your baby is at least 6 months old. Younger infants lack the neck strength to hold their heads upright and to support the weight of safety helmets.

c You might also want to consider purchasing a treadmill, stair stepper, cross-country ski machine, or other piece of fitness equipment for home use. These machines are great for getting back into shape in the privacy of your own home, at your own pace, and in your own time with the baby nearby.

d Another option is to use an exercise video at home. Chances are your baby will get a kick out of watching you jump around puffing and panting. If you are using an exercise video in the first 6 weeks, be careful to choose one that is approved for postnatal use.

■ **Watching me watching you:** *Your baby can lie back and look on, or even drop off to sleep while you work out at home.*

275

ARE YOU READY FOR ABDOMINAL EXERCISES?

Before beginning abdominal exercises, make sure the gap in your stomach muscles has closed following birth. Otherwise you could impede your abdomen's healing. Here's how to check to see whether you're ready to begin abdominal exercises:

1. Lie flat on your back with your knees bent.

2. Place the fingers of your left hand, palm facing you, just above your belly button.

3. Inhale, then exhale, and as you do lift your head and shoulders off the floor and slide your right hand up your thigh toward your knee. This will make your abdominal muscles tighten, and you should be able to feel a gap between the two edges of the muscles. If the gap is three or more finger widths, you'll need to start with pelvic tilts and leg slides. Once the gap narrows to only one to two finger widths and you can easily manage 16 head and shoulder raises, it's safe to proceed to sit-ups.

Simple exercise routines

HARD TO BELIEVE, but you won't always look pregnant, even though you may feel that way immediately after giving birth. It takes time, patience, and physical activity to get back in shape. The gentle exercises below are perfect for easing your body back into an exercise routine.

Start out with 5 minutes of movement 2 or 3 days per week, and work up to 20 minutes of brisk walking and some stretching and muscle toning. As you feel stronger and less sleep-deprived – usually from around 4 to 6 weeks after the birth – you can add sets and do more repetitions to increase the level of difficulty, or you may want to try more advanced exercises.

INTERNET

ghc.org/web/health_
info/self/children/
bdaynews/bdn_9a.jhtml

This site is a wonderful source for learning how to do a variety of exercises for getting back in shape.

■ **It doesn't get simpler than this!** *A brisk walk through the countryside is a great way to get back into regular exercise, and your baby can enjoy the view too!*

Pelvic tilts

You can do pelvic tilts immediately following birth. Even if you had an episiotomy or vaginal tearing during birth, this exercise will speed healing by increasing blood flow to the pelvic area. Pelvic tilts can also help relieve symptoms of incontinence, haemorrhoids, and perineal pain.

1. Lie on your back with your knees bent and your feet flat on the floor.

2. Inhale and allow your abdomen to expand.

3. Exhale and lift your tailbone towards your navel.

4. At the top of the tilt, tighten your buttocks, then release. Repeat eight to ten times.

Pelvic floor exercises

Earlier in the book I said pelvic floor exercises are for life – before and after birth. If you had an episiotomy or if your perineum feels bruised or swollen, then doing your pelvic floors will improve circulation to the area and help avoid problems such as incontinence. These muscles tire easily, so it's best to do several contractions repeatedly throughout the day rather than in one session. Pelvic floor exercises are the best way to keep the vaginal canal in shape. Here's a review of how to do them:

1. Lie on your back or sit in a chair with your knees bent and your feet on the floor.

2. Tighten the muscles of the vagina as if trying to interrupt the flow of urine when going to the bathroom.

3. Hold for a count of four, then release.

Try to do your pelvic floor exercises every time you feed your baby.

Leg slides

If you choose to get right back into an exercise routine, this exercise is a gentle and effective way to tone your abdominal muscles in the early days following birth. Here's how to begin:

1. Lie with your back on the floor and your knees bent.

2. Tighten your abdominal muscles and press the small of your back against the floor as you breathe out.

3 Slide both legs away from your body slowly, using your abdominal muscles to keep your back flat on the floor.

4 When your back starts to arch, bring your legs back to the start position – keep your stomach tight. Repeat eight to ten times.

5 Pay attention to your breathing throughout this exercise. Remember to tighten your abdominal muscles and flatten your back before you start sliding your legs away from you. As your stomach muscles strengthen, you'll find you can push your legs out further.

INTERNET

www.mylifepath.com

Click here to find more exercise routines to help you regain your former shape.

Cat stretch

This is another great exercise to strengthen your lower back and abdomen. You can start doing this exercise in the early days following birth.

1 Kneel on all fours, hands under shoulders, knees under hips, back straight.

■ **Keep your back straight**, *your feet slightly apart, and your hands flat on the floor.*

2 Round your spine up towards the ceiling, tuck your tailbone down, and relax your head and shoulders. Hold for 5 seconds, then return to the starting position and repeat four or five times. While in the same position, inhale and pull your abdomen in towards your spine while keeping your back straight.

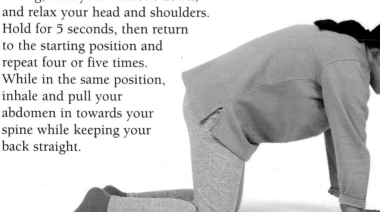

■ **Arch your spine upwards** *and push up on your arms, making sure you don't lock your elbows.*

3 Release and repeat ten times building up to two sets of ten repeats.

Push-ups

Push-ups are a good way to strengthen the upper-body muscles needed for carrying your little one and also for avoiding posture problems such as a rounded back and resulting aches common in breastfeeding mothers. If you have time to do only a few exercises, make sure this is one of them.

1 Start on all fours with your knees directly below your hips and hands slightly more than shoulder-width apart.

2 Keeping your back flat and your stomach in, gently bend your elbows and then straighten again. Keep breathing normally, and don't lock your elbows when you straighten them.

3 Repeat ten to 12 times. Work up to three sets.

Head and shoulder raises

Another good way to tone your abdominal muscles is through these head and shoulder raises. Here's the proper way to proceed:

1 Lie on your back with your knees bent and your arms by your side.

2 Take a breath and, as you exhale, tighten your abdominal muscles, flatten the small of your back against the floor, and raise your head and shoulders off the ground. Slowly lower and repeat the entire sequence eight to ten times.

■ **Raise your head and shoulders on your out-breath** *and hold for a few seconds before relaxing. With regular practice, you'll be able to get your head up higher and your abdominal muscles nicely toned.*

Shoulder and back stretch

Neck pain and posture problems are a common complaint of all new mothers. You need a lot of upper body strength to deal with all the lifting, carrying, and bending over required with the care of a little one – not to mention supporting those milk-filled breasts and breastfeeding positions. The following is easy to do even if you have only a minute or two break between activities:

1 Stand against a wall, feet shoulder-width apart, arms relaxed by your side.

2 Inhale, contracting your abdomen while pinching your shoulder blades together and down. Then bring your shoulders together in front.

3 Repeat ten to 15 times at first and build to two sets of 20 repeats.

A simple summary

✓ Exercise is at least as important after you give birth as it was while you were pregnant.

✓ Exercise restores energy, health, your figure, and mental alertness. It is important for restoring muscle tone and balance.

✓ Exercise will help you return to your original body shape, but you also must lose all that excess weight. Eat sensibly to lose weight gradually. Do not diet, especially if you are breastfeeding. Plan to shed 0.5 kg (1 lb) a week.

✓ If you had a surgical delivery, do not exercise beyond pelvic floor exercise until your doctor or midwife has cleared you. Limit activity to walking, increasing your pace gradually.

✓ For the first 6 weeks after a normal delivery, begin exercising slowly and gradually. Stick with approved postnatal exercises. Avoid high-impact leg and back exercises.

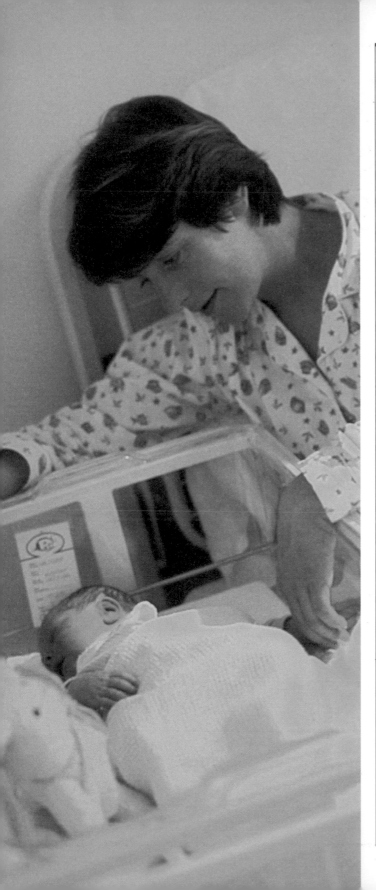

PART SIX

YOU AND YOUR BABY'S WELL-BEING

WITH SO MUCH EMPHASIS on the medical aspects of pregnancy, we sometimes forget that it's a natural event, not an illness. *Complications* do arise for mothers and their babies but most are relatively mild, and there is relief for almost any ailment or condition, either for you or your newborn. Simply knowing what to *anticipate* during pregnancy, childbirth, and the first few days of your baby's life will help you cope with the unexpected.

Over the next 9 months, maybe more so than at any other time, natural products, non-invasive treatments, and drug-free pain relief might be especially appealing to you. Even if *complementary* therapies never crossed your mind, discovering their advantages may help you to better enjoy childbearing and birthing, and unlock the secret to a lifetime of mental and physical *well-being*.

Chapter 19

Coping With Complications

PREGNANCY IS NOT ALWAYS a simple, blissful experience. It can be complicated, difficult, scary, and even sad. Problems can range from the very minor to the very serious. Among the serious, we might include miscarriage, illness, premature labour, and depression. Solutions range from dietary changes, to total bed rest, to emergency surgery. Nobody wants to talk about complications of pregnancy. During this incredibly life-changing event, we all want to be positive and optimistic. Still, you should be aware of the danger signals, and that the best course of action is to call your doctor or midwife without delay if you think *anything* is wrong.

In this chapter...

✓ Kinds of trouble

✓ Signs of trouble

✓ High-risk pregnancy

✓ Losing a baby: emotional grief

✓ Depression after childbirth

DON'T BE AFRAID TO CALL YOUR DOCTOR IF SOMETHING DOESN'T SEEM RIGHT

Kinds of trouble

SOME OF THE TROUBLES *connected with pregnancy relate to risky physical ailments or conditions that beset the mother. Most of these troubles respond to medical treatment such as dietary changes, bed rest, surgical intervention, and medication. Other troubles, those that do not culminate in the birth of a baby, particularly miscarriage and ectopic pregnancy, must be classified as irreparable troubles, though they do not preclude another try.*

Miscarriage

Bleeding in the early months of pregnancy signals the possibility of a miscarriage. As many as 25 per cent of pregnancies end in miscarriage. Sometimes miscarriage occurs so early following conception that you may not even know you were pregnant. Sometimes you may have had signs of pregnancy but no embryo can be found during an early ultrasound. If this is the case, the body has probably reabsorbed the embryo. This is called a blighted ovum. If the embryo has died but remains in the uterus, and is seen on an ultrasound scan, it is known as a missed abortion. Miscarriage in the first trimester of pregnancy is most commonly due to chromosomal defects or hormonal problems. Bleeding, clots, and cramping are the usual signs. Your body may completely expel the pregnancy, or surgery (a *D&C*) may be required to empty the uterus of any remaining tissue.

DEFINITION

D&C, *or dilation and curettage, is a surgical technique in which the cervix is widened (dilated) and the tissue lining of the uterus is gently scraped or suctioned. A D&C may be required if bleeding does not stop after a miscarriage. Continued bleeding after miscarriage indicates that tissue is remaining in the uterus and must be removed.*

INTERNET

www.fertilityplus.org/ faq/miscarriage/ resources.html

An invaluable web site for miscarriage support and information resources.

After the first trimester, a miscarriage is not so straightforward. The only warning sign you may have that the baby has died is the lack of heartbeat or lack of fetal movement. The miscarriage is usually diagnosed conclusively by an ultrasound. The cause of some late-term miscarriages is never known. Others may be the result of complications or illness. If you have a second- or third-term miscarriage, you are generally given two choices for delivering the baby. You may undergo either chemical induction during which you deliver, or a D&E (dilation and evacuation) during which you are put under anaesthesia and the baby is removed.

Ectopic pregnancy

If a fertilized egg has not made its way into the uterus, a woman may test positive for pregnancy, yet she is not truly pregnant. This is a "no-win" pregnancy. The embryo must reach the uterus in order to flourish. Typically the embryo attaches and starts growing in a Fallopian tube. The organ to which the embryo has attached itself stretches unnaturally, tearing delicate structures and blood vessels. The symptoms of an ectopic pregnancy are bleeding, lower back pain, fainting, nausea, lower abdominal pain or cramping, and the usual signs of pregnancy. This can turn quickly into an emergency requiring surgery to remove the malpositioned, non-viable embryo.

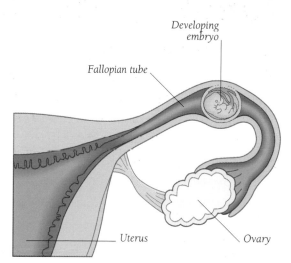

Developing embryo

Fallopian tube

Uterus

Ovary

■ **In an ectopic pregnancy,** *the fertilized egg becomes implanted in tissues outside the uterus. Most ectopic pregnancies occur in a Fallopian tube.*

An ectopic pregnancy in the Fallopian tube may require removal of part or all of that Fallopian tube and ovary along with the ectopic pregnancy itself. If this happens to you, do not despair that you will be unable to concive again. The body is a wonderful mechanism. If its partner is not there to take its turn, the remaining ovary will take over the job and release an egg every month. A single ovary may be so efficient that a woman may become pregnant as soon as her doctor signals that it is safe to try again.

Signs of trouble

YOUR BODY GOES THROUGH *so many changes during pregnancy that it's simply hard to distinguish between what is normal and what should raise alarm. Heartburn and fatigue, while troubling, are just the expected discomforts of pregnancy. But some signs of trouble are not a routine part of pregnancy, and should prompt you to make an urgent call or visit to your doctor or midwife.*

Premature birth

Premature labour and delivery is a common problem of pregnancy. About 11 per cent of all pregnancies end in delivery before 37 weeks of gestation have been completed. Thirty-seven weeks is considered the cut-off for premature labour. The problem is serious or less serious depending on how many weeks before term you go into labour. A change in vaginal discharge, leakage of fluid from the vagina, menstrual-like cramps, dull backache, abdominal cramping for more than 1 hour, or a feeling of having to push, may all indicate premature labour. The consequences of early delivery can be serious for your baby. Seek care and advice immediately.

Decreased movement

For various reasons, some babies have trouble getting enough oxygen in the womb. They may manifest this by a decrease in activity. Some doctors recommend that mothers do "kick counts", counting the number of times the baby kicks inside the uterus within a set time period. If your baby becomes unusually less active for more than a few hours, you should call your doctor or midwife.

WARNING SIGNS

If you experience any of the following at any time during your pregnancy, call your doctor or midwife:

a Sudden weight fluctuations

b Failure to gain weight

c Sudden swelling of the face, hands, or feet

d Vaginal bleeding

e Persistent headache

f Blurred vision or spots before your eyes

g Excessive nausea and vomiting

h Leaking fluid from the vagina

i Fever

j Increased frequency of urination or a burning sensation during urination

k Abdominal pain

l Regular or frequent contractions (more than 4 to 6 per hour)

m Decrease in fetal movement

High-risk pregnancy

WOMEN WHO HAVE *health problems before pregnancy or who develop conditions during pregnancy can have healthy babies, but they do require special care and extra monitoring. If you have a condition that might complicate your pregnancy, you may require special or extra testing and more frequent visits to your health care practitioner, or you may be required to stay in a hospital or in bed at home.*

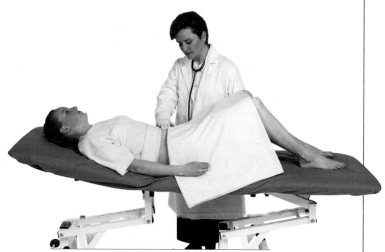

■ **If you have a history** *of health problems or develop complications in your pregnancy, it will be in your best interests to make frequent visits to your doctor.*

Multiple pregnancy

If you are carrying more than one fetus, you automatically fall into the high-risk category even though both you and the babies may be quite normal and progressing well. The most common multiple pregnancy is of course twins, found in about one in 43 pregnancies. Twins occur either when two separate eggs are fertilized (fraternal, or non-identical, twins) or when a single egg divides (identical twins). Identical twins are much rarer – fewer than one in every 100 pregnancies results in the birth of identical twins.

Rarer still are pregnancies in which there are three or more fetuses. However, with the use of fertility drugs and IVF (in-vitro fertilization), multiple births are becoming more common.

Multiple pregnancy carries some high risks for you and your babies. Mothers are considered at higher risk for developing high blood pressure or anaemia, and are also more likely to go into premature labour. The mother having a multiple birth needs special monitoring during labour and delivery.

EXPLAINING AND UNDERSTANDING INFERTILITY

For some women, the increased risk of multiple pregnancy associated with fertility treatments does not act as a substantial deterrent. A woman who is having difficulty conceiving will grasp at straws and try every new method for which she could possibly be a candidate. Sure, we've all heard the stories of our friends getting pregnant on birth control or other seemingly easy, unplanned events. And we agonize over the accidental, unwanted babies who are discarded like trash by their immature mothers. But this may not be the story for many of us who find that conceiving is a long, uphill battle. If you are like me and at the upper end of your reproductive years, infertility may be easy to understand – the body is simply shutting down many of the functions essential to conceiving and maintaining pregnancy. But if you are between the youthful ages of 20 and 35 and thus at the peak of what should be your fertile years, the inability to conceive can be a cruel and mysterious saga. Presumably, if you have bothered to buy this book, you have overcome your infertility through hard work and, more likely, good luck. For plenty of us, and perhaps for some of your friends who are still searching for a magic answer, what follows is a brief rundown of the ever-growing field of fertility treatments.

Reproductive technology

In this era of rapid advances, reproductive technology is on the fast track towards solving many human reproductive problems. Charting your basal body temperature and using ovulation predictor kits can also help you take charge of your fertility and calculate the optimum time when you are likely to conceive. Positive results are also possible through artificial insemination, in-vitro fertilization (IVF), gamete intra-Fallopian transfer (GIFT), and other assisted fertility techniques, though some of these may result in multiple pregnancies.

■ **If you and your partner** *are having trouble conceiving, your doctor will be able to help you decide upon the best way of increasing your chances of becoming pregnant.*

Fertility drugs

Fertility drugs are sometimes given bad press following the media hysteria when a woman gives birth to six babies or more. But multiple pregnancies are not necessarily the norm, nor are they the end result of many fertility drugs prescribed these days. If used as directed, drugs such as Clomid and Pergonal can be a welcome aid for many who are having trouble conceiving naturally.

www.inciid.org

The best place to start your infertility research is at INCIID (pronounced "inside"). The InterNational Council on Infertility Information Dissemination is a non-profit organization located in Arlington, Virginia, USA. This site provides the most current information regarding the diagnosis, treatment, and prevention of infertility and pregnancy loss.

■ **Chinese therapies** *are hard to verify scientifically, but may positively affect your state of mind.*

Alternative therapies

You may find your greatest hope for conceiving lies with dietary change, Chinese herbs, acupuncture, and other alternative therapies. Naturopaths, homeopaths, Chinese doctors, and herbalists enlist a variety of supplements and procedures that, while scientifically hard to verify, may result in a positive pregnancy. Actually, your mental state has a great deal to do with your physical condition. If you truly believe that an alternative therapy will help, you will relax, and your body may become more receptive to fertilization.

High blood pressure

High blood pressure is a condition that can be present before pregnancy or it can arise during pregnancy. High blood pressure that begins during pregnancy is the leading cause of caesarians, premature births, and low birth-weight babies. Chronic high blood pressure, depending on its severity, can also affect mother and/or child in different ways.

Blood pressure is reported as two readings separated by a slash. The first number is the pressure in the arteries when the heart contracts. This is called systolic pressure. The second number is the pressure in the arteries when the heart relaxes between contractions. This is the diastolic pressure.

You may hear a sequence like 115 over 80 when your blood pressure is measured. (This is a very good reading.) Typically a nurse or doctor uses a stethoscope and a sphygmomanometer (an inflatable cuff with a pressure gauge) to measure your blood pressure.

Some women have high blood pressure before they become pregnant. Lifestyle, genetics, weight, and diet all play a role in this condition. During pregnancy, high blood pressure puts you at a higher than normal risk for complications including a low birth-weight baby and *abruptio placenta*, premature separation of the placenta from the uterus before the baby is born.

■ **It's important** *to monitor your blood pressure throughout your pregnancy. Higher than normal levels can increase your risk of birth complications.*

> ### DEFINITION
>
> **Abruptio placenta** *is a condition in which the placenta separates from the uterine wall before the baby is born. This condition sometimes results in bleeding and often requires emergency surgery to deliver the baby.*

It's best to bring chronic high blood pressure under control through diet, losing weight, and sometimes medications before becoming pregnant. During pregnancy your doctor or midwife will be checking you regularly for signs of more trouble.

Pre-eclampsia

High blood pressure that occurs for the first time in the second half of pregnancy, and is accompanied by protein in the urine, fluid retention, and swelling, is called pre-eclampsia. Seven out of 100 pregnant women develop this condition. Women with chronic high blood pressure are thought to develop pre-eclampsia more easily, although women who have never had high blood pressure can also develop it. The cause is unknown in these cases. Pre-eclampsia in a woman without a history of high blood pressure generally occurs during a woman's first pregnancy and seldom recurs in later pregnancies unless her blood pressure does not return to normal after pregnancy.

Symptoms of pre-eclampsia may include swelling of the hands, feet, and face, protein in the urine, and higher than normal blood pressure.

Typically, a woman who develops pre-eclampsia is confined to bed rest in a hospital or at home. Resting often lowers blood pressure and brings it back to normal. The woman with pre-eclampsia should lie on her left side. This helps improve blood flow to the uterus and kidneys. Hopefully bed rest will help control the situation and allow the pregnancy to continue until the baby is old enough to be born without complications.

According to a recent study published in the Journal of American Medicine, consuming sufficient calcium during pregnancy can reduce the risk of pregnancy-induced hypertension (PIH) and pre-eclampsia.

Eclampsia

Severe pre-eclampsia is rare, but it can be dangerous to the mother. This condition can affect almost all of the mother's organs causing convulsions known as eclampsia. If this happens, the baby must be delivered by emergency surgery to save the mother's life.

Symptoms of eclampsia may include visual changes such as spots before the eyes, flashes of light, and blurring, headache, and pain in the area above the stomach. Seizures may result.

What is HELLP Syndrome?

HELLP syndrome is characterized by liver compromise during or after a pregnancy that has been complicated by hypertension and/or pre-eclampsia. The letters stand for Haemolytic anaemia (when red blood cells break down), Elevated Liver transaminases (sign of liver problems), and Low Platelet count (causing problems in blood clotting).

This condition usually appears in the third trimester and most commonly in first-time pregnancies, but it can begin as early as 20 weeks and recur in subsequent pregnancies. A simple explanation of the disease is that it is a more complicated form of pre-eclampsia. About 15 per cent of women with pre-eclampsia go on to develop HELLP.

HELLP syndrome is diagnosed by blood tests for clotting factors and liver function. This condition can be mild – requiring only close observation and rest – or it can be life threatening to mother and baby. In severe cases, micro blood clots form in maternal vessels and decreased clotting factors can lead to haemorrhage. The cause of this whole complex syndrome of pre-eclampsia and HELLP has not been identified. It tends to be decreasing in frequency, which may indicate that better screening and antenatal care, and improved nutrition, are having some impact.

Placental problems

Placenta praevia, whereby the placenta covers part or all of the cervix, is a common placental problem. About one in 250 pregnant women develop this complication, which can cause severe, often painless, bleeding, usually towards the end of the second trimester or later. Uncontrolled haemorrhage can jeopardize the mother's life and the life of her baby, although this is rare. If the bleeding doesn't stop or if placenta praevia causes premature labour, the baby will be delivered by caesarian even if the due date is weeks away.

If an early ultrasound (between 12 and 14 weeks) shows the placenta near, or covering the cervix, don't be alarmed – it is most likely not placenta praevia. As the uterus grows, it naturally pulls the placenta away from the cervix. Medical intervention generally is necessary only when the placenta persists in covering the cervix in later pregnancy.

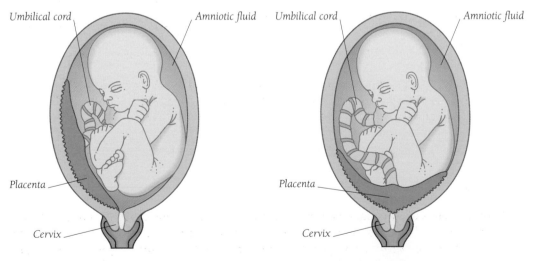

Umbilical cord   *Amniotic fluid*   *Umbilical cord*   *Amniotic fluid*

Placenta   *Placenta*

Cervix   *Cervix*

PARTIAL PLACENTA PRAEVIA   **COMPLETE PLACENTA PRAEVIA**

Treatment depends on whether you're bleeding and how far along you are in your pregnancy. If the condition is diagnosed after week 20 but you're not bleeding, you'll probably be asked to cut way back on your activity level and increase the amount of time you spend in bed. If you're bleeding heavily, you'll have to be hospitalized until you and the baby have been stabilized. If the bleeding stops or is light, you'll have to continue bed rest until the baby is ready to deliver.

AN INCOMPETENT CERVIX

Cervical incompetence is the technical term describing a cervix that is too weak to stay closed during pregnancy. Such a cervix opens without labour or contractions, resulting in a premature birth and possibly the loss of the baby. This complication generally shows up in the early part of the second trimester, but sometimes as late as the early third trimester, and is believed to be the cause of 20 to 25 per cent of all second trimester miscarriages. Factors that may increase your likelihood of having an incompetent cervix are:

a Your mother was given the drug DES while pregnant with you

b An incident of cervical trauma

c Hormonal influences

d A congenitally short cervix

e A history of one or more forced D&Cs

f Other uterine anomalies

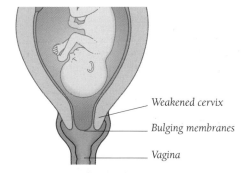

Weakened cervix

Bulging membranes

Vagina

If it is suspected that you will have problems with the strength of your cervix, a cerclage (stitching the cervix closed) can be performed at approximately 14 to 16 weeks of your pregnancy. This may help you continue to term.

Bed rest is best

Many women with pregnancy complications such as an incompetent cervix, high blood pressure, multiple babies, or early, preterm contractions are ordered by their doctors to go on bed rest. Bed rest means just that: resting in bed. But each pregnancy situation differs. You may be prescribed strict bed rest or a less-limiting kind of rest.

Whether you've been sent to bed for 2 weeks or 6 months, take some comfort in knowing you are not alone: each year, as many as one-fifth of all pregnant women are prescribed bed rest for a variety of reasons. Bed rest itself is a controversial prescription because its benefits have not been backed up by much medical research. Even so, the goal of bed rest is to keep your baby inside you, developing in your uterus for as long as possible, so it's best to follow doctor's orders.

Pregnancy and HIV

In some centres in the UK, it is routine for all pregnant women to undergo an HIV test, provided they give consent, and all women who are particularly at risk may ask to be tested. If you are HIV positive, become pregnant, and decide to have your baby, the most important thing you can do is get good antenatal care. The chances of passing HIV to your baby before or during birth are about one in four, or 25 per cent. As a general rule, treatment for HIV infection in pregnant women is the same as for others who are not pregnant. You should have a cervical smear test during your pregnancy, and your doctor will probably recommend a *CD4* count as soon as antenatal care begins. Depending on the results, you may not need another CD4 count during your pregnancy.

> **DEFINITION**
>
> **CD4** *lymphocytes are a type of white blood cell needed to fight infection and certain types of cancers. If CD4 levels fall, treatment must begin at once.*

After birth, your baby will be tested regularly for HIV infection, whether or not HIV is present at birth. HIV infection can be passed through breast milk, so if you are HIV positive, you should not plan to nurse your baby.

Gestational diabetes

During pregnancy, your body is under continuous demand to supply an ever-increasing amount of insulin: two to three times higher than before pregnancy. In about 3 per cent of pregnant women, insulin resistance, or gestational diabetes, occurs. Gestational diabetes is thought to be caused by a hormone from the placenta. It differs from other forms of diabetes in that gestational diabetes usually disappears after the birth of the baby, whereas the other forms of diabetes last a lifetime. Also, diet and exercise can control more than 85 per cent of gestational diabetes cases, while other forms of diabetes often require medication.

If carefully managed, gestational diabetes seldom has any permanent effect on the baby.

When gestational diabetes is not controlled, the risks to the baby include jaundice, premature birth, and excessive birth weight caused by excess glucose from the mother being stored as fat in the unborn baby.

If the mother develops gestational diabetes during pregnancy, she is suspected of having a predisposition to diabetes and a 25 to 60 per cent chance of developing type 2 (non-insulin dependent) diabetes later in life. The child is also at risk of developing juvenile diabetes.

Premature labour and delivery appear more frequently in women with gestational diabetes than with other pregnancies. Caesarean deliveries are also more common for women with gestational diabetes, especially when the baby is very large. Another complication of diabetes during pregnancy is pre-eclampsia. Urinary tract infections (UTIs) are also more prevalent in women with gestational diabetes. UTIs are characterized by pain and fever, and a need to urinate often, with or without a burning sensation. Sometimes, however, they have no symptoms at all.

Controlling gestational diabetes

Daily monitoring of blood glucose levels is a must. This is done by drawing a small amount of blood and placing it on a test strip used with a glucose monitor. Although gestational diabetes is a special type of diabetes, you can gain insight and useful tips from information about type 2 diabetes at a library or on the Web. Your doctor may recommend that you receive nutritional counselling. If you develop this condition, you must be responsible and follow your treatment plan on a daily basis to ensure that you and your baby remain in good condition.

A closely monitored diet can control blood sugar levels, and good nutrition along with an exercise programme can, in most cases, control gestational diabetes.

Losing a baby: emotional grief

IT'S A HORRIBLE BUT NOT UNCOMMON fact of pregnancy that sometimes a baby can die inside the womb, often for no obvious reason. When this happens, there is shock, anguish, sadness, and pain, no matter if the event is an early miscarriage or if a full-term child is stillborn. You may feel singled out for this terrible tragedy, and no matter when miscarriage occurs, depression can take over your life. It is okay to go into mourning over a person you have never met. Becoming attached to your baby before it is born is very natural and is to be expected. The loss of a baby at any stage is a tragedy, and you should allow yourself to go through the normal stages of grief. You will want to blame yourself; you'll feel anger and shock and look for any reason to explain the loss.

No one can tell you what it feels like; every woman's experience of miscarriage is personal. Some women bounce right back and go on to have a successful pregnancy, especially if the loss was early. For some women experiencing late miscarriage or stillbirth, another pregnancy may be unthinkable, either for the near future or the rest of their days, though most will try again. Some women end up with a high ratio of miscarriages to successful births, but one stillbirth most certainly does not guarantee another. You can find support from a counsellor or from mothers' groups, all of which can help relieve your pain and help you understand and accept what has happened. You are not alone, so be sure to reach out if you feel the need.

No matter when or how you lose your baby, do not feel guilty. Sad, yes; guilty, no. It is not your fault. Sometimes tragedies just happen. We cannot question and cannot understand.

Depression after childbirth

MOST WOMEN EXPERIENCE the "baby blues" about 3 days after the birth, and this state may last as long as 2 weeks. This mild condition is not unexpected. With the baby blues, many mothers feel sad, afraid, angry, or even anxious. Other baby blues are characterized by crying, irritability, exhaustion, tension, restlessness, and possibly insomnia. Hormones play a large part in this situation. Considering the stress and strain of having a new baby, you shouldn't be too hard on yourself if any of these signs present themselves.

■ **Mild depression** *is a common and quite normal reaction to the stresses involved with giving birth.*

A small percentage of women have true postnatal depression. This is generally characterized by a worsening of the normal symptoms, possibly postnatal panic or mania, even obsessive-compulsive disorders (including repetitive thoughts that might be repulsive). Some women experience post-traumatic stress disorders, particularly after a traumatic birth. This very serious condition requires counselling and treatment by a professional. If the baby blues turn deep purple and don't go away, seek help from your doctor.

A simple summary

✔ Most pregnancies are smooth and without complications, but some pregnancies are complicated by maternal illness. Some complicated pregnancies do not have successful outcomes.

✔ Miscarriage (loss of the embryo or fetus, usually in the first trimester) and ectopic pregnancy (implantation of the embryo at a location other than the uterus) are the most common complications from which the result is no baby.

✔ You must be alert for danger signals outside of the normal discomforts of pregnancy. Your doctor or midwife should know at once if you gain weight suddenly, have vaginal bleeding, have blurry vision or spots before your eyes, run a high fever, find your face and extremities swelling rapidly, or sense that your fetus has stopped moving.

✔ High-risk pregnancies require special management to assure a satisfactory outcome. Multiple pregnancies qualify in the high-risk category. High blood pressure, gestational diabetes, an incompetent cervix, placenta praevia, HIV, and pre-eclampsia all create special risks for mother and baby. Dietary changes, bed rest, and medication may all be used to counter the risks.

✔ Losing a baby is always painful, whether by early miscarriage or full-term stillbirth. Feel free to mourn and seek counselling or help from support groups, but do not feel guilty.

✔ Mild depression is normal in the first few days after giving birth. Hormones need time to stabilize. Heavy, long-lasting postnatal depression requires medical attention.

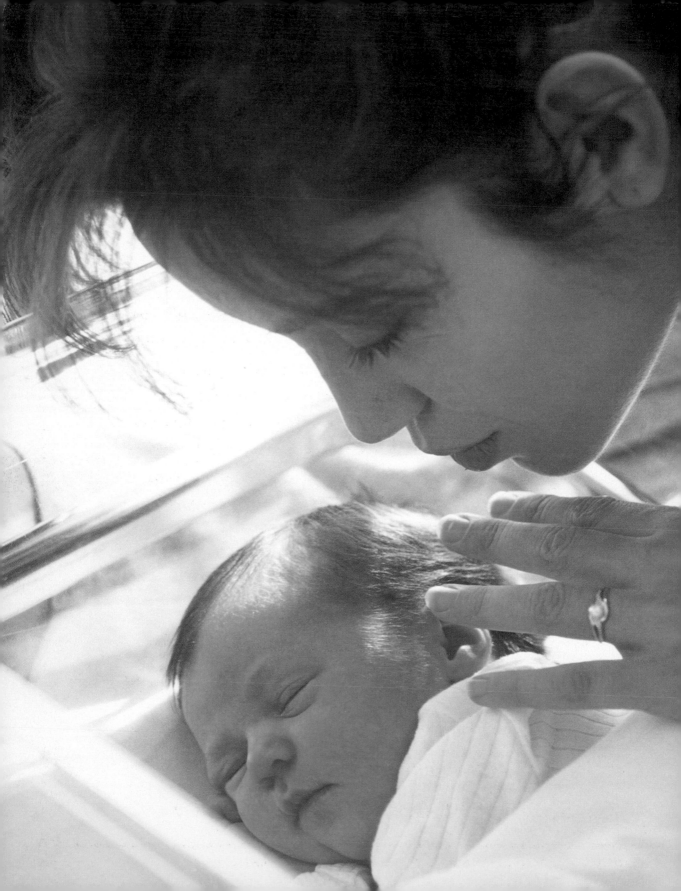

Chapter 20

If Your Baby Needs Extra Care

THE ARRIVAL OF A NEWBORN is a challenging and rewarding experience. The challenge can be overwhelming for parents whose newborn has a health problem. And there is no way to completely prepare yourself for the baby you love and the handicap that you and the baby must deal with. But some problems can be corrected and will not dominate your child's life. Antenatal testing and education can provide valuable information in preparation for your newborn's arrival, but be prepared to make decisions. In this chapter we aim to help prepare you by describing some of the problems you need to be aware of.

In this chapter...

✓ What to do if there is a problem at birth

✓ Health problems common to premature babies

✓ Serious problems not related to prematurity

✓ Common problems of healthy newborns

✓ Sudden infant death syndrome (SIDS)

IN ADDITION TO A MOTHER'S LOVE, UNWELL NEWBORNS RECEIVE GREAT CARE THESE DAYS

What to do if there is a problem at birth

FEW BABIES ARE BORN WITH SERIOUS health problems. If your baby is one of the few, you and your partner can be facing a difficult time. A hospital's medical team is trained to offer professional recommendations and to discuss options with you. If you are not up to talking with a doctor, don't be afraid to ask your partner or another close relative to step in. The medical staff will be sensitive to your needs. Many parents find that talking with a counsellor or clergy member brings some added comfort.

Problem or no, your baby is your baby, and no matter how helpless you feel, you can offer love. Every newborn, healthy or otherwise, benefits from a parent's soothing voice and loving touch. Every baby needs its parents' love. Many support groups are available to give you the emotional backing you'll need. Don't hesitate to ask for help.

Premature babies

The single most common source of complications for infants is premature birth. Many health problems are the direct result of the baby's being born too soon, before all its systems have matured sufficiently. Premature infants come into the world too early, usually at fewer than 37 weeks, while full-term infants are born 38 to 42 weeks after they are conceived. Premature infants, especially very early and very small ones, have many special needs that make their care different from that of full-term infants. This is why they often begin their lives following delivery in a special care baby unit (SCBU). The SCBU is designed to provide an atmosphere that limits stress to the infant and meets its basic needs for warmth, nutrition, and protection to assure proper growth and development. Furthermore, by giving hospital staff the chance to detect and treat early problems, their long-term effects can be limited.

Thanks to recent medical advances, more than 90 per cent of premature babies who weigh more than 800 grams (2 pounds) survive, though some will have serious physical handicaps.

Premature delivery may stem from one of many causes. Sometimes it is related to the mother's lifestyle choices during pregnancy: smoking, drinking alcohol, using drugs, eating poorly, not gaining enough weight, exposure to physical stress, or poor antenatal care. Often, however, the cause is not within the mother's control. The mother could

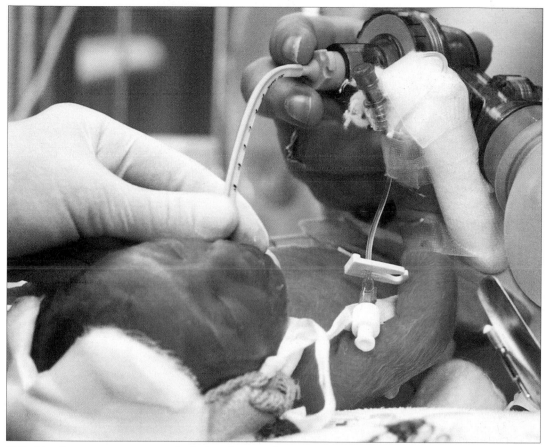

■ **Babies born 5 or more weeks** *before they are due are considered premature, or pre-term, and often spend their first few weeks in an intensive care unit, where they are closely monitored.*

have a hormone imbalance, a structural abnormality of the uterus, a chronic illness, or an infection. A life-threatening condition may lead doctors to risk problems of prematurity in preference to loss of the mother's life.

Premature delivery is more likely when the mother is over age 35 or under age 19 or when she is carrying multiple fetuses. But sometimes the cause is simply unknown.

Pre-term babies look different from term babies. They are often red and skinny because they have little body fat and their blood vessels are close to the surface of the skin. Obviously, the earlier a baby is born the less developed it is. This lack of development often leads to respiratory and breathing troubles, feeding problems, and increased risk of infection.

Incubators

Premature babies lack the body fat necessary to maintain their body temperature, even when they are swaddled with blankets. Therefore, incubators are used to keep the babies warm. These special beds are made of transparent plastic. They completely surround the infant to keep him or her warm and limit water loss. A premature baby may be fed through a tube and may be connected to a respirator to aid breathing.

Feeding

Premature babies have special nutritional needs because they grow at a faster rate than full-term babies, yet their digestive systems are immature. Breast milk is an excellent source of nutrition, but sometimes premature infants are too immature to feed directly from the breast or a bottle until they are 32 to 34 post-conception weeks old. Most premature infants have to be fed slowly because of the risk of developing necrotizing enterocolitis (NEC), an intestinal infection unique to premature babies. Breast milk can be pumped by the mother and fed to the premature baby through a tube that goes from the baby's nose or mouth into the stomach. Breast milk has an advantage over formula because it contains proteins that help fight infection and promote growth. Special fortifiers may be added to breast milk for premature infants, or, if breast milk is not desired, these fortifiers may be used alone. Premature babies have greater vitamin needs than do full-term infants, so they are given vitamin supplements. A number of blood chemicals and minerals, among them blood glucose (sugar), salt, potassium, calcium, phosphate, and magnesium, are monitored regularly, and the infant's diet is adjusted to keep these substances within a normal range.

Kangaroo care

Baby kangaroos, which are called joeys, are always born prematurely. Immediately after birth, a joey climbs into its mother's pouch. There it self-feeds and clings to its mother until it is mature enough to survive on the outside.

In the last few years, medical professionals in some parts of the world have recognized that the kangaroo protocol can be applied to humans.

Kangaroo care is simple. Using a baby sling, the mother wears her baby skin-to-skin and close to her breasts. Her body, and blankets, keep the premature baby warm and the closeness to its mother's breasts allows the baby to feed as often as his or her tiny stomach needs to. Giving kangaroo care, mothers can contribute to helping their own premature babies thrive. Premature human babies who receive kangaroo

Trivia...

You may think that it is strange that mere closeness of baby will stimulate milk-producing hormones. This does happen. In fact, there are more than just a few cases in which love, devotion, and emotion have served to produce milk in adoptive mothers. Nature works in wondrous ways, and these adoptive mothers were actually able to breastfeed their adopted babies.

care gain weight faster, have fewer stop-breathing episodes, and experience shorter hospital stays. If the baby is too young to breastfeed, the closeness of kangaroo care will stimulate its mother's milk-producing hormones and allow for more productive pumping of milk for the baby. All the while, the mother is holding, rocking, and wearing the baby as though he or she were still in the womb. Neonatal specialists also believe that the mother acts as a rhythmic-breathing pacemaker for the baby and that this is one of the main reasons that the baby thrives from this method. The mother's rhythmic breathing, voice, and heartbeat all seem to act as reminders to the baby to breathe and also help mother and baby attach and bond with each other.

■ **Learning from nature:** *By adopting a modified version of the way in which kangaroos care for their young, it is now thought that we can help our own premature infants to thrive.*

Health problems common to premature babies

PREMATURE INFANTS *are prone to a number of problems, mostly because their internal organs are not completely ready to function on their own. In general, the more premature the infant, the higher the risk of complications.*

Infection

Infection is a big threat to premature infants because they are less able than full-term infants to fight germs that can cause serious illness. Infections can come from the mother before birth, during the process of birth, or after birth. Practically any body part can become infected. Frequent handwashing is mandated in the SCBU to reduce the risk of infection. Bacterial infections can be treated with antibiotics, even for tiny premature babies. Other medications also can be prescribed to treat viral and fungal infections. Breast milk, an important source of antibodies for the baby, can also help ward off infections.

Handwashing makes for good hygiene whatever the age or condition of your baby. Hands spread germs.

GET INTO THE HABIT OF WASHING YOUR HANDS OFTEN

Clean hands spread fewer germs.

Hands acquire germs by coming in contact with germ-laden objects. Germs are everywhere, so wash often – and always before handling your infant.

Neonatal jaundice

Hyperbilirubinaemia – that is, neonatal jaundice – is a common treatable condition of premature babies. Infants with neonatal jaundice have high levels of bilirubin, a compound that results from the natural breakdown of blood. This high level of bilirubin causes infants to develop jaundice, a yellow discoloration of the skin and whites of the eyes. While mild jaundice is fairly common in full-term babies, it can be more severe in premature babies. Extremely high levels of bilirubin can cause brain damage in any baby, so premature infants are monitored for jaundice and are treated quickly, before bilirubin reaches dangerous levels. Jaundiced infants are placed under lights that help the body eliminate bilirubin. In rare cases, severe jaundice must be treated with blood transfusions.

Apnoea

Apnoea is another common health problem in premature babies. During an apnoea spell, a baby stops breathing, its heart rate may decrease, and its skin may turn pale, purplish, or blue. Apnoea is usually caused by immaturity in the area of the brain that controls the drive to breathe. Almost all babies born at 30 weeks or less will experience apnoea, although kangaroo care has been found to help prevent this condition. Apnoea spells usually become less frequent with age; by 50 weeks post-conception, apnoea is rare.

In the SCBU, all premature babies are monitored for apnoea spells. Treating apnoea can be as simple as gently stimulating the infant – by rubbing the feet, for example – to restart breathing. However, when apnoea occurs frequently, the infant may require medication (most commonly caffeine or theophylline) or a special nasal device that blows a steady stream of air into the airways to keep them open.

Anaemia

Many premature infants lack the number of red blood cells necessary to carry adequate oxygen around the body. This complication, called anaemia, is easily diagnosed using laboratory tests. These tests can determine the severity of the anaemia and the number of new red blood cells being produced.

Premature infants may develop anaemia for a number of reasons. In the first few weeks of life, infants do not make many new red blood cells. Also, an infant's red blood cells have a shorter life than those of an adult. And the frequent blood samples that must be taken for laboratory testing make it difficult for red blood cells to replenish.

Some premature infants, especially those who weigh less than 1 kg (2.2 pounds), require red blood cell transfusions.

Low blood pressure

Low blood pressure occurring shortly after birth is a relatively common, but not too problematic, complication in premature babies. It can be caused by infection, blood loss, fluid loss, or medications given to the mother before delivery. Low blood pressure is treated by increasing fluid intake or prescribing medication. Infants with low blood pressure due to blood loss may need a blood transfusion.

Respiratory distress syndrome

One of the most common and immediate problems facing premature infants is difficulty breathing. Although there are many causes of breathing difficulties in premature babies, the most common is called respiratory distress syndrome (RDS). With RDS, the infant's immature lungs do not produce enough **surfactant**. Fortunately, RDS is now treatable, and many infants do quite well. When premature delivery cannot be stopped, most pregnant women can be given medication just before delivery to help prevent RDS. Then, immediately after birth and several times later, artificial surfactant can be given to the infant.

> **DEFINITION**
>
> **Surfactant** *is an important substance that allows the inner surface of the lungs to be slippery and to expand properly when the infant makes the change from the womb to breathing air after birth.*

While most premature babies who lack surfactant will require a breathing machine, or ventilator, for a while, the use of artificial surfactant has greatly decreased the amount of time that infants spend on the ventilator.

Serious problems not related to prematurity

THEIR NUMBERS ARE FEW, *fortunately very few, but their problems create a heavy burden for the children and their parents. These are the babies born with severe handicaps. Some handicaps are genetic in origin, some stem from illness or problems during fetal development, and some stem from accidents in the birth process. Regardless of the reasons for these problems, these babies need extra care and extra love.*

Some problems can be treated, and even cured, by surgery in the first few weeks of the infant's life. Malformations in the urinary system or digestive system, and even some heart defects fall into this category. Others, such as spina bifida and cerebral palsy, can be alleviated but not cured. These children will require special care and training, as will those born blind and deaf. We have all seen courageous youngsters who struggle to live normal lives with these handicaps. None of these misfortunes happens often, but parents of handicapped children can find support from organizations bearing the names of the problems and from parent support groups. We will discuss only a couple of the more common, though still infrequent, problems.

Self-pity — okay, a little bit; compassion for the baby — you bet, a lot; guilt — no! Whether the problem comes from your genes, happened at some stage of fetal development, or developed in the process of birth, it is not your fault. Do not waste energy blaming yourself. You will need every ounce of energy for coping with the problem and for helping and loving your child.

Babies with Down's syndrome

Infants born with Down's syndrome are at increased risk for certain health problems. Congenital heart defects, increased susceptibility to infection, respiratory problems, obstructed digestive tracts, and childhood leukaemia occur with greater frequency among children who have Down's syndrome. However, advances in medicine have rendered most of these health problems treatable, and the majority of people born with Down's syndrome today have a life expectancy of approximately 55 years. Down's children respond readily to love and tend to be extremely affectionate. If their affection is returned, they tend to have happy lives within their limitations.

Feeding the infant

An infant with Down's syndrome can be breastfed. Breast milk is generally easier to digest than formulas of all types. Breastfeeding also enhances oral motor development, which is the foundation of speech. The emotional benefit derived from breastfeeding can also be extremely important for both the mother and the Down's baby. Even if the baby is unable to breastfeed directly, and some cannot, expressed breast milk given another way will be beneficial.

Sucking problems in Down's infants may make breastfeeding initially difficult, particularly if the baby is also premature. If the baby can't suckle, the mother is encouraged to feed expressed milk by other means, perhaps a bottle. The patient mother may find that after several weeks the baby's sucking ability may improve.

Maintaining milk supply

Many infants with Down's syndrome tend to be "sleepy babies" in the early weeks. Consequently, feeding only on demand may be inadequate both for the calorific and the nutritional needs of the baby and for stimulation of the mother's milk supply. The sleepy Down's infant should be awakened to feed at least every 3 hours, or every 2 hours if breastfeeding is the sole feeding being used. The mother may need to pump her breasts to stimulate the production of an adequate supply of milk.

Babies with cleft lip or cleft palate

Cleft lip, once called hare lip because the lip is divided like that of a hare, and **cleft palate** comprise the fourth most common birth defect. One of every 700 newborns is affected by cleft lip and/or cleft palate.

Cleft lip and cleft palate can occur on one side (unilateral cleft lip and/or palate) or on both sides (bilateral cleft lip and/or palate). Because the lip and the palate develop separately, it is possible for the child to have a cleft lip, a cleft palate, or both cleft lip and cleft palate.

The majority of clefts appear to be due to a combination of genetics and environmental factors. The risks of recurrence of a cleft condition are dependent upon many factors, including the number of affected persons in the family, the closeness of affected relatives, the race and sex of all affected persons, and the severity of the clefts.

> **DEFINITION**
>
> *A **cleft lip** is a separation of the two sides of the lip. The separation often includes the bones of the upper jaw and/or upper gum. A **cleft palate** is an opening in the roof of the mouth in which the two sides of the palate did not fuse, or join together, as the unborn baby was developing. Both of these conditions are considered congenital defects, or birth defects, which occur very early in fetal development.*

A child born with a cleft frequently requires several different types of medical attention including surgery, dental/orthodontic care, and speech therapy, all of which need to be provided in a co-ordinated manner over a period of years. Interdisciplinary cleft palate/craniofacial teams, comprised of professionals from a variety of health care disciplines who work together on the child's total rehabilitation, provide this co-ordinated care.

Always keep in mind that the baby's cleft condition is correctable in time. Try to put everything in perspective. Give the baby plenty of love and cuddling, and develop a lot of patience.

As with most infants, the first few months are the hardest, and, of course, this is a time when mother needs her rest too. If this is a first baby, remember that firstborns cause additional anxieties anyway; you are adjusting to many things at once. If the baby cries excessively or is extremely fussy, call your doctor as you would with any baby. If you have specific questions or worries about the specific care of the cleft or about feeding, feel free to ask for help from your doctor or from others who have shared this experience.

Common problems of healthy newborns

MOST BABIES ARE HEALTHY *and happy for their first year and struggle only with an occasional cold, teething problems, allergies, or ear infections. However, there are some conditions that can cause you to worry, such as jaundice, or that can make you frantic for yourself and the baby, particularly colic.*

Jaundice in newborns

About one-third of all newborns develop jaundice or a yellow tinge to their skin by their third day. Sometimes doctors can predict which babies are more likely to develop jaundice by knowing the mother's and the baby's blood types. When your and your baby's blood pass each other in utero, some of your antibodies pass to the baby. If your blood types are not compatible, a reaction may occur that causes the red blood cells to break and release a substance called bilirubin. If the baby's liver is overwhelmed with this substance, the yellow bilirubin accumulates in the skin and jaundice appears.

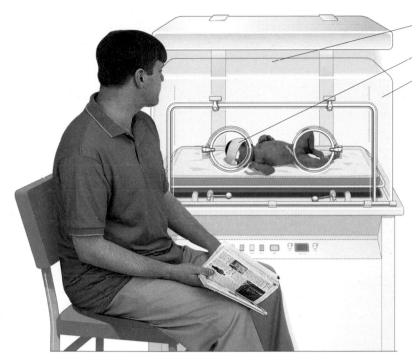

Blue fluorescent light

Eye shield

Incubator

■ **Neonatal jaundice** *is often treated with blue fluorescent light in a process called phototherapy. The baby is "bathed" in the light, wearing nothing but an eyeshield to prevent damage to the eyes, until blood tests show normal levels of bilirubin. However, there is a move towards using indirect natural light, when possible, by placing the baby near a window letting in sunlight.*

Don't be alarmed if you are told your newborn is a little jaundiced – it's not a disease.

The nurses will draw small samples of blood from your baby's heel two or three times a day. No treatment is necessary unless the bilirubin is over 20 milligrams per deciliter of blood (20mg/dl), which is unusual. Although jaundice cannot be diluted, so is not remedied by giving excess amounts of water, the doctor may ask you to nurse and feed the baby more often, hoping bowel movements will soon follow. In that way some of the bilirubin can be excreted.

Another treatment for jaundice is based on the fact that a certain wavelength of light that is found naturally in sunlight can help to eliminate bilirubin from the skin by breaking it down so it can excreted in the urine and faeces. A little indirect sunlight, or "sunlight" created by special artificial lights, can break down the bilirubin so that the baby's liver doesn't have to do all the work.

Babies who develop jaundice soon after delivery are often kept in the hospital an extra day or two, but in most cases jaundice doesn't begin until the third day. It generally takes that long for the bilirubin to collect in the skin. It's also possible that jaundice may not be discovered until after discharge: the baby's doctor can handle this easily. If your baby appears yellow any time before its first check-up, call the doctor.

Since many infants tend to have a bowel movement after each breastfeeding, the best way to treat jaundice is by breastfeeding more frequently. Frequent breastfeedings throughout the day and night may help prevent jaundice. The mother's fluid intake should also be increased to eight to ten large glasses of fluid per day.

Colic

Colic in newborns was for many years thought simply to be indigestion. But today there is no complete agreement on what colic is, what causes it, or how to treat it. The most widely accepted definition of colic today is "unexplainable and uncontrollable crying in babies up to 3 months old, more than 3 hours a day, more than 3 days a week for 3 weeks or more, usually in the afternoon and evening hours".

It has been widely estimated that between 8 and 49 per cent of newborns suffer from colic. Or, an estimated average of 22 per cent of all newborns suffer from colic at some time.

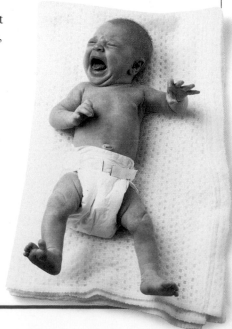

The condition is regarded as self-limiting, disappearing spontaneously at 3 months of age; however, studies have shown that many cases of colic will persist until 6 and even 12 months of age, causing considerable distress and frustration for both babies and parents. The crying that is so typical of babies with colic may also have a higher frequency – that is, pitch – than that of non-colicky babies. Another frequent symptom is motor unrest (flexing of the knees against the abdomen, clenching of the fists, and extension or straightening of the trunk, legs, and arms).

Treatment of colic is as widespread as the theories about its causes. Chiropractors, Chinese medicine practitioners, paediatricians, and other mothers may all suggest possible remedies and cures. Go ahead and try them. Some work, and some don't, depending on your child. Ultimately there is no known cure. As the mother of a colicky baby, you need patience and you need to give yourself breaks. If you can afford competent help, get out of the house periodically. And don't hesitate to ask your partner to take over occasionally. Hopefully the condition will pass quickly, and you and your baby can move on to happier times.

■ **The most common feature** *of colic is "excessive crying" – more hours of crying and more stretches of crying per day than is typical of non-colicky infants.*

Sudden infant death syndrome (SIDS)

SUDDEN INFANT DEATH SYNDROME, or SIDS, *is among the greatest fears of parents with newborns, but it is rare. Despite its rarity, SIDS is the leading cause of death in children 1 to 12 months old. In England and Wales, 279 infant (aged up to 1 year) deaths were attributed to SIDS in 1999.*

Although doctors still don't know what causes SIDS, there are a number of precautions you can take to significantly reduce the chances of your baby becoming a victim. In fact, the number of cases in England and Wales has dropped around 70 per cent since 1991, when the "Reduce the Risk" public-awareness campaign was launched.

SIDS is not a disease, nor can it be a diagnosis for a living baby. While most babies who die of SIDS give no warning signs, there are certain factors that define the high-risk groups: premature infants; infants who have had apnoea or stop-breathing incidents; infants of poor mothers who had little or no antenatal care; and siblings of a previous SIDS baby. Still, even in these high-risk groups, the chance of SIDS is less than 1 per cent.

Among the diverse theories regarding the cause of SIDS, the prevailing one is that the baby has an undiagnosed sleep disorder wherein it stops breathing. Some babies seem to have an immature breathing regulating system deep inside their brains, and this breathing signal may click on and off. The human organism has a back-up system that automatically wakes us up and restarts breathing should the oxygen in our blood fall below an acceptable level. It seems that in some SIDS babies, a disorder of the arousal-from-sleep mechanism complicates the situation caused by the immature breathing system, and these babies never wake up when their breathing clicks off.

> **DEFINITION**
>
> *Formerly known as cot death,* **SIDS** *is the sudden and unexpected death of an apparently healthy infant, whose death remains unexplained after an autopsy, investigation of the scene and circumstances of the death, and exploration of the medical history of the infant and family. SIDS is a classification that describes an infant whose death cannot otherwise be explained.*

> **INTERNET**
>
> **www.sids.org.uk**
>
> *You can find research studies, tips for preventing SIDS, support for families of SIDS victims, publications, and events at this web site.*

HOW TO REDUCE THE RISK OF SIDS

There are several ways to reduce the risk of your newborn suffering from sudden infant death syndrome. The following list is not totally comprehensive, but if you *always* follow ALL of these pointers then you will be on the right track.

1. Always have your baby sleep on its back unless your doctor instructs you otherwise for medical reasons. Having the baby sleep on its back is the official advice you will find at the SIDS web site where the focus is solely on SIDS. However, contrary medical advice recognizes the danger of a baby's choking to death on vomit and recommends putting the baby to sleep on its side. Some baby-care shops sell a special firm bolster, sort of a sandbag for your baby, against which you can prop the baby on its side. The bolster keeps the baby from rolling onto its tummy while sleeping. Putting the baby to sleep on its tummy is against all current medical advice.

2. When putting your baby to sleep in a cot, make sure that his or her feet are at the bottom of the cot, and keep his or her head uncovered.

3. Breastfeed your baby. New research shows that breastfed babies have a lower incidence of SIDS.

4. Keep pillows, comforters, and large toys made of soft materials out of the crib.

5. Keep the baby's sleep environment safe. Don't put the baby to sleep on soft surfaces such as a couch, waterbed, pillow, or any other surface that can conform to the infant's face.

6. Avoid overheating a baby during sleep. Dress the baby lightly.

7. Don't smoke or allow anyone to smoke in the same room as the infant. When compared with babies who live in a smoke-free environment, those exposed to smoke are at an increased risk of developing colds and upper respiratory illnesses as well as SIDS. Here's another good reason to give up smoking.

8. If the baby seems sick, call the doctor.

A simple summary

✔ Babies that are born prematurely are often born with immature body-temperature controls, respiratory systems, and digestive systems. They may require treatment in a special care baby unit (SCBU) where they may be kept warm in incubators, and may be given assistance with breathing and nutrition.

✔ Premature babies are especially susceptible to infection, neonatal jaundice, apnoea, anaemia, low blood pressure, and respiratory distress syndrome. With proper care, all of these problems can be avoided or overcome.

✔ Some newborns are born with serious problems not related to prematurity. Among these problems are malformed organs, Down's syndrome, cleft lip and cleft palate, spina bifida, and cerebral palsy. Some of these problems can be treated and cured, some can be alleviated but not cured, and some must simply be managed with special care and support, and with lots of patience and love.

✔ Healthy babies can also have problems that, while not serious, can be upsetting and worrisome. Jaundice usually disappears very quickly; if not, it is readily curable. Colic is not curable. It disappears in time, but requires much love and patience and family support to allow the mother to rest.

✔ Sudden infant death syndrome (SIDS) is frightening, but rare. Lower the possibility by sleeping your baby on its side on a firm surface with no soft objects into which it might burrow. Breastfeed if possible, and do not permit smoking anywhere in the baby's space.

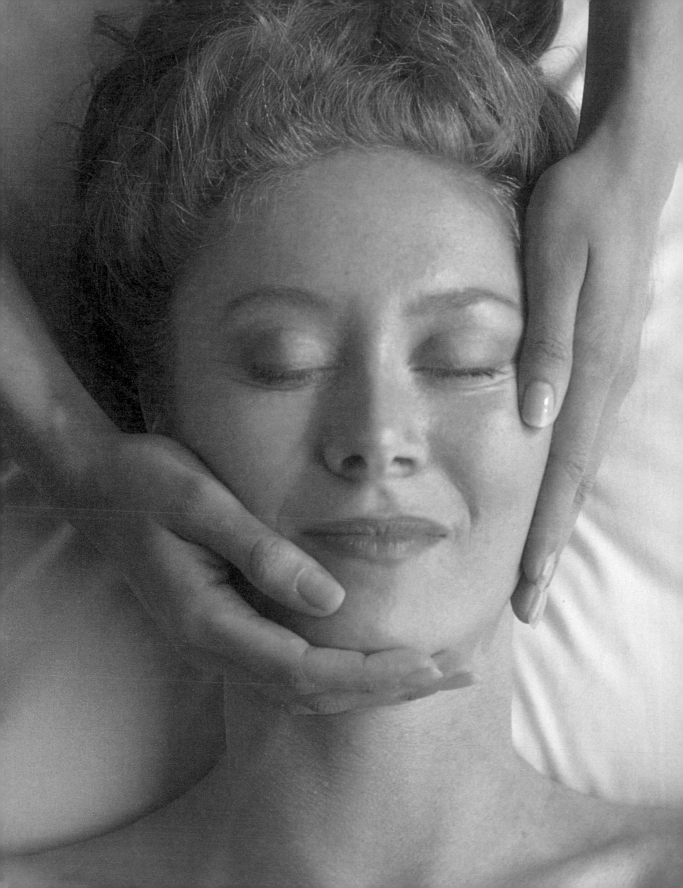

Chapter 21

Consider the Alternatives

BEFORE BECOMING PREGNANT most of us don't think twice about taking tablets for pain relief or a cold. When you are pregnant, however, you quickly realize that almost every drug in your local chemist's carries a warning alerting you to seek a doctor's advice before using it. Most pregnant women choose to suffer through various conditions rather than face the risk of unexpected side effects from medications. But there is no need to suffer pain or discomfort during pregnancy: most pregnancy and postnatal ailments can be relieved by using a combination of alternative therapies. In this chapter we take a very broad approach to natural therapies, to give you a glimpse into alternative health solutions for a few common pregnancy ailments. Read on to discover more.

In this chapter...

✓ Why should I choose alternative therapies?

✓ What is alternative medicine?

✓ Complementary treatments for common ailments

DON'T WANT TO TAKE PILLS? LIE BACK, RELAX, AND FEEL THE HEALING EFFECTS

Why should I choose alternative therapies?

STRANGELY ENOUGH, if doctors or drug companies claim they can cure gestational diabetes, relieve morning sickness, end constipation, or induce labour, most of us are likely to believe them. But what if these claims were posted in the fruit or vegetable section of your local supermarket, or emblazoned on an aromatherapist's door around the corner?

When it comes to addressing specific health issues of pregnancy, most of us are more likely to trust a pill prescribed by a doctor in a white coat than the powerful, alternative healing remedies and treatments that have been used in China and many other places around the world for thousands of years. In fact alternative, or complementary, medicine can provide safe and effective relief from many of the common ailments of pregnancy without harmful side effects to you or your baby.

What is alternative medicine?

WHILE THE TERM ALTERNATIVE MEDICINE may conjure up exotic images, many of these therapies are more familiar than you think. If you've ever massaged your temples to ease a headache, applied an icepack to a sprained ankle, or closed your eyes to relax after a long day at work, you've already practised some simple natural healing techniques.

Alternative treatments and medicines generally work in harmony with natural rhythms, recognizing the human body's innate ability to heal itself. Typically these therapies fall outside the scope of generally accepted Western medical standards of care. Alternative medicine's approach to antenatal care and childbirth is no different. Most practitioners start with the premise of giving women a choice and helping them gain a feeling of control over their bodies.

Where do alternative therapies come from?

Most of what is labelled alternative medicine comes to us from other cultures or from ancient healing traditions. Some, such as traditional Chinese medicine, have been used to treat pregnancy and other conditions in the East for as many as 4,000 years. While the use of herbs, to treat everything from infertility to breech babies, is an ancient practice found all over the world, you may be surprised to learn that chiropractics and naturopathy were developed in the United States.

■ **Alternative medicine** *is not as bizarre as you may think. A simple technique such as forehead self-massage is a form of natural medicine.*

Never put off seeing your doctor or midwife during pregnancy when you are sick with a fever. High temperatures in pregnant women can lead to birth defects and other complications.

Are there any risks involved with alternative approaches during pregnancy?

In general, no. If you are seeing a high-quality provider of alternative therapies, who delivers professional care and has experience with treating pregnant women, you should not be in harm's way. In general, it's probably best to combine alternative approaches with more conventional care by a doctor or midwife.

If you suspect that you might be about to miscarry, seek immediate medical attention. Alternative therapies are intended to complement, not replace, medical advice.

Are there any natural or whole substances that are dangerous during pregnancy?

Yes. In general you should not self-prescribe any drug, vitamin, or herb during pregnancy. You should always be under the care of or seek the advice of a professional health practitioner before ingesting anything that is not just plain wholesome food.

Certain plants are known to be dangerous to either you or the fetus during pregnancy. For instance the oils of clary sage and rosemary should only be used just before or during labour.

■ **When used in concentrated forms,** *such as oils, generally safe plants such as rosemary can be detrimental to the health of you and your developing baby. It is best to seek professional advice before using any new substance.*

HOW DO I CHOOSE A PROVIDER?

Finding an alternative medicine provider may not be an easy task. You need to find someone who suits your needs and, most importantly, can assure safety:

1. Learn your options. Add to your doctor's recommendations by researching the latest resources to get all your treatment options.

2. Get good referrals. Find referrals through various sources and verify that those referrals are capable of really helping you.

3. Screen the practitioner. Make use of an alternative practitioner's staff to get reliable information about the provider and how he or she works.

4. Interview the provider. Ask the provider for all of the pertinent information you want, so that you'll feel confident working with him or her.

5. Form a partnership. Maximize your healing potential by developing an active alliance with your alternative health care provider.

Complementary treatments for common ailments

YOGA, TRADITIONAL CHINESE MEDICINE, *homeopathy, flower remedies, and simple diet and nutrition are just a few of a long list of natural remedies and treatments available for conditions that may give you trouble during pregnancy.*

We have chosen some common ailments to give you a sense of how complementary methods achieve results. If you are suffering from any conditions not listed here and have not found relief through orthodox methods, it might be beneficial to consult with a qualified alternative medicine professional and discuss your symptoms.

Morning sickness

About half of all pregnant women experience morning sickness and most conventional doctors assume that it will pass after the first trimester. However, rather than suffering through 3 months of nausea, you may find relief from acupuncture, acupressure, reflexology, yoga and meditation, Western herbalism or homeopathy.

Acupuncture

What is popularly known today as acupuncture and Chinese herbal medicine is part of a complete medical system called traditional Chinese medicine (TCM). The ancient Chinese believed that there is a universal life energy called *chi* or *qi* present in every living creature. This energy is said to circulate throughout the body along specific pathways that are called **meridians**. As long as this energy flows freely throughout the meridians, health is maintained, but once the flow of energy is blocked, the system is disrupted and pain and illness occur. Imagine rivers that flood and cause disasters or an electrical grid short-circuiting that causes blackouts. Acupuncture works to "re-programme" and restore normal functions by stimulating certain points on the meridians in order to free up the *chi* energy.

> **DEFINITION**
>
> **Meridians** in traditional Chinese medicine are channels running through the body that transport chi, or energy. Chi in traditional Chinese medicine is the life energy that flows through the body.

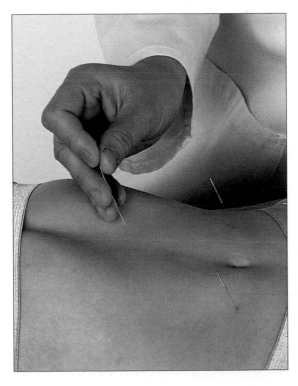

When treating morning sickness, an acupuncturist will insert needles into acupoints on your body, depending on the history and nature of your problem. Disposable acupuncture needles are used to attract or disperse energy along the meridians. They are very thin – 8 to 10 times thinner than hypodermic needles that are used for injections – and are barely felt when inserted. You should experience a pleasant and relaxing state of being and may even fall into a restful nap. Between four and six weekly acupuncture treatments may be needed to relieve morning sickness.

■ **Acupuncture** *can be a pleasant and relaxing way of treating morning sickness, but be prepared to engage in up to six treatments in order to feel relief.*

Acupressure

Based on the same ancient TCM principles as acupuncture – that sickness arises out of the blockage of life energy or *chi* – an acupressure practitioner treats your morning sickness by stimulating acupoints. In fact, you can learn these points yourself, and find some relief in treating yourself. The Pericardium 6 acupoint on your forearm, just beneath your wrist, can relieve nausea. Also, special acumagnets can be worn on the same acupoint to bring relief.

■ **By learning about** *the Pericardium 6 acupoint on your forearm, you may be able to relieve nausea by treating yourself.*

Chinese medicinal herbal therapy

After diagnosing a pattern of disharmony in a pregnant woman and administering acupuncture treatments, a doctor of TCM often writes a prescription from over a thousand common herbal formulas or from more effective traditional family prescriptions. Medicinal herbal therapy works in concert with acupuncture by providing the nourishing support for the energetic "re-programming" and "re-balancing" efforts of acupuncture.

There are many herbs that should not be used at all during pregnancy because of their potentially dangerous effects on you or your baby. Most herbs should be used only under the guidance of a professional medical herbalist. Be careful not to self medicate but seek the advice of your doctor, midwife, or a qualified herbalist.

Ginger is a key herb used in the treatment of morning sickness. It is rich in zinc, which helps combat the symptoms of nausea. In clinical studies, ginger has been shown to reduce nausea and vomiting attacks. It is preferable to drink a warm infusion of ginger tea made with fresh ginger. Drink one cup two or three times a day, or sip the tea frequently throughout the day.

■ **Fresh ginger tea** *taken frequently may have the effect of reducing nausea and vomiting attacks. Ginger's effectiveness in combating morning sickness is due to its high zinc content.*

323

Other herbs that can help morning sickness include chamomile, fennel, spearmint, or peppermint. Made into gentle, soothing teas, they offer safe, effective relief from nausea during pregnancy.

FENNEL AND CHAMOMILE TEA

Reflexology

Reflexology is related to the ancient techniques of foot massage. It is based on the theory that reflex points on the feet act as nerve receptors for all organs of the body, to which they are linked by energy pathways.

Nausea and morning sickness may respond to reflexology in combination with other treatments such as acupuncture, homeopathy, and diet and nutrition changes. For relief of your symptoms, a reflexologist will gently massage the solar plexus zone of the left foot.

■ **A reflexologist will massage** *the solar plexus reflex point on your left foot in order to relieve the symptoms of morning sickness and nausea.*

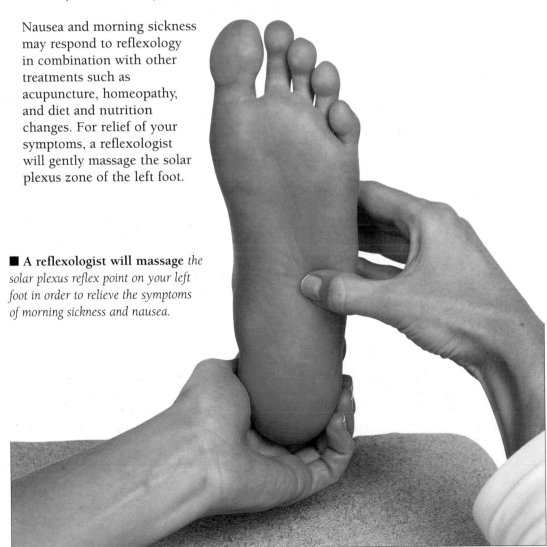

Yoga and meditation

Yoga is an ancient, complex system of physical and mental training that can be highly beneficial during pregnancy. For morning sickness, yoga and meditation theory concentrates on encouraging you to relax your diaphragm. To achieve this, a yoga teacher demonstrates a series of postures (asanas) that aim to integrate mind and body, thus relieving tension.

Homeopathy

With a strong following in Europe, homeopathy is guided by a law of similars: "that which makes you sick shall heal". Homeopaths view symptoms of illness as signs that the body is using its powers of self-healing to fight a disease.

There are many doctors of homeopathy in this country with whom you can consult, or you may choose self-help by procuring some remedies from your local healthfood shop or pharmacy.

For morning sickness and irritability try Nux vomica 6c. If you have nausea that is not relieved by vomiting, try Ipecac 6c. And for evening sickness and tearfulness try Pulsatilla 6c.

Heartburn

The sensations of burning acid in the throat and nausea are just some of the symptoms of heartburn. Many pregnant women suffer from this condition, which is caused by the greater elasticity of the abdominal muscles, which, in turn, causes the valve at the entrance to the stomach to remain slightly open instead of closing. My heartburn worsened as pregnancy progressed and I wish I had had the information below to help relieve my suffering.

Acupuncture

According to TCM, heartburn is linked to excessive heat in the stomach. To help you achieve balance, an acupuncturist examines your tongue first. The tip of the tongue is a window on the heart and is often red in women suffering from heartburn. The middle area of the tongue represents the stomach and digestive system, and it too may be very, very red. Treating specific acupoints on your arms and feet can clear excessive heat. An acupoint below the breastbone can also be treated on your own to help relieve heartburn. Ask your practitioner to show you exactly which point to press and for how long. According to TCM, the stomach should rest between 7 p.m. and 9 p.m. While you are pregnant, this is also a time to rest, relax, and not eat, in order to avoid heartburn.

Homeopathy

There are many homeopathic remedies for heartburn. It's best to consult with a practitioner to select the most appropriate one for you, based on your specific symptoms.

Western herbalism

To alleviate heartburn, there are many herbal self-help remedies. Seeds such as caraway, dill, and fennel may help you. Peppermint, lemon balm, and chamomile taken as soothing tea throughout the day can also help.

FENNEL SEEDS

Skin problems

Nothing can be as devastating as watching your perfectly healthy skin develop acne or become dry and itchy. Stretch marks, dermatitis, psoriasis, and eczema are a few of the ailments that can afflict the skin during pregnancy.

Most skin-related problems are the result of the vast hormonal changes of pregnancy and the fact that the body must work harder to eliminate toxins, as well as change and stretch as your baby grows.

Your skin is a good window on the state of your overall health. The alternative methods below aim to help you bring your system back into balance as well as relieve specific problems.

Diet and nutrition

A balanced diet can help prevent and protect you against skin problems during pregnancy. Eating plenty of protein and foods high in vitamin C promotes skin health and healing. Dryness is best relieved by consuming essential fatty acids like those found in nuts, seeds, and oily fish. Consuming foods high in zinc such as ginger, cheese, and whole-grains may prevent stretch marks.

Hydrotherapy

Water immersion has been used to promote health and well-being for thousands of years. It has also increased in popularity among expectant mothers as a means of gently exercising and easing the pain of childbirth. To ease psoriasis during pregnancy (or at any other time in your life), add oak and lime blossoms to warm bathwater and soak in it for a while. These herbs can be placed in equal quantities in a muslin bag (like a tea bag) directly into the bath. Mashed cucumber enclosed in a muslin bag and then added to a warm bath can also soothe and soften your skin.

■ **Bathing with certain herbs** *or mashed cucumber contained in a muslin bag can help ease skin complaints such as psoriasis.*

Aromatherapy

The wonderful and powerful healing properties of plant oils have been well documented for hundreds of years.

There is a great debate about which oils should or should not be used during pregnancy. Some people believe it is not advisable to use certain oils during the first trimester, although some oils are known to be perfectly safe. Be careful. Consult with a fully qualified aromatherapist before self-prescribing any plant oil during pregnancy.

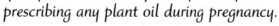

To treat acne, a homemade remedy of diluted tea-tree or lavender oil may help reduce inflammation. It is best not to use this remedy indefinitely: try it for a week or two. If symptoms persist seek professional advice.

Massaging the skin with gentle oils such as mandarin, diluted in a carrier oil such as wheatgerm oil, may help reduce stretch marks.

■ **Massage with oils** *may be beneficial in reducing stretch marks, but check with an aromatherapist before self-prescribing any plant oil when you are pregnant.*

Depression, stress, and anxiety

Vast hormonal changes both during pregnancy and following childbirth are the most likely cause of your mood swings. Having a baby is also one of the most radical changes you will undergo in life. These emotional and physical changes can make you depressed, stressed-out, and anxious. But prolonged depression, stress, and anxiety can affect you and your baby adversely, so it is important to find ways to relax, let go of buried fears, and sleep and eat well, rather than let your feelings take control of your life. Below are some natural methods to help you cope.

Yoga

Yoga is a particularly good treatment for depression, stress, and anxiety. Deep breathing exercises, which are the cornerstone of all yoga practice, will help lead you to deep physical relaxation and improved spiritual well-being. Yoga breathing is especially beneficial in the third trimester when tiredness and anxiety about giving birth can test your emotional fortitude. These breathing techniques will also help you cope with the pain of contractions during labour.

■ **The deep breathing exercises** *fundamental to yoga practice are helpful in combating feelings of anxiety and tiredness, and can help you deal with the pain of contractions during labour.*

Flower remedies

The use of gentle flower remedies were first recorded in ancient Egypt. Over the ages, flower remedies have become especially popular for easing stress and emotional problems. Flower remedies can be taken individually or combined with up to five essences. Distillations are made by infusing plant parts in spring water and preserving their essences in alcohol. They are often prescribed (by homeopaths) for an individual, rather than for a disease.

Flower remedies are usually available in healthfood shops and pharmacies under the trade name of Bach Flower Remedies.

There are a number of flower remedies that can be used for depression, stress and anxiety: elm eases a sense of overwhelming responsibility; gentian counteracts despondency and negativity; holly eases anger and feelings of not being loved; mimulus calms fearfulness; and borage soothes depression.

Acupuncture

Acupuncture is a wonderful way to help heal yourself and is also excellent in the treatment of depression, stress, and anxiety. Stimulating your acupoints along key meridians encourages the release of neurotransmitters in the brain that in turn relieve symptoms of depression, stress, and anxiety.

If you are feeling depressed, you should not be reluctant to tell your doctor or midwife. Sometimes a reassuring conversation can be as effective as an antidepressant drug in relieving mild to moderate depression. Do not suffer alone. Seek out help.

Problems with breastfeeding

Everyone now recognizes that the breast is best for baby and mother. However, breastfeeding is not always straightforward and intuitive. It's important to find help straight away if you have any problems with feeding. If you find breastfeeding painful or difficult, these complementary therapies can help.

Western herbalism

Sore nipples, engorgement, and acute mastitis can be relieved through plant therapy. To prevent sore nipples and to help keep them supple, try applying buttermilk and honey or comfrey ointment.

For breast engorgement (especially during the first days of breastfeeding) you can try an old folk remedy: place a well-washed fresh rhubarb or cabbage leaf inside your bra for 3 hours. After this time your breast should return to normal and you can easily nurse again.

A poultice made from a mixture of chopped comfrey leaves and crushed flaxseed, pounded into a paste with hot water and put into a muslin bag, can be applied to the engorged area. This is an age-old secret the midwives in Switzerland taught me following the birth of my daughter.

AN OLD FOLK REMEDY: THE CABBAGE LEAF

Homeopathy

Homeopathic remedies for breastfeeding problems are very thorough and helpful if you are experiencing any trouble. Insufficient milk flow, slow milk flow, cracked nipples, engorgement, and mastitis can all be relieved with advice from a knowledgeable homeopath.

If milk flow is unsatisfactory because you are emotionally distressed a homeopath will likely recommend *Ignatia*. *Lac defloratum* is useful if your breasts are getting smaller and you are feeling thirsty all the time. *Belladonna*, *Phytollaca,* and *Bryonia* are often recommended for engorgement, depending on particular symptoms. In general, it is best to seek professional attention rather than self-prescribe these remedies.

> *Trivia...*
>
> In traditional Chinese medicine the ear is highly significant and said to resemble an inverted fetus. The ear has more than 120 acupoints and is crossed by all major meridians.

Western massage

A system of healing through touch has deep roots in many cultures, most notably in Asia. Western massage therapists usually combine the best of different Eastern theoretical styles with our Western knowledge of physiology. Massage can be very soothing for relieving the pressure on the breasts from engorgement. The warmth of warm water either in the shower or bath is often recommended in combination with massage.

You can massage your breasts on your own by using your fingers to gently apply pressure in a downward motion from the chest toward the nipples, thus encouraging the milk to flow down the ducts.

A simple summary

✓ You do not need to suffer pain or discomfort during or after pregnancy. Most minor ailments of pregnancy and postpartum such as morning sickness, heartburn, headache, backache and sciatica, fatigue, sleeplessness, constipation, edema, stress, anxiety, postnatal depression, and breastfeeding problems can be relieved safely and effectively by using a combination of alternative therapies.

✓ One of the most important principles of holistic or complementary medicine is that it doesn't prescribe magic pills or simple fast-acting solutions to problems.

✓ Alternative treatments and medicines typically work in harmony with natural rhythms, recognizing the human body's innate ability to heal itself.

✓ Whether you were aware of it or not, it is likely you have already used alternative medical techniques in your own life, pregnant or not.

✓ Complementary medicine's approach to antenatal care and childbirth starts with the idea of giving women a feeling of control over their own bodies by giving them choices about how to relieve pain.

✓ In general you should not self-prescribe any drug, vitamin, or herb during pregnancy. You should always be under the care of, or seek the advice of, a professional health practitioner before ingesting anything that is not just wholesome food.

✓ Always use your judgment. It's probably best to combine alternative approaches with more conventional ones that are administered by your doctor or midwife.

Further resources

Recommended Books

The Birth Partner: Everything You Need to Know to Help a Woman Through Childbirth
Penny Simkin, Harvard Common Press, 1989

A Child Is Born
Lennart Nilsson, Bantam Doubleday Dell Publishing (Trd), 1990

The Complete Book of Pregnancy and Childbirth
Sheila Kitzinger, Knopf, 1996

Dr. Miriam Stoppard's New Pregnancy and Birth Book
Dr. Miriam Stoppard, Ballantine Books, 2000

Drugs in Conception, Pregnancy and Childbirth
Judy Priest with Kathy Attawell, Thorsons, 1998

Eating For Two: The Complete Guide to Nutrition During Pregnancy
Mary Abbott Hess RD, MS and Anne Elise Hunt, IDG Books Worldwide, 1992

Fit and Pregnant: The Pregnant Woman's Guide to Exercise
Joan Marie Butler RNC, CNM, Acorn Publishing, 1995

Getting Pregnant and Staying Pregnant: Overcoming Infertility and Managing Your High-Risk Pregnancy
Diana Raab BS, RN, Hunter House, 1999

A Good Birth, A Safe Birth: Choosing and Having the Childbirth Experience You Want
Diana Korte and Roberta Scaer, Harvard Common Press, 1992

Natural Childbirth the Bradley Way
Susan McCutcheon, Plume, 1996

The Pregnancy Journal: A Day-to-Day Guide to a Healthy and Happy Pregnancy
A. Christine Harris PhD, Chronicle Books, 1996

1000 Questions About Your Pregnancy
Jeffrey Thurston MD, Summit Publishing Group, 1997

The Womanly Art of Breastfeeding (A La Leche League International Book)
Gwen Gotsch and Judy Torgas, Plume, 1997

Organizations

Active Birth Centre
25 Bickerton Road
London N19 5JT
Tel: (020) 7482 5554
www.activebirthcentre.com
Provides information and resources
to help you gain the knowledge and
confidence to make informed choices
and be actively in charge of your
pregnancy and birth.

The Association of Breastfeeding Mothers
PO Box 207
Bridgwater
Somerset TA6 7YT
www.home.clara.net/abm
Supplies names and numbers of
breastfeeding counsellors across
the country.

Association for Postnatal Illness
25 Jerdan Place
London SW6 1BE
Tel: (020) 7386 0868
www.apni.org
Provides support to mothers suffering
from postnatal illness, increases public
awareness of the illness, and encourages
research into the cause and nature of
the illness.

The British Medical Acupuncture Society
BMAS London Teaching Clinic
Royal London Homeopathic Hospital
London WC1N 3HR
Tel: 0800 01 55226
www.medical-acupuncture.co.uk
Offers modern Western acupuncture
treatment by trained acupuncturists
who are registered practitioners

Foresight
The Old Vicarage,
Church Lane
Withey, Goldalming
Surrey GU8 5PM
Provides guidance in planning for
pregnancy and preconceptual care.

Gingerbread
7 Sovereign Close
London E1W 3HW
Tel: (020) 7488 9300
www.gingerbread.org.uk
Offers lone parents and their children
practical and emotional support. Campaigns
to improve the lot of lone parents.

Independent Midwives' Association
1 The Great Quarry
Surrey
GUI 3XN
Tel: (014) 8382 1104
www.independentmidwives.org.uk
An organization of fully qualified midwives
working outside the NHS. Deal with home
births as well as planned hospital births.

La Leche League
PO Box 12
West Bridgford
London, WC1N 3XX
Tel: (020) 7242 1278
www.laleche.org.uk
The UK branch of the international
organization supporting breastfeeding
mothers.

MAMA (Meet-a-Mum Association)
26 Avenue Road
South Norwood
London SE25 4DX
Tel: (020) 8771 5595 (office)
www.gn.apc.org/womeninlondon/MAMA.htm
Provides friendship and support to
mothers and mothers-to-be who may
feel alone or isolated after the birth
of their baby.

The Miscarriage Association
c/o Clayton Hospital
Northgate
Wakefield
West Yorkshire WF1 3JS
Tel: (019) 2420 0799 (helpline)
     (019) 2420 0795 (admin.)
Staff offer support and understanding
from the perspective of having been
through miscarriage or ectopic
pregnancy themselves.

The National Childbirth Trust
Alexandra House
Oldham Terrace
Acton
London W3 6NH
Tel: (020) 8992 8637
Fax: (020) 8992 5929
www.nct-online.org
An organization run by parents for
parents, the Trust provides information
and support on pregnancy, childbirth,
and early parenthood.

National Council for One Parent Families
255 Kentish Town Road
London NW5 2LX
Tel: (020) 7428 5400
Fax: (020) 7482 4851
E-mail: info@oneparentfamilies.org.uk
www.oneparentfamilies.org.uk
Offers parents the means to help
themselves and their families by providing
information and advice, and by developing
new solutions to meet changing needs.

SANDS (Stillbirth and Neonatal Death Society)
28 Portland Place
London W1N 4DE
Tel: (020) 7436 5881
Fax: (020) 7436 3715
www.uk-sands.org
An organization that provides support for
bereaved parents and families that have
suffered the death of a baby at or near birth.

The Vegetarian Society
Parkdale
Dunham Road
Altrincham
Cheshire WA14 4QG
Tel: (0161) 925 2000
Fax: (0161) 926 9182
www.vegsoc.org
Provides nutritional advice for vegetarians
wishing to conceive as well as pregnant
women who are vegetarians.

Pregnancy on the Web

THERE IS A HUGE AMOUNT *of information about pregnancy on the Internet. The following list contains some of the sites that I think are most useful. Please note that due to the fast-changing nature of the Net, some of the below may be out of date by the time you read this.*

www.alternativeparenting.com
For families and families-to-be interested in a more natural parenting lifestyle.

www.ausoft.com/pregnancy
Comprehensive chart compares the signs of pregnancy such as nausea and food cravings with other conditions that might cause similar symptoms.

www.babydata.com/demo.html
Create your own ovulation calendar and pregnancy timetable at this site conceived by a practising physician. Browse pregnancy information and links.

www.baby-place.com
Library of articles on pregnancy, childbirth, and parenting.

www.babycentre.co.uk
Advice and information for expectant and new parents, covering every conceivable topic to do with pregnancy, babies, and family life.

babyzone.com/stages.htm
Explains what happens to your body (and your baby) during the three trimesters of pregnancy, including foetal development and maternal health.

www.bloomingmarvellous.co.uk
A one-stop online shop, offering maternity clothing, nursery furnishings, and baby gear. You can also pick up tips for improvising or creating your own clothing.

www.bradleybirth.com
Contains information on the Bradley method of natural childbirth.

www.childbirth.org
Provides many links to information and resources related to pregnancy, giving birth, and newborns.

www.childbirth.org/articles/faqs.htm
Extensive list of frequently asked questions covering such topics as foetal monitoring, vaginal birth after caesarean (VBAC), labour support, and amniotomy.

www.childbirth.org/section/VBACindex.html
Excellent web site for those considering a VBAC.

www.cnm.wa.org/pregnv.htm
Find out what causes nausea during pregnancy and learn about prevention and relief tactics. Includes a list of danger signs.

www.content.health.msn.com/living_better/hpr
Ask the experts or read articles and advice.

*www.cs.ruu.nl/wais/html/na-dir/misc-kids/
pregnancy/anesthesia/epidural.html*
Compilation of research and opinions from professionals and women who have had epidurals during childbirth.

www.cyberdiet.com
Diet and nutritional information for pregnant women.

www.ds-health.com
Information for parents of Down's syndrome children.

www.efn.org/~djz/birth/resources.html
Guide offering details on midwifery educational programs as well as recent news articles.

www.familyweb.com/pregnancy/natal/natpt101.htm
Outline of the physical and emotional changes you and your family might experience when you become pregnant.

www.fertilityuk.org
Provides comprehensive and objective information to the general public and health professionals on all aspects of fertility awareness.

www.fertilityplus.org/faq/miscarriage/resources.html
Good site for miscarriage support and information resources.

www.fitnesslink.com
Contains great ideas for exercise during pregnancy.

www.fitnesszone.co.za/pregnancy.htm
Information for pregnant women on what exercises to do and how to do them. Features recommended sites and related links.

www.fitpregnancy.com
Articles offering advice to women on how to remain in shape during pregnancy. Includes nutrition tips, a chat room, and discussion forum.

www.gentlebirth.org/archives/pih.html
Explore the causes and treatments for pre-eclampsia (also known as pregnancy-induced hypertension). Access medical journals and research reports.

lifematters.com/medicalinfo.html
Precautions you should take during pregnancy to ensure your exercise programme does not lead to complications.

www.maternityzone.com
A US site offering a full line of simple, stylish, and sensible maternity clothes.

www.maxpages.com/babynames
One of the most complete sources for baby names on the Web.

www.mayohealth.org/mayo/common/htm/pregpg.htm
Helpful site covering the latest news, reference articles, and answers to common pregnancy questions.

www.miscarriage.association.care4free.net
National support group with branches around the country. Offers information and services to women and their families on all aspects of pregnancy loss.

www.momdays.com
Get customized pregnancy and baby calendars with daily updates containing age-appropriate parenting advice and ideas.

www.motherandbaby.co.uk
Covers pregnancy, birth, and parenting issues, and provides a free online advice service.

www.motherisk.org/recomm/folic.htm
Explains how folic acid helps prevent birth defects, and lists the recommended amounts needed.

www.nal.usda.gov/fnic/pubs/bibs/topics/pregnancy/pregcon.html
Provides links to articles and books relating to nutrition during pregnancy and breastfeeding.

www.parenthoodweb.com
Expert advice on pregnancy, child care, and parenting issues.

www.parentsoup.com/pregnancy
Click on the link for UK women to access the pregnancy and parenting online community.

www.parentsplace.com
A good general web site for pregnancy and parenting issues.

www.plainsense.com/Health/Womens/TUBPREGY.htm
Offers a brief list of warning signs for ectopic pregnancies, together with information about treatment.

www.pregnancyguideonline.com
Takes the pregnancy couple through foetal development and maternal changes for each of the 40 weeks of pregnancy.

pregnancy.miningco.com
Provides articles on antenatal care, a week-by-week report on pregnancy, what to buy for a new baby, and much more.

www.pregnancytoday.com
Forum for expectant mothers and new parents to meet with each other, and to exchange coping and lifestyle advice

www.salon.com/mwt
Online magazine featuring articles and information for new and expectant mothers.

www.storknet.org
Fun site for parents to be and new parents, featuring information on pregnancy and childbirth, plus tips and hints.

www.storknet.org/complications
Provides links to feature articles, news, drug information, and support groups relating to pregnancy complications.

www.thelaboroflove.com
Features a collection of pregnancy and parenting related articles. Includes a pregnancy and parenting search engine.

www.webbaby.co.uk
Good general web site dealing with most pregnancy and parenting issues. Offers a free newsletter and an online medical advice clinic.

www.womens-health.co.uk
Contains details on pregnancy complications, miscarriage, infertility and other women's health issues.

A simple glossary

Abruptio placenta A condition in which the placenta separates from the wall of the uterus and causes bleeding.

AIDS Acquired Immunodeficiency Syndrome.

Albumin Protein in the blood that can leak into the urine. During pregnancy, protein in the urine can be a sign of pre-eclampsia.

Alveoli Milk glands in the breast.

Amniocentesis A medical procedure in which amniotic fluid is extracted from the womb by needle, and the fluid is analyzed for fetal defects.

Amniotic fluid The liquid surrounding the fetus in the womb.

Amniotic sac The membrane that surrounds the fetus and retains the amniotic fluid inside the uterus.

Anaesthesia Medication to relieve or deaden pain sensation.

Apgar score Evaluation of a newborn immediately following delivery to determine its well-being or to note signs of distress.

Areola The dark pigmented circular area on the breast that surrounds and contains the nipple.

Braxton-Hicks contractions Warm-up contractions of the uterus, usually beginning around the eighth month of pregnancy.

Breech presentation The head-up position of the baby in the uterus at the time of labour and birth. This position makes delivery more difficult.

Caesarean section The surgical delivery of a baby, accomplished through an incision in the lower abdomen and uterine wall.

Cephalopelvic disproportion A condition in which the baby is too large to pass safely through the mother's pelvis during delivery.

Cervical incompetence A condition in which the cervix opens too soon during pregnancy, possibly resulting in miscarriage. This condition is sometimes treated by stitching the cervix closed until delivery.

Cervix Entrance from the vagina to the uterus. The cervix is normally closed but is stretched open during labour to allow passage of the baby out into the world.

Chorionic villi Microscopic, finger-like projections that make up the placenta.

Chorionic villus sampling (CVS) A medical procedure in which a small sample of cells is taken from the placenta and tested for genetic and birth defects.

Chromosomes Structures within each cell in the human body. Chromosomes contain the genes that determine heredity.

Circumcision A surgical procedure to remove the foreskin of the penis.

Cleft palate A congenital birth defect creating an abnormality of the roof of the mouth.

Colostrum The pre-milk secreted by the breasts in the first 2 or 3 days after delivery and nursed upon by infants before true milk comes in. Colostrum is yellow, creamy, and rich in protein and antibodies.

Congenital disorder A birth defect usually resulting from a damaged gene, exposure to drugs or chemicals, or the effects of illness during pregnancy.

Contractions The regular tightening of the uterine wall muscles to dilate the cervix during labour and to help push the baby down the birth canal.

Crowning The appearance of the baby's head through the opening of the vagina.

Cystitis Infection of the bladder.

Diabetes Failure of the body to properly metabolize sugar.

Dilation and curettage (D&C) A surgical procedure in which the cervix is dilated and tissue is gently scraped or suctioned from inside the uterus.

Down's syndrome A genetic disorder caused by the presence of an extra chromosome, usually causing mental retardation, abnormal features, and medical problems.

Ectopic pregnancy A pregnancy that occurs when a fertilized egg implants outside the uterus, usually in a Fallopian tube.

Edema Swelling caused by fluid retention.

Electronic fetal monitor (EFM) Instrument used to record the heartbeat of the fetus and contractions of the mother's uterus.

Embryo The term used to describe the developing

organism following conception until the twelfth week of pregnancy, at which time it becomes known as a fetus.

Engaged The position of the fetus when it has settled into the deep area of the pelvic cavity, usually in the last month of pregnancy.

Engorgement The over-congestion of a woman's milk glands leading to pain if the breasts are not emptied through feeding or pumping.

Epidural Anaesthesia injected into spinal cavity; used to numb the lower part of the body.

Episiotomy A surgical cut made into the perineum (area between vagina and anus) to widen the vaginal opening for delivery.

Fallopian tube The duct or tube through which a mature egg travels on its way to the uterus after expulsion from the ovary. Also the site of conception.

Fertilization Meeting of sperm and egg to begin a new life.

Fetal alcohol syndrome Specific set of physical abnormalities and mental retardation in a baby that are thought to result from the mother's abuse of alcohol during pregnancy.

Fetus The term used to describe a developing human in the uterus from about the twelfth week of conception until delivery.

Folic acid A nutrient necessary in elevated quantities during pregnancy for the production of blood cells. Folic acid deficiency can lead to neural tube defects. Folic acid is easily supplemented through food or vitamin tablets.

Follicle stimulating hormone (FSH) Female hormone produced by the pituitary gland that helps eggs in the ovaries mature and be released.

Forceps Medical instrument used to assist and help guide a baby down through the birth canal during delivery.

Fundus The upper part of the uterus.

Gene A DNA "map" that codes the specific traits of humans, including hair and eye colour among many others.

Gestation The length of time between conception and birth.

Gynaecologist A medical doctor who specializes in female reproductive issues and conditions.

Haemorrhoids Swollen veins around the anus.

Hormones Chemical messengers in the bloodstream produced by various glands in the body and serving to stimulate organs.

Human chorionic gonadotrophin (HCG) The hormone produced during pregnancy by the placenta that is the basis for most pregnancy tests.

Hydramnios A condition during pregnancy in which there is an excess of amniotic fluid in the sac containing the fetus.

Induction (of labour) The artificial augmentation of labour, usually accomplished with the help of medication.

Insulin A hormone that controls the levels of glucose (sugar) in the blood.

Jaundice A toxic build-up of bilirubin – a chemical produced by the breakdown of red blood cells – that gives babies a yellowish appearance.

Lanugo Fine hair that covers a newborn baby. It usually disappears 2 to 3 weeks after birth.

Linea Nigra The line running from the navel to the pubis; it usually darkens during pregnancy.

Lochia Vaginal discharge following birth and delivery.

Luteinizing hormone (LH) The hormone produced by the pituitary gland that helps an egg mature and be released from an ovary.

Maternal serum screening A group of blood tests to check for birth defects.

Meconium A greenish substance that builds up in the bowels of the fetus and is passed in babies' first stools.

Miscarriage The spontaneous loss of pregnancy before the fetus can survive outside the womb.

Multiple pregnancy A pregnancy in which there is more than one fetus.

Neural tube defect (NTD) A birth defect in which there is improper development of the brain and spinal cord.

Oestrogen Female hormone produced in the ovaries. Oestrogen helps regulate fertility and pregnancy, and stimulates growth in the lining of the uterus.

Ovary One of two female glands that contain eggs (ova) and regularly release matured ones. The ovaries secrete the hormone oestrogen.

Ovulation The release by an ovary of a ripe ovum, or egg.

Oxytocin A naturally occurring hormone that

stimulates contraction of the uterus and stimulates milk production. Can be administered as a drug to help start uterine contractions.

Paracervical block An injection of anaesthetic into the tissue surrounding the cervix to help relieve pain during labour.

Pelvic floor The muscles strung hammock-like in the pelvis for supporting the uterus, the bladder, and the bowel.

Perineum The area between the anus and vagina.

Perineum massage Massage technique used to help stretch and soften the perineum. This technique is beneficial in helping to avoid an episiotomy during delivery.

Pituitary gland A gland located at the base of the brain that produces a number of hormones, including those that control reproduction.

Placenta Organ that connects a mother and her fetus. The placenta transports nutrients to the fetus and carries away its waste.

Placenta praevia A condition in which the placenta is located very low in the uterus, completely or partially covering the cervix.

Pre-eclampsia A condition of high blood pressure combined with excessive fluid retention and/or protein in the urine during pregnancy that results in swelling and can lead to kidney dysfunction.

Presentation Part of the baby to be delivered first, e.g., breech presentation.

Progesterone A female hormone produced in the ovaries after release of an egg that builds the tissue lining of the uterus in preparation for pregnancy. When levels fall, menstruation results.

Pudendal block An injection of an anaesthetic to the perineum area to help relieve pain during delivery, but not during labour.

Quickening A mother's first sensation of fetal movement.

Respiratory distress syndrome A condition of premature babies caused by immature lung development.

Rooting A baby's instinctive reflex that leads it to turn its head towards the breast.

Sacrum The big bone at the base of the spine forming the back of the pelvis.

Show Vaginal discharge prior to beginning of labour.

Spinal block A form of anaesthesia that numbs the lower half of the body.

Stillbirth Delivery of a baby that shows no sign of life.

Sudden infant death syndrome (SIDS) The sudden, unexpected, and unexplained death of an infant.

Term The end of pregnancy or 38 to 42 weeks from the date of the last menstrual period.

Toxoplasmosis Parasitic disease spread by cat faeces that can cause blindness in the fetus if the parasite passes through the placenta in the first 12 weeks of pregnancy.

Trimester Any one of the 3-month periods that mark the stages of pregnancy.

Ultrasound A medical test in which sound waves are used to produce images of internal structures for evaluation by a radiologist or other doctor. During pregnancy, it is used to monitor the health of the fetus and to confirm the due date.

Umbilical cord Cord connecting the navel of the baby to the placenta.

Uterus Hollow muscular female organ in which a fertilized egg embeds itself and matures.

Vagina The canal between the uterus and the external genitals that receives the penis during intercourse and serves as the passageway for the exiting baby during delivery.

Vernix Greasy, whitish coating of a newborn.

Vulva The external part of the female reproductive system including the labia and clitoris.

Yolk sac Sac containing the nutrients for the developing fertile egg.

Index

Acknowledgments

Author's acknowledgments
I am indebted more than I can say to Imre Molnar, Barbara Travis, Tom Ong, Jocelyn Fried, and my editors at DK, Jill Hamilton, Jennifer Williams, and LaVonne Carlson for believing in me and helping bring this book into being. Also to Karla Iacampo, M.D., who in her very special way has taught me about healing and the ups and downs of pregnancy.

Publisher's acknowledgments
Dorling Kindersley would like to thank the following for their help and cooperation in this project: Sue Davidson MB BS MRCP MRCGP DRCOG for her consultancy work; Hilary Bird for the index; Martin Dieguez for design assistance; and Nikki Thompson for editorial assistance.

Picture credits

a	above	l	left
b	below	r	right
c	centre	t	top

The publisher would like to thank the following for their kind permission to reproduce their photographs:

AKG London: Erich Lessing 21, 42.
Britstock-IFA: Gerald Schorm 44; Option Photo J. Gordon OPP 74, 120bl.
Bubbles: Anthony Dawton 186; Angela Hampton 120tr; Daniel Pangbourne 110; Frans Rombout 269; Peter Sylent 197.
Bruce Coleman Ltd: John Cancalosi 305.
Empics Ltd: Andy Heading 28.
Mary Evans Picture Library: 181, 202.
Family Life Picture Library/Angela Hampton: 206, 259.
Sally & Richard Greenhill: 64, 70.
Hutchison Library: Nancy Durrell McKenna 242.
Image Bank: Romilly Lockyer 282.
Mother & Baby Picture Library: 38, 45, 92, 182, 272; Ian Hooton 8, 35, 250; Ruth Jenkinson 33bl, 217, 228, 239; Paul Mitchell 100, 165; Caroline Molloy 126.
Photodisc: 22.
Powerstock Photolibrary / Zefa: 34, 210, 226, 264.
Rex Features: Tang/Williams 102.
Science Photo Library: D. Phillips 14-15, 16-17, 20, 54; Petit Format/Nestle 166.
SOA Photo Agency: Raith/Picture Press 248; Rueffler/Picture Press 180; Rueffler 203, 245; St. Buettner/Picture Press 270.
The Stock Market: 277.
gettyone stone: Elie Bernager 142; Celande Bobbe 90; Paul Chesley 33tr; Frank Clarkson 124; Owen Franken 214, 230; Chris Harvey 72, 154; Peter Lorrez 266; Charles Mason 225; Laurence Monneret 300; Dennis O'Clair 168; Ian O'Leary 60; Lori Adamski Peek 50; Bob Thomas 284; Roger Tully 113; Mark Williams 2.
Telegraph Colour Library: D. Waldorf 194.

Jacket:
Science Photo Library: Petit Format/Nestle back cover tl.